D1029284

COME TO THE PARTY

Previous Books by Hugh Scott

The Golden Age of Chinese Art (*1966*)
How To Go into Politics (*1949*)
Law of Bailments (*1931*)

Come to the
PARTY

By
Hugh Scott

PRENTICE-HALL, INC.

ENGLEWOOD CLIFFS

NEW JERSEY

47,006

TO MARIAN

ACKNOWLEDGMENTS

In the nature of things, the writing of a book involves a draft not upon the energies of the writer alone.

The author is aided by many people in a number of ways.

My wife is often asked whether she helps me with my writing. Her overly modest reply is simply: "I keep quiet." It is much more than that. I lean frequently upon her recollection of shared events. Her judgment as to style and content has been invaluable. Moreover, she fought every battle with me.

I am greatly indebted to that skillful journalist, Donald Irwin of the Los Angeles Times, Washington Bureau, for assistance in organizing and writing this book and for his invaluable help in overhauling those difficult passages that obstinately refused to move properly into place.

For the wise and penetrating suggestions of my friend, Albert N. Leman, of Rockport, Massachusetts, I am so grateful. From his vantage point in the Eisenhower Administration he counseled well and recounts with wit and sagacity.

My special thanks go to my associates Eugene S. Cowen, Edith V. Skinner, Margaret Lynch, Grace E. Hussie and Mary Ellen Pinkasavage, not only for much hard work contributed but for useful suggestions all along the line. My thanks, too, to Juanita Shields and Josephine Good for help from the Republican National Committee.

I wish to express my appreciation to all those who confirmed recollections or helped in checking data and references.

Finally, thanks to the editors of Prentice-Hall for their suggestions, their assistance, and above all, for their patience with a writer constantly distracted by the various demands which press upon a working legislator and politician.

FOREWORD

For a quarter of a century Senator Hugh Scott has struggled to make the Republican party a constructive force in American public affairs. This book is his candid account of disappointments and triumphs in those efforts.

In the past thirty-four years, a Republican has occupied the White House for only two terms. Those eight years were a persuasive demonstration of the creative moderation in national politics for which Hugh Scott has worked. The nation experienced no wars. Threats to the peace were courageously resolved without recourse to gunfire. The NATO alliance was unified, formidable, and effective. SEATO and CENTO were conceived and remained intact. Shackling price and wage controls were eliminated. Employment burgeoned. The gross national product increased. Money costs were moderate. Fiscal integrity was restored and serious inflation was brought under control. The first civil rights act since the Civil War was passed. Massive research, especially in the health and space sciences, was inaugurated. The greatest road-building program in the history of the nation was begun. The St. Lawrence seaway, a cooperative project with Canada, was built. Alaska and Hawaii were granted statehood. The national and international legal bases for the

Alliance for Progress were enacted. Ten million persons were brought under Social Security.

Political moderation was demonstrated as a blend of logic, realism, and dreams.

The presidential campaign which occurred in the last year of that Republican period concentrated on three blatant misrepresentations, for evidently truth would not be advantageous.

Democrats, speaking at all the crossroads of the country, asserted that the reputation of the United States had tobogganed to an all-time low. Dare we compare the lamentable reputation of the United States now to what it was as 1960 drew to a close?

Speakers struck fear into the voters by the claim that a dangerous missile gap existed—that the Soviet Union was far in advance of us in the development of new sophisticated weapons. Only six months after the Democratic Administration took office, the Secretary of Defense announced that no gap existed and, only recently, in reviewing the increased military posture the administration sought to achieve in 1961, he indicated that this effort enhanced the arms race and caused both the United States and the Soviet Union to become overburdened with armaments, much beyond what either needed or could afford.

And, third, it was claimed that the Republican Administration had fostered dear money, thus retarding economic development and increasing unemployment. Today, the cost of money is the highest in this century.

I do not condone, and certainly Senator Scott, originator of the Republican "Truth Squad," does not condone, a national campaign based upon such blatant misrepresentations. A national campaign should be a massive program of adult education to enlighten voters on the critical issues and the candidates' views on these issues. The Republican candidate and the Republican party as a whole must, as Senator Scott insists, be *responsible* while also being *responsive* to the needs of the people.

Extremism may have its place in a democratic society so long as its contribution is limited to the prevention of smugness by the moderates. But moderation, in philosophy and programs, must be the standard of the Republican party if it is to merit and win the support of a vast majority of the American voters.

Hugh Scott is a moderate and in this book he tells with pride how he has tried in the House of Representatives, in the Senate, and in national, state, and local elections to induce the Republican party to win with creative but moderate proposals and candidates. He personally has won his numerous election victories on this basis and has played a key role in electing the only Republican president of this era. All members of the Republican party, all independents, and discerning Democrats should read this book, consider what Senator Scott has done, and then emulate his attitude and methods.

Milton S. Eisenhower
Baltimore, Maryland

PREFACE

SAID Congressman John Scott Harrison to his son Ben: "I do not believe that there is anything in the future of the Republican Party that would justify a man in making very great sacrifices to sustain its falling fortunes."

Youth must have its fling, and Benjamin Harrison, young Republican, chose to reject the paternal adjuration, rising with the party's fortunes and becoming President of the United States at the last cresting of the party's first high tide.

Controversy is built into any free discussion of the falling fortunes of the Republican Party before November 1964. Its current comeback struggles, yet holds inestimable promise, quite as much for the Nation as for the Party. For crisis haunted America urgently needs a responsible and responsive Republican Party as the alternative governing force to a Democratic Administration— bogged down by fatigue and failure.

To this end, I hope the proceeds of a quarter century invested in public and party office rubbing elbows with most of this period's political gnats and giants may hold interest for today's voters.

As this book is written in candor tempered with mercy, the United States is engulfed in the worst national up-

heaval since the Civil War. In the volcanic eruptions of
pent up racial frustration, our laws are broken, order dis-
rupted, and property sacked. The end is not in sight.

America is encompassed by other problems of mounting
magnitude for which Republicans now have the best answers. We live in history's greatest hour of hope and horror, with unlimited opportunities to wage peace and end
racial injustice or sink into irreparable failure. It is toward that challenge in the political sector that this book is
oriented.

Republicans too long have stood mute while demagogues have twisted the record, smeared party leadership
and claim-jumped credit for Republican innovations and
reforms.

"Mum's the word" never yet has been a victorious political slogan. I intend to take the opposite course in these
pages. My credentials are seniority in long Congressional
service, as a former Chairman of the Republican National
Committee, as a team-member of the victorious Eisenhower crusades, as the participant in numerous Republican summit planning and action sessions and—I am
proud to add—as the target of years of hit-and-run political bully ragging.

Right now our war wounded generation huddles with
increasing apprehension under the lengthening shadow of
the hydrogen mushroom. That ominous portent jitters the
stoutest nerves. Should the Red Chinese chimaera harden
its nuclear muscle and employ it in military strikes, millions everywhere now living would perish in atomic cin-
ders.

On the near horizon also are exploding portions of fid-
gety Africa, Latin America, Asia and the Middle East.
With colonial pressures removed, former captives often
have burst into lurid rebellion against their own founding
governments or into overt aggression against their neigh-

bors. Uncle Sam has become their favorite patsy. Plagued by internal fickleness they are often rent asunder by local upheavals, preyed upon by home grown demagogues and tyrants, tempted by Communist bait and enticed by nationalistic pipe dreams.

Among such are the restive Middle East and the chauvinist Viet Cong, where escalating military commitment drains American military resources and devours precious American lives.

At home we are challenged as never before by a Pandora's box of problems especially in urban areas where the ingredients of racial despair fester toward explosion.

Stygian pictures are not the entire landscape. We Americans live in a land of optimism where climbing is our unbreakable habit. Under the joint aegis of private enterprise and government, we have measured the miniscule neutron and plumbed the reaches of space to produce the boundless miracles of modern science. We can muster the know-how and the production mix to help banish ignorance, hunger, disease and war from this tension-plagued earth and to generate a continuous flood of blessings for all mankind.

To meet such breathtaking challenges, Americans of all political backgrounds need and want wisdom in government equal to the crisis.

Republicans now are best equipped to meet that public demand.

We can ignore the mockery of loud-mouth cynics who scoff at everything Republican. We can save America from civil war. We can make a U-turn in government policies that have ground to a halt. We can spurn ideological extremes and press forward to better times for all on the popular and unifying middle course.

We can, if we are wise. We will, if we are ready. We must, if we are to serve the national purpose.

To such a Republican quest I marshal these pages.

CONTENTS

I speak truth,
not so much as I would,
but as much as I dare,
and I dare more as I grow older.

MONTAIGNE

PROLOGUE

SAN FRANCISCO: AT BAY

. . . extremism in the defense of liberty is no vice!
And let me remind you also that moderation in the pursuit of justice is no virtue!

BARRY GOLDWATER
July 16, 1964

BEDLAM.
On the terrace of a hillside home in Sausalito, the enveloping chill I felt did not come from the breeze moving inland across San Francisco's lovely bay. The other refugees from yesterday's trauma were sight-seeing the cliffside house or enjoying the sweeping vista of the hills of Marin County. Alone I was still a party to the turbulence of the Cow Palace.

I could still see the televised image: the handsome bronzed man from the desert country grinned pleasurably as he savored these two defiant sentences, remembering perhaps the praise he had expressed to his speechwriters for their resonant challenge. "I like those lines." The harsh, uncompromising words were to cut many ways before the campaign was over.

1

Yet surely, at this moment of triumph, he could hardly have imagined the irreversible impact. This was the ungloved slap which was to have such dire consequences. Many members of his party, listening across the country, had expected to hear in the first speech of the candidate the accustomed generosity to the losers and the normal plea for union and solidarity in the face of the strongest opponent in years. Instead they were dazed and humiliated.

In the history of both political parties, there had occurred quarter turns, changes of direction toward more or less conservatism or toward greater or less liberalism. Here was something new—something called "a choice, not an echo." The "choice" offered was a 180-degree change of course away from decisions made by the American people under presidents of both parties, ratified and reratified by them over more than half a century. The "echo"—intended to convey repudiation of majority policy—sounded rather more like reverberations from the dead days of *laissez faire*.

The Republican Party, born in the struggle for human rights and equality of opportunity, nurtured upon its belief in a just distribution of responsibilities between the individual, the states and the federal government, was about to become a party ashamed of its own past and afraid of the Nation's future.

This was no quarter turn to starboard navigated by men with challenging new ideas and realistic new hopes for the future. This was a summoning of the fearful, the frustrated and the newly taxed to move together in a nostalgic retreat to an imagined past, a past which had never really existed in the heritage of the venturesome American spirit.

Was this, I wondered, the Republican Party within

which and for which I had worked for more than twenty-
five years? The new radicalism was in the saddle and
riding hell for leather on a course far to the right of both
Eisenhower and Taft and largely out of step with the
records and positions of most of the Republican Governors. I wondered whether such a party could hold the allegiance of true conservatives and moderates and yet appeal to essential new recruits such as those who had come
into the party as Citizens for Eisenhower and Nixon.

The trend of 1964 made the picture bleak. From the
end of the 1960 campaign, those who called themselves
"conservatives" or "constitutionalists" had welcomed the
zealous workers of the far right. In the Deep South they
had allied themselves with the white supremacists, such as
the Mississippi Republican State organization. They had
grown comfortable with the simplistic beliefs of the John
Birch Society, even though Senator Goldwater himself
had expressed disapproval of the more appalling comments by its authoritarian leader, Robert Welch.

The constitutionalist fears of federal expansion had received little sympathy at the national level. Frustrated by
their failures, therefore, these conservative radicals and
extremists refused to attribute changing concepts of federal responsibility to the free choice of a majority of the
American public. Because they could not tolerate the
thought that they comprised a minority, they singled out
scapegoats whom they accused of conspiracy and sabotage.

The favorite extremist thesis was that the United
States is in the grip of a massive Communist conspiracy,
which directed executive actions and dominated legislative
decisions. For those to whom this medicine was a little
strong, there was the explanation that control was in the
hands of combinations of minority groups. This had its

conveniences because one could reshuffle the alleged combinations to stack the cards against those whom he feared or hated most.

Obviously, the more thoughtful constitutionalists, and certainly most elected officials, could not intellectually justify dissatisfactions with the Republican Party on either of these grounds, which furnished such grist for the gullible rank and file. But there was one scapegoat, already tethered and branded—the so-called "Eastern Establishment." A lot of persuasive hay could be stacked by attributing all past frustrations to its machinations.

The "Establishment" was the mystical "power group," never fully identified, which purportedly embraced Republican moderates and liberals, candidates, officeholders and contributors who lived in the wicked East (especially naughty New York) or who shared their views. The Eastern Establishment was blamed for all national Republican defeats. All candidates who had not sworn in for Goldwater were automatically included, even if they came from Oregon or Michigan.

The primaries, until California in June 1964, were another story. Why the middle-of-the-roaders, with a clear preponderance of Republican opinion behind them, missed every opportunity, calls for some detailed examination. The moderate governors, Members of Congress and state officials engaged in a tiptoeing minuet while all around the listening ear could catch the sound of delegates plopping to Goldwater.

On the last day of the San Francisco Convention, we prepared to return home by Canadian Pacific. Ordinarily, I love Western trains, but it was a long time before I could relax. I needed time to reach my own decisions, to announce and defend them. I was worn and weary after the defeat of the moderates' amendments to the platform offered by me and of the amendments offered at the insistence of Governor George Romney of Michigan on behalf of a number of delegates in opposition to the Goldwater Platform.

The most disturbing memory I left with was of the barbarism of the lunatic fringe in the Goldwater ranks. At the convention they had offended and embarrassed all of the twenty-five Negro delegates. The most blatant incident involved William P. Young, Pennsylvania's dignified and much-respected Secretary of Labor and Industry who then held the highest ranking position ever occupied by a Negro in the Commonwealth of Pennsylvania. Young was being interviewed when, in the full view of the television audience, his coat smouldered and caught fire. Someone in the pressing, hooting crowd had lighted a match against his coat pocket.

Then there was the horrifying incident on the night of the balloting when Governor Bill Scranton and I were standing side by side with Pennsylvania State Attorney General Alessandroni in Scranton's Communications Trailer. We were talking about the loyalty of his supporters in so many parts of the country, especially the young people, when we noticed a glow outside the window. The most alert member of my staff, Gene Cowen, public relations man extraordinaire, with the peripheral vision of his trade, suddenly yelled: "Get everybody out of the trailer. I think we're on fire!" Everyone rushed out. The trailer was not on fire but a ramp a few feet away leading into the Cow Palace was. The fact that Mary Scranton had just reached the bottom of the ramp seconds before was perhaps a coincidence. The fact that someone deliberately had set a fire only a few feet from the Scranton trailer was not a coincidence. A policeman told me: "I saw a dim figure move away from the side of the ramp only a minute before the fire."

I concede that people who set fire to the clothes of other people comprise the worst element of a political movement. No movement, however respectably motivated, can control every one of its followers. Yet, at no time did the Goldwater leaders either apologize for the uncivilized behavior of some of their followers or publicly urge their zealots to temper their actions. Perhaps it would have been too much for the original followers of Barry Goldwater to repudiate the infiltrators of the hard-line right, since many of these fanatics were the Senator's most articulate and active missionaries.

I remembered this when in the course of the following month I publicly upbraided the Goldwater button wearers who insistently heckled Republican speakers, including myself, at an outdoor rally in Montgomery County, Pennsylvania. At the end of my speech, I said to the handsome young man on the speaker's stand, Barry Goldwater, Jr.: "What does your father think of this kind of impudence?" He replied that his father was disturbed by it and entirely disapproved. I suggested that the Goldwater campaign managers ought to take public steps promptly to disavow these extremists. But nothing was ever done.

Certainly it looked as if the Republican Party would have to go to the voters with a rapidly eroding minority, with a candidate who was the choice of a minority. The implications of this were unfortunately far-reaching. I recalled what Arthur Larson wrote eight years before the 1964 convention. His unheeded statement in his book, *A Republican Looks at His Party*, was indeed prophetic:

> If, as seems likely, the Republican Party in 1956, 1960 and later years puts forward candidates who represent the New Republicanism, while Democratic spokesmen are obliged to attack from one extreme

position or another, and if some cataclysmic event does not come along which calls all bets off, the Republicans should have a strong chance of staying in power as representatives of the great majority of the voters. But if, as seems unlikely, the Republicans were some day to nominate a candidate for the presidency who was identified with an extreme conservative position, and if, as seems equally unlikely, the Democrats were to seize that moment to choose a nominee who took over the formula of the great middle way, the Democratic candidate would almost certainly win, and thereafter it would be difficult indeed for the Republicans to get back in.[1]

With the Republican Party at the edge of this disaster, grave questions arise: How did this 1964 debacle come about? Did an historical division in the Party foreshadow this? Was there precedent? Were the moderates never aware of the growing strength of the Goldwater candidacy or of the means being used in state after state to advance that candidacy?

These questions are part of history, but the answers to them have overwhelming significance for the future. They raise, in turn, subsequent queries: Can the Republican Party retain the united loyalty of the *true* Conservatives and Moderates who hold the essential human values sacred? Can the Party re-establish political rapport with the American people who were also traumatized by the San Francisco disaster? In other words, how difficult will it be, in Larson's words, "for the Republicans to get back in?"

For me, these complex matters have paramount importance. My 25 years of involvement with the Republican Party and my commitment to moderation and political sanity press me to come to grips with the historical causes and future possibilities.

The French have a saying: "Vaut le detour"—worth the trip. Have Republican detours of the last quarter century been worth the trip? If not, how to return to the main line?

I

ELWOOD, INDIANA, U.S.A.

Only the productive can be strong, and only the strong can be free.

WENDELL WILLKIE

HAVE Republicans lost touch with the people? Are they condemned forever to the minority's inglorious role? As an observer of the national Republican scene for nearly three decades, I think the answer to both questions is: Not necessarily!

The party's 1964 downfall makes one wonder why Republicans have so often "done the things they ought not to have done and left undone those things they ought to have done." But its comeback two years later showed once again that the party can command public confidence when it leads where the voters will follow.

Three decades back, when people spoke of being "turned on," it was the radio, not themselves they referred to. Those who cared what the Republicans were doing in the fourth year of the New Deal heard the name of the Republican challenger in the November election from a radio announcer describing him as: "Governor Alfred M. Landon of Kansas, a progressive Republican."

That is not how he is remembered today, even in Maine and Vermont, the only states to plop into Alf Landon's G.O.P. bag. What were the Republicans doing that they ought not to have done?

Landon had in fact been a good and progressive Governor. He was a man of good will, strong motivation and decent principles. What happened to bring about such wholesale rejection of man and party? Briefly, Landon was shackled by a reactionary platform, overly conservative advisers, poor public relations and some unfortunate public statements to match.

He was, of course, well nigh hopelessly under-matched against the gay and charming incumbent, champion of the people, just beginning to turn on the golden blessings at the Washington faucet. F.D.R. was in process of forging the coalition which was to endure for thirty years: The South, the labor unions, the intellectuals, the beneficiaries of the Federal bounty.

Four years later, reduced in ranks and in regard, the G.O.P. party machinery still languished in the hands of the Old Guard, themselves unable and unwilling to put together a winning combination of the faithful within their ranks and of the discontented and the disillusioned beyond their willful walls.

Of candidates, there were a few, but hardly of championship material. Vandenberg was still becalmed in the doldrums of isolationism, Taft was new on the scene, Dewey young and untried. Republican rank and file were ready for new leadership, even as their party leaders contended among themselves for a prize few thought they could grasp.

The stage was set for a new man, a leader who could

rally more than they had and who would summon those
who were deaf to the voices of the old status quo anti-
Roosevelt. The political scene was ready for the emer-
gence of such a man. As was the wont of the old regulars,
when he did appear, they did not wish to let him show his
wares.

For Wendell Willkie was of the business world rather
than a denizen of the cozy confines of the professional political club members. Worse than that, he was a Democrat.
A less likely leader of the Republican Party would have
been hard for these standpatters to imagine.

So it became the lot of the few true believers in what
Willkie had to say to bring him forward and present him
to an unwilling party as the one public person who could
unlock for them the doors of the promised land of electoral
office.

The professionals held back. The regulars squared off
for a fight. Unaware that it could not be done, the inno-
cents, the Willkie volunteers, zealously buckled on the
righteous armour of their faith.

By the time Willkie's nomination had been achieved,
elders had been frozen into positions no longer tenable in
a changing America. Willkie himself was suspect, an un-
known quantity: a nonprofessional, a man regarded by
many regulars as an interloper at best and, at worst, an
unsound crypto-liberal.

The far right conservatives—the Tories, as F.D.R.
loved to call them—totally opposed Willkie's receptivity
to governmental reform. They refused to admit the existence of any abuses which the government had any right to
correct. Since 1938 it had been Willkie's thesis that the
intelligent businessman was confronted not by theories
but by the *fait accompli* of the new federal economic laws.
Ask not, he said, "How can we fight this legislation?" but,

"How can we make it workable?" [1] The outraged tyran-
nosauric types condemned the Willkie stand as sheer socialism.

Willkie's articulate logic revived public appreciation
for the enlightened industrial empires without which there
would be no means to expand employment and raise the
level of individual prosperity.

Hard-shelled conservatives recoiled at Willkie's admis-
sions that the federal government had a responsibility to
intervene in areas where historic abuses festered untreat-
ed. Yet Willkie slashed through layers of ideological
clichés to expose the basic conflict between free enterprise
and the fully planned society.

The true issue was, he argued: How much government
can the people, to their real advantage, do without?

To Wendell Willkie the subjection of individual enterprise to a paternalistic government was not the way to
freedom. Such a road could only lead, in his judgment, to
an economy less and less productive, less and less able to
provide the only true security, full employment.

Willkie, articulate in opposition to the bludgeonings of
the New Deal, sounded an alert to all who believed that
the right to produce and to sell the fruits of their production was as integral a part of freedom as the right to be
paid for the labor of head or hand. Government, he insisted, had no right to diminish these returns except as
necessary for the general welfare.

Order must limit freedom by equalizing the rules but
not by repression of the right to risk.

As close to the convention as early May 1940, however,
Wendell Willkie was not being taken seriously as a candidate. An article by him, "We, the People" was published
in the April issue of *Fortune* magazine, at the insistence
of the editor, his friend Russell Davenport. His major
theme also was drawing favorable attention: "Only the

productive can be strong, and only the strong can be free."

People were beginning to ask each other: "Why don't the Republicans put up somebody like Willkie?" So far, it was just parlor and commuter talk, but Willkie's admirers set themselves to supply the answer: "Why not Willkie?"

Then, as was to happen again with Eisenhower and Scranton, the young nonpoliticians began to get excited. From Princeton, New Jersey, twenty-nine-year-old Oren Root, Jr., began by correspondence and telephone to put together "Willkie for President" Clubs. Russell Davenport became Willkie's preconvention manager. Influential publishers and business leaders stepped in to help.

I decided to work for Willkie, even though I knew of only two among the seventy-two Pennsylvania delegates who favored him in a delegation committed to back Governor Arthur James. Willkie was clear of the isolationist debate in Congress; he was a man of ideas and great personal magnetism. He was the strongest candidate in public view. Would the Republicans see that at their convention?

In mid-May, I located a modest office serving as the first Willkie headquarters in Philadelphia. I introduced myself as a Republican Congressional nominee, the first candidate in the State to declare for Willkie.

It was too late for any campaign in depth, so I proposed emergency tactics aimed at persuading the delegates who would soon start trickling into town for the June 24 opening of the convention. The delegates would support Willkie if they were convinced there was a Willkie ground swell in Pennsylvania. All of the uncommitted (and many of the committed) were presumably interested in the reality and depth of public sentiment for Willkie. On this premise, I advised our volunteers:

"Take off your Willkie buttons and circulate in the hotels. Get acquainted with the delegates as they check in. Eat with them, drink with them, offer to show them the town. Don't talk politics until they ask what you hear. Then let it slip that everybody seems to be talking about this man Willkie. Keep a record of their names and states and report back to this headquarters."

Once they had a mission, our volunteers recruited others, and the headquarters was swarming by convention time. Morale zoomed as Willkie supporters converged from across the country dispensing zeal along with buttons, pamphlets and petitions.

There is a legend that the galleries were purposely packed for Willkie at Philadelphia in 1940. They weren't. His volunteers lacked the organization to pull off such a coup, and in any event, it was not necessary. Convention planners were naturally anxious to avoid the appearance of empty galleries and there was little effort to limit seats to ticket holders as long as there were seats available.

Unlike the inflexible Pinkerton guards at later conventions, the doorkeepers were mostly Pennsylvania party workers who liked to do favors for friendly people. They gave no preference to those who wore Willkie buttons—there were just so many more of the Willkie people. They came in by the thousands from the city, its suburbs, from other parts of Pennsylvania and from other states. There were no cheerleaders, no organized groups, no noisemakers. There were a few placards—but none of the fake preplanned demonstrations that have blocked progress at later party conventions. Their fervor probably infected less committed spectators, who arrived without a candidate and stayed to yell: "We want Willkie!"

The spectacular success of the Republican grass roots

revolt was at once a tribute to Willkie, who won on the convention's sixth ballot, and a rejection by the Republican rank and file of the narrow isolationism of the party's legislative leaders. Unfortunately, the leaders controlled the platform committee and their reactionary principles shaped the vital foreign policy plank.

Not until 1964 would the party again write such a narrow, backward-looking platform. Not until 1964 would reaction again prove so blind to reality. The situations differed in that in 1964 the party had a much stronger record in Congress and a much weaker Presidential nominee.

The nomination of Willkie was, in itself, a repudiation of the platform, which expired without mourners the week it was born. As Dillon notes:

> It [the nomination] forecast the future program of the Republican Party. It reversed the Republican policy of isolationism. It connoted aid to the Allies and especially succor to England for the Battle of Britain. It meant Republican support for foreign trade and lowering of the tariff barriers. It also meant a reinterpretation by the Republican Party of the meaning of free enterprise. It was the Republicans' answer to the New Deal.[2]

Or would have been—had Willkie won.

Brave, tough-minded Wendell Willkie, in seeking to lead the nation along Republican paths in 1940, failed narrowly, mostly for reasons beyond his control, though his internationalist views cost him the votes of isolationists. He fired millions of Americans, some of whom had not been Republicans, with new confidence and high hopes. He left behind a heritage of realistic belief in the individual which the party has mislaid at times, but has never wholly lost.

When Republicans named Willkie as their candidate, the party had recovered in the main from the economic disaster of 1929 and the New Deal landslides of 1934 and 1936. The Willkie campaign fostered an expedient union for common goals. Its failure unloosed divisions that reached their climax in the hollow victory for a faction that led inescapably to the party-wide disaster of November 1964.

I entered national politics during the sparring that helped Willkie take the 1940 convention by storm, when in January of that year, octogenarian Representative George P. Darrow announced that he would not run for reelection.

Determined to enter politics as a boy of thirteen attending committee hearings in the Virginia House of Delegates, I scoured the newspapers for political doings, state and national. By the time I was eighteen, I was an eager listener in the U.S. Senate Gallery, and I intended to serve some day in the Congress of the United States. Entering legal practice in Philadelphia at the age of twenty-one, politics had been sidelined until the Congressional race beckoned.

Several persons had already hinted at their "availability" if the Darrow seat fell vacant. After his announcement, I went directly to Darrow, told him of my long-held desire to go to Congress, and solicited his support. I learned at once that the Congressman had done past favors for the two leading claimants to his seat (one of them had been his appointee to a service academy). Neither had thought to ask his support. Naturally, he resented their jumping the gun on his announcement.

I found the Congressman nostalgically leafing through the scrapbooks recording his career. I told him how, at the age of eight and again when twelve years old, I had followed Presidential election campaigns as zealously as my compeers collected cigarette card pictures of baseball greats.

Unlike most young lawyers who looked ahead to a chance to interpret laws as a Judge and who regarded legislative office as a political job valued chiefly for its emoluments, I wanted to be a maker of the laws, a sharer in the operation of the legislative process which had commanded my interest as student and observer.

After a pleasant visit, I left gratefully with Representative Darrow's personal endorsement.

This was only the beginning.

One of the other candidates had lined up most of the political leaders and another was backed by a number of businessmen in the district. With the help of the politically-wise Judge Harry S. McDevitt, I obtained the solid support of the Republican members of the Philadelphia County Board of Judges. This Board, then as now, was empowered to appoint the members of several commissions who, in turn, controlled a great deal of political patronage.

Word of Judge McDevitt's backing got around. It was generally believed by the pols that five Republican leaders of the District's wards would pick the candidate after the 57th annual banquet of our Germantown Republican Club, of which I was a life member. A good conspiratorial friend, the late Judge Theodore Rosen, slipped me his ticket of admission to the head table. Guests so honored consisted of party officials and elected officeholders or candidates selected for elective office. Only head table guests wore dinner jackets and Judge Rosen's seat was next to that of the Republican District Chairman, David E. Watson. Watson was the only one of the five leaders whom I believed to be in my corner.

Politics has considerable similarity to poker. I held a fair hand but not necessarily a winning one. Before the

banquet I paced the floor for an hour, trying to decide
what to wear. I opted for the dinner jacket of those who
had "arrived" politically. No sooner had I settled myself
into the strategic Rosen seat, when some of my friends
rushed up ostentatiously to congratulate me. Who shall
say how coincident was this verbal confetti? Committeemen anxious to be among the first to sniff out a winner,
joined the foofaraw. After a decent interval, one of my
principal opponents came up to extend his congratula-
tions. A small smile played about the lips of the District
Chairman.

Next day's decision was 5 to 0 in favor of the man in
the tuxedo.

I began my first campaign with the conviction that is
the freshman candidate's greatest asset. I described myself, and I still do, as a "liberal when it concerns people's
rights and a conservative when government tries to take
away their property."

As the campaign progressed, however, even Roosevelt's
assault on the hitherto inviolable tradition limiting Presidents to two terms was eclipsed as an issue by the growing
menace of war in Europe. To millions the basic question
was whether F.D.R. or Willkie was best qualified to avert
war if possible and to lead the nation to victory if war became inevitable.

Republicans were handicapped by the outspokenly isolationist views of those in the party who so distrusted
Roosevelt that they ignored the realities of the situation.
They could and should have made a strong case of the
failure of the Roosevelt Administration to arm and prepare the nation to face the consequences of the drift toward war which was implict in F.D.R.'s policies, but they
missed the bus.

To the growing alarm of some Republicans, those policies shifted the Democrats away from the posture of rigid

neutrality assumed by both parties in the mid-1930's to the extension of active aid "short of war" to the democracies engulfed by Hitler's aggression.

Mistrust of Roosevelt led most Congressional Republicans to vote indiscriminately against defense appropriations.[3] It was a reflex which distressed some in the party, including the former Presidential candidate Alf Landon, but they elected to keep silent rather than risk a split with the Senate leaders, Arthur H. Vandenberg of Michigan, Charles McNary of Oregon and Robert A. Taft of Ohio.

Their ceaseless battle with the New Deal involved these men so deeply in domestic affairs as to befog their view of foreign policy. It made them obtuse to the public's mounting alarm at the prospect of a Nazi Europe. By their failure to realize that the public was far ahead of them in accepting the risk of war, Republicans hazarded their future. They offered no constructive proposals either to keep out of the war or to strengthen the national defense against the emergency.

Republicans might have cut their losses somewhat if they had been more sagaciously selective, supporting that which could be found good in Democratic proposals or at the least offering constructive amendments to the laws they could not stop. Republicans fell into the delusion that they could not stay in the minority. But to win, a party should deserve to win.

Republican rank and file always have favored kindness to older people as proven by their long personal records of family duty, private charities, church benevolence and public aid. Yet too often their front row leaders seemed to have the taint of Scrooge. So after three decades, for example, the Republican Party still suffers from the obtuseness of its earlier spokesmen to the demand for social security for the elderly. At every step of the Congressional hearings most Republicans doggedly fought the concept.

Here was an opportunity to examine the proposed new system, face the inevitability of its adoption, and seek to make it more workable fiscally and administratively. The need is attested by the many revisions soon added to the system. Republicans of the 1930's could have won both respect and political credit if they had tried as hard to improve the original bill as they did to kill it.

Some hold that the Republicans could not have supported such a "socialistic" system and should therefore have fought it to the bitter end. Not so. A large majority of the Republicans who found flaws in the bill along most of its route voted *for* the social security system when it finally passed in 1935. The Republican vote in the House was: For: 77; Against: 18.

It is more than thirty years since Republicans helped approve social security, but Democratic orators still deny any Republican compassion and still declaim with calculated elision of the facts that "the Republicans voted *against* social security. They had no heart for the people!"

Overshadowing all domestic issues, however, were the clouds of war.

I recall listening on the radio to F.D.R.'s pledge in Boston at the end of the campaign, that no American soldier would ever have to fight on foreign soil. I knew the promise could never be kept, just as I knew it would have a telling effect. I went immediately to keep a speaking engagement in my Congressional district. I repeated the words I had just heard, and branded the assurance as an act of deceit.

To prepare Americans for possible entry into war would have been an act of high statesmanship. To promise to stay out, against growing evidence of the risk of involvement, was sheer political guile.

In re-examining these confusing times, we look back to ask ourselves, did Willkie feel that war was inevitable? In any event, perhaps imminent? Did he fail to draw an issue of credibility for fear the public would take the President's word? Did he share with Roosevelt the feeling that the American people were not yet ready to be told that war for the U.S. was just around the corner?

In the campaign Willkie was a big shaggy bear of a man in rumpled clothes whose rather boyish charm, engaging candor, and obvious sincerity won him large, admiring audiences across the country.

On election night at Willkie headquarters in Philadelphia, the returns from the bellwether Connecticut towns signaled defeat. Willkie and the third term issue lost by about five million votes. The people had decided to keep the same hand at the helm, hopeful of its sureness of purpose, fearful of change in the face of imminent danger.

That election sent me to Congress for my first term by a majority of 4,170, a margin of 51.5 percent. Willkie had carried my district by 3,007 votes. My wife and I headed for the Republican City Committee headquarters. I was the only Republican to survive the landslide in a city which had rooted for Willkie in June and voted for Roosevelt in November. As we entered the city headquarters, Jay Cooke, the City Chairman, broke the tension by shouting: "We ought to have you stuffed."

My wife's mixed reactions came out like this: "Oh, thank you, but isn't it awful!"

At the back of the room a lady volunteer with a plate on her lap was saying between sobs, "This is the *hardest* ice cream I ever ate."

Early in December 1940, Willkie addressed 3,600 persons assembled at the National Interfraternity Conference in New York City. He counseled his listeners and nationwide radio audience to put aside personal bitterness, then offered a frank, clear-eyed appraisal of the American role on the darkening world scene.

"I believe it is necessary," he said, "for America to give that aid to the British as to build armaments for itself."

He added that "America within the next few years must make some very fearful and some very fateful decisions . . . not the ordinary type of decisions. They are decisions that will determine whether or not democracy shall survive."

One year later America was at war.

II

CAPITOL HILL TO TOKYO

"I say to you fathers and mothers of America, and I say it again and again and again, no American boy is going to die on any European battlefield."

F. D. ROOSEVELT

It was bitter cold for President Roosevelt's third inaugural on January 20, 1941. We in Congress viewed the scene from the platform on the steps of the Capitol. We heard the President speak of the faith of America, of the Magna Carta, the Mayflower Compact, the Constitution, the Declaration of Independence, the Gettysburg Address, the hopes of the Republic, the spirit and destiny of America, and the First Inaugural Address.

He concluded that we do not retreat. We are not content to stand still.

Not a word about peace—or war. There was no mention of the national crisis nor of preparedness. Despite the ringing Rooseveltian promises to keep the country out of war, he did not choose to deal with the menacing dilemma

23

of involvement or non-involvement in the growing conflict.

The President did not seize the opportunity to take the people into his confidence. Had he made his Inaugural Address a clear statement of those American decisions which he would ask the Congress to support, he would have had less trouble with a Congress fired up by his step-by-step progression toward our inevitable ultimate commitment. This was not the President's way. He enjoyed too much his successes in the game of cat and mouse.

Few in Washington expected the war to begin at Pearl Harbor, for few fully appraised the level of Japanese audacity. Yet war was in the crisp fall air. As an amateur student of Japanese history and art, I became alarmed after Japan's envoys frostily rejected on November 26 a U. S. peace formula that would have required Tokyo to forswear the expansion into East Asia from which it hoped to gain so much in power and "face." The men who ran Japan were asking concessions, not making them, and there were warnings of a sudden Japanese attack from our embassy and from the British. The gloom deepened with the news on the evening of December 6 that the President had addressed a personal appeal to the Emperor.

To me such a message, routed deliberately over the head of the Prime Minister, could only mean war in the very near future—one little knew how soon. I reasoned from the knowledge that the Emperor was a deity to Japanese officialdom, sacred in his person and in his privacy. Mere existence of a statement to him that bypassed the Prime Minister and his Cabinet, particularly the military staff, would present them with three possibilities: [1]

(1) Abject submission to a foreign power, which would call for surrender unconditionally [totally unacceptable];

(2) Hara-kiri of Prime Minister and Cabinet because of loss of face [unlikely] ;

(3) Strong military action.

I therefore expected war in a matter of days, but it had never occurred to me that the enemy would attack the Hawaiian Islands. Of course, no one outside of the Administration knew that our cryptographers had much earlier broken the Japanese code, and thus had deciphered the famous "winds" passage signalling the coming attack upon Pearl Harbor.*

I took my oath in January, 1941, as a freshman member of the Seventy-seventh Congress. Within eleven months, the war we had debated so hotly during the campaign became a reality. Normal interplay between the parties atrophied in the face of the grim necessity to develop policies that would win the war.

Despite the war's pressures, that old devil, isolationism, clouded the views of most of the Republican Congressional leadership and of the party's highly insular National Chairman, crusty old Harrison Spangler. Facing backward, they shrank from affirmative commitments in a world of wholesale change.

Change was breaking about our ears. F.D.R., withholding any specific blueprint of the future direction of foreign policy, drew increasing fire from Republicans.

I arrived in Washington as a Republican committed to affirmative answers to the great question propounded by the fourth chapter of Genesis: Whether we were comfortable about it or not—and I was not entirely comfortable —at the national level, we *were* our brother's keeper in some areas of responsibility. Differing on method, I would question the constitutionality of some legislative ap-

---

* As late as 1944, candidate Tom Dewey refused to reveal and exploit the broken code, believing such tactics divisive of the war effort.

proaches, but I would support the concept of a federal
sharing of responsibility in the advancement of the general welfare. I would want to provide for the poor and the
needy and the unemployed where the need existed and to
the extent that other governmental units had failed or fal-
tered.

It wasn't long before I realized it was easier to have a
program as a candidate than it was to make a constructive
record as a freshman Congressman. At the first meeting of
the Pennsylvania delegation in 1941, I made my first mistake in Congress. At issue was our stand on the acutely
controversial Lend-Lease Bill. Twelve of the delegation
announced their opposition to the Bill, which authorized
transfer of arms to foes of the Axis virtually as gifts. I
was one of three for Lend-Lease. We strongly argued that
the public was ready for this legislation and that no alternative had been offered as a means of defending the
United States by aiding the Allies, particularly Great
Britain.

The Bill's foes warned that it would bring us closer to
war. To my argument that to help Great Britain was to
help freedom, they retorted that there would be less risk of
U. S. involvement if we gave Great Britain outright
grants to buy munitions. Moreover, the Bill contained no
limit on expenditures—and there was then no precedent
for open-ended appropriation bills. Republican seniors
insisted that opposition in the House, fully explained in
debate, would surely bring the Senate to correct its glar-
ing defects. (At that time I lacked the experience to know
that House Bills do not necessarily return from the Senate in a more healthy state.)

One by one our arguments were rebutted. Ranking
members argued cogently for a unanimous delegation vote
against the Bill.

I was the last to be persuaded. I agreed to "go along."

("To get along, go along," Speaker Sam Rayburn used to advise his flock.) In a speech on February 8, 1941, I surrendered my inner convictions to the pressure to conform. Although I retrieved my position by voting for the final version of the Bill when it returned from the Senate, I have always regretted that I permitted the expedient to determine my initial vote on that crucially important Bill.

Returning from Naval Reserve sea duty off Iceland aboard the *New Mexico* in August 1941, I was appalled to learn that the House Republican Leadership had "paired" me against the draft extension. This action was completely unauthorized by both House rule and party custom. The "pair" system permitted some absent member who wished to vote for the extension to be matched on the roll call with me as one who, if present, would have voted against the draft extension. The device removed the risk that the other member might return to Washington to cast an effective vote for continuance of the draft law.

This arbitrary action and the myopic thinking behind it resolved any doubts I might have held then about measures to prosecute the war. I supported them all.

When the Republican National Committee met at Chicago on April 20, 1942, despite continuing mistrust among remnants of the Old Guard, the Willkie influence prevailed. A resolution was adopted calling for full participation in the war and an end to isolationism.

By the summer of 1943, Republican members of Congress had begun to demand that the President take the country into his confidence as to the future direction of foreign policy. Characteristically, Roosevelt ignored these rumblings.

Some Republicans saw opportunities and obligations for postwar leadership. Demands for a strong Republican position on the emerging issues of foreign policy came

from an influential party segment that included Warren
R. Austin of Vermont, the assistant Minority Leader of
the Senate, and Representative Charles A. Eaton of New
Jersey, ranking Minority member of the House Committee on Foreign Affairs. They stated their views force-
fully in and out of Congress. They lent their prestige to
the newly formed Republican Policy Association, a citizens' group committed to multinational organization for
maintenance of international order.

Realistically focusing its efforts toward the coming
1944 campaign, the Council aimed to break the isolationist grip on the party machinery by influencing selections of convention delegates and nominations of Congressional candidates.

On July 19, 1943, Republican anti-isolationists from
twelve Eastern states met in New York to form an Eastern Division of the Association. The speakers, including
Christian A. Herter, later Secretary of State, foretold
Roosevelt's election to a fourth term unless the Republicans offered the nation a candidate and a platform
pledged to international postwar cooperation to keep the
peace. A resolution was adopted, calling upon each Republican member of Congress "immediately after the re-
convening of Congress to sponsor and support Congressional action pledging cooperation by the United States
in world affairs." [2]

President Roosevelt was campaigning as Commander in
Chief (the title he now used rather than that of President) and many in Congress felt he should face an accounting for blunders as well as achievements. I was
among those who demanded the true story of Pearl Harbor, thus profoundly misjudging the mood of the people.
The theme of the Administration was "Give Roosevelt a
Democratic Congress." Responding patriotically, even

Republicans shelved their mistrust of Roosevelt, fearful of a change in the White House in wartime. Roosevelt avoided Woodrow Wilson's direct appeal for a Congress of his party—but left it to his adherents to carry the message. Republicans like myself abetted his cause by playing down our bipartisan support of most Administration measures since the advent of war. We compounded this error of omission with criticism, which the public rejected while the war continued. I know of Republican contributors (and their wives) who furnished funds for the election of Republican Congressmen and then voted the Democratic ticket.

Although the loyal opposition is forced to play the lesser role in Congress, it can still be valuable, and should exploit its duties. There was such an instance in March 1943, when the House Banking and Currency Committee met in an abruptly-summoned joint session with the now-disbanded Coinage Committee.

The topic was a new monetary stabilization bill. The witness was the Secretary of the Treasury, Henry J. Morgenthau, Jr., appearing with a squad of advisers. Morgenthau had an aversion to testifying personally, so, as was his custom, he called on an aide to explain plans to manage an international stabilization fund through a new world agency. This witness was Harry Dexter White, the enigmatic economist whose relations with Soviet agents later came under scrutiny.

White's highly technical presentation roused questions from every Congressman. As the committee's junior member, I was the last interrogator, which gave me time to study the bill, none of us having seen it in advance.

"This bill," I told White when my turn came, "would give the Russians a veto over any devaluation, in fact over any change in the value of any other nation's currency."

White retorted that I had missed the entire intent of the bill. Patiently, I disagreed.

Our prolonged interchange was followed by a colloquy on the House floor on April 8, 1943, with the late Representative August H. Andresen (R.-Minn.). To my questions about the plan's unexplained veto provision, Andresen agreed that power to devalue the currencies of participating nations could definitely be "read into" the Treasury plan.

The Treasury plan was thereafter quietly abandoned. No record of this hearing remains in the files of the House Committee.

The story behind this curiously suspicious proposal seems to have died with Harry Dexter White, who suffered a fatal heart attack in 1948, three days after he testified at length before the House Un-American Activities Committee. There was talk of an inquiry, but the attention of Congress and the country was focused elsewhere.

Political careers can be built on the lessons of defeat. In November 1944, I learned the perils of inviting attack without strengthening fences in my own district. The moral is there for every brash Congressional sophomore to ponder. Republicans should mark it well, for G.O.P. legislators are still too scarce.

I fell into a brash blunder as I was settling down to my second term. On April 11, 1943, a group of junior members attended a White House briefing on the progress of the war. After optimistic reports by miltary and Naval officers, the President chatted with his visitors in groups. One topic in addition to war was a strike threat by the United Mine Workers.

I asked what Mr. Roosevelt planned to do about John L. Lewis, the flamboyantly militant president of the UMW. "Oh," the President chuckled, "I've got John L. Lewis behind the eight ball."

Tactlessly, I blurted: "Do you think you can keep him there?"

There was silence and a long, unwavering, baleful glare that seemed to miss nothing about me—past, present or future. It may have lasted fifteen seconds. To me, it seemed an hour.

One does not challenge any President to his face with impunity. Roosevelt in particular brooked no naysayers. Worse yet, I was questioning his power of persuasion, in which he took great pride, and doing it in the presence of others.

The tension dissolved in a small Rooseveltian laugh. The President addressed his next remark to someone else. But the moment was remembered.

In 1944, the President saw fit to campaign in the Sixth Congressional District of Pennsylvania—for my opponent. I could have done without the honor.

As a Naval Reservist, I had chafed at the compulsions that kept me a civilian. I tried twice to return to the fleet by pulling the wires available to a Congressman, but was balked both times by a Presidential order against accepting members of Congress for active duty, whatever their reserve status.

On my second try, I went all the way to Secretary of the Navy, Frank Knox. His letter of rejection, dated June 16, 1942, advised me that he and the Secretary of War had just received a military directive from the President ". . . to return all members of the Senate or the House, who are now serving with the military forces, to an inactive status on July 1, or in case they are outside the continental limits of the United States, to restore them to an inactive status immediately upon their return to the United States."

On June 17, Secretary Knox telephoned to say I could serve a limited period of active duty. I had to settle for that. I went to serve in Naval Intelligence until all members of Congress serving with the armed forces were ordered to return.

The Representatives ordered returned to Congress included the promising young Texas Democrat, Lyndon B. Johnson. I never understood why Congressman Johnson was able to remain on active duty for a number of months after the effective date of the order until I recently reread Secretary Knox's letter. The recall affected those officers outside the continental limits of the United States "immediately upon their return." Congressman Johnson just did not *return* to the United States!

Since I had been rebuffed in three requests for active duty, I ran in 1942 for a second term and was re-elected. During the 1944 campaign, I made very few speeches in my District and they seem to have been the wrong ones.

In some of them, I told my constituents to decide whether they wanted to return me to Congress or to the Navy. By some 2,300 votes, they elected me to the Navy. Suddenly, I became one of the few officers in the armed forces to arrive there by that unique route.

The day after the Seventy-Eighth Congress expired, I returned to active duty, this time with the Third Amphibious Force in the Pacific aboard the U.S.S. *Mt. Olympus.*

On the day of the surrender ceremonies aboard the U.S.S. *Missouri,* I was junior deck officer on our flagship's bridge, leading a 14-mile parade of occupation troops into Tokyo Bay. We steamed past the *Missouri* at the moment the Japanese were signing the surrender document. Thus I eyewitnessed the end of a war I had voted to declare.

During service in the Navy I came to realize more than I ever had as a Representative how deeply our military personnel felt about their hopes for a better postwar world.

I listened at long evening sessions in officers' wardrooms

to endless talk, born of frustration, about what "they" (i.e. "the politicians") ought to do about defense, peace, the home front. Many an officer spoke of going into politics. Some of them did, including Commander Harold Stassen and Lt. Richard Nixon.

I had been one of those politicians. One wished fervently that many of those who had known war at firsthand would commit themselves to careers of public service. I decided to write a book, a sort of how-to-do-it book on going into politics.

I reached another decision. I would return to Congress —if I could.

III

NOT QUITE WASHINGTON

"I'm going to give them hell."

HARRY S. TRUMAN

"They have . . . reached a new low in mud-slinging . . . That is the campaign I have refused to wage and I never will."

THOMAS E. DEWEY

FOR Republicans, the party's stunning setback in the 1948 Presidential election was a shocking reminder of the campaigner's first commandment: Take nothing for granted. I played a part in that classic exercise in over-confidence, although I neither expected nor asked for the role.

I was on my way to keep a standing engagement with my father to watch a telecast of the heavyweight championship bout between Joe Louis and Jersey Joe Walcott when I received a surprising telephone call. It was Mason Owlett, our National Chairman, urging me to hurry to a conference in his suite at Philadelphia's Bellevue-Stratford Hotel.

Dewey was preparing to choose a National Chairman to succeed the ultraconservative Representative B. Carroll Reece of Tennessee. Owlett said Dewey wanted to name a Pennsylvania Congressman, partly in recognition of Pennsylvania's key role in nailing down his nomination, and also as a link with Republicans in Congress, where he had never served. In addition, he said, the new chairman should have had experience with a state-wide election and have seen active service in World War II.

"I think you're the only one who fits the qualifications," were Owlett's startling words. "I've talked to Governor Dewey and he is very favorable to you."

At about that time Louis knocked out Walcott. Jersey Joe's work in Philadelphia was over. Mine was just beginning.

When I was released from the Navy in April 1946, my only thought had been to regain my seat in Congress. I had buckled down full time to turning the tables on Herbert J. McGlinchey, the Democrat who had defeated me two years before. I returned as a third term "mustang" in the House, enthusiastic about serving for the first time with the Republican majority.

Without ever anticipating the Chairmanship, I had already begun to work for Dewey's nomination. His demonstrated competence, recognition of America's international responsibilities, and vigorous campaign to unseat Roosevelt in 1944 earned him, I felt, the right to a peacetime try for the Presidency. I had recommended to him the strategy that eventually won him the bulk of Pennsylvania's convention votes that swung the tide in his favor on the third ballot.

Some time after 3:00 A.M., I went alone to Dewey's suite. I found the Governor unwilted by the hour. His thinking was as ordered as his well-pressed suit. His dark eyes focused on me continuously. In his controlled bari-

tone he cross-examined me in a manner that was thorough
even for the former racket-busting District Attorney of
New York.

In spite of the hour, another conference began with the
arrival of Dewey's running mate, Earl Warren, California's Governor; big Bill Knowland, then the Golden
State's only Republican Senator; Herb Brownell and
Owlett.

Dewey put me forward for the Chairmanship with a
commendatory reference to the sea duty as a source of
good future publicity. I would be the only war veteran on
the National Committee. In 1948, the vote of recently
returned war veterans was important. He remembered
that many of them had written on their absentee ballots in
1944: "But Tom Dewey in '48."

Of the others, Tom Dewey inquired: "Is Hugh Scott
acceptable to all of you?" There was no dissent.

My friend, Frank McGlinn, who sat up all night with
me when I was notified of my selection as National Chairman, reminds me that just as dawn was breaking, I arose
without explanation, left the hotel and walked the eight
blocks to Independence Hall and found, somewhat to my
surprise, that the old doors were open.

I walked in and for perhaps half an hour stood by the
Liberty Bell, reflecting on the night's surprises, groping
for guidance and inspiration from the sturdy old walls
that cradled the Constitution and witnessed the first stirrings of our two-party system. I wondered what sort of
impact my Chairmanship might have on the evolution of
that system. Like most Philadelphians I seldom saw the
Liberty Bell unless visitors came to town. But there was
reassurance in the cracked bronze bulk of the great bell
that sonorously voiced the birth of American freedom.

Later in the day, I received more insight into the terms
and conditions of my new job at a meeting with a group

of Dewey associates headed by J. Russel Sprague, the New York National Committeeman.

I was told, in effect, that I was to be a contact man exclusively. Sprague passed the word in his blunt, abrasive way in an exchange with shaggy Ed Jaeckle, the most powerful G.O.P. leader in upstate New York. Pointing a monitory finger at me, he instructed: "Let's give it to him straight. *You* keep the party happy. Brownell runs the campaign."

I was to cultivate and maintain friendly ties between national headquarters and elements in a Republican spectrum, ranging from those to the right of Reece on over to the left of Dewey. I was to do a lot of traveling, working to keep party leaders informed and, I hoped, happy. But I was on notice that the harmonious strategy of the campaign was in the hands of the (till-then) successful Republican team in New York.

Under an agreement without precedent in the party's history, Brownell and a task force drawn largely from Dewey's confident New York organization were to run the campaign staff from a command center in Washington.

In four grueling months, I visited all the forty-eight states then in the Union; but I was asked to attend only one meeting of the strategy committee. Brownell presided and most of the dozen other participants were New York professionals. Brownell, always calm and businesslike, was on the telephone during much of the meeting and reported conditions good around the country. He said nothing then or later to indicate anxiety, except one uncomfortable passing comment late in October that sticks in my memory: a wish that the election were that very day.

It must be recorded that I missed the one chance I might have had to influence the 1948 campaign. It arose when I met with Tom Dewey to report on the twenty-eight states I had already visited. I told the Governor I had advised party gatherings everywhere to wait until the campaign got underway; that Dewey and Warren, both former prosecuting attorneys, were preparing to draw a stinging indictment against the Administration and then lay it on the line to the voters. I told Dewey I had been spreading the word that he was going to come out fighting. His pattern, I suggested might be a much-discussed speech he delivered in 1944 at Oklahoma City just as his first Presidential campaign was warming up. He beamed that speech straight against Roosevelt, accusing the President of "frivolous mudslinging tactics . . . ridicule, demagogy and wisecracks" used to cover a "desperately bad record." [1] In political terms, it was a "strong" speech, and it drew strong reactions.

"That was the worst speech I ever made," Dewey replied, thereby shooting down my working model for 1948.

The Governor said the decision had been reached to wage a low-keyed campaign, using rather bland speeches, position papers and statements focused toward moral issues. It was not his intention, he said, to help raise the level of excitement to the pitch toward which Truman seemed to be working.

By ignoring Truman, it was argued, Dewey would deprive his opponent of the publicity that grows out of controversy. He left me with the feeling that he hoped to muffle Truman's impact by waging his own affirmative campaign. This strategy was developed by the inner circle of Dewey's Albany administration: Brownell, Sprague, Jaeckle and Superintendent of Banks Elliot V. Bell.

Dewey's blueprint for the celebrated "high-level" campaign of 1948 disquieted me and I said so, briefly and respectfully. The Governor asked me to come back later in the evening to discuss my reservations with him in New York's Victorian Executive Mansion. I begged off—rack-

ing up what I now feel was my greatest single error of the
1948 campaign.

Perhaps, as a still-junior Congressman, I was too much
in awe of the decisive Governor, with his piercing black
eyes, crisp manner and reputation for carefully considered action. I erred when I failed to point out that this
tactic blithely overlooked the access to publicity that is
built into the modern White House—especially when the
incumbent is a picturesquely out-spoken scrapper. In
Dewey's previous career he had no glass chin. He was un-
rivalled as a champion slugger both in court, State House
and on the stump. He won his former political fights by
fighting. But this time he switched. I now suspect that
Dewey's inner circle had no stomach for a battle of personalities with Harry Truman. There was an acute sensitivity to ridicule in the Dewey camp.

Together these were fatal miscalculations. Truman was
grabbing headlines with assaults on what he dubbed the
"Eighty-worst Congress." Yet, I believed then, as I still
do, that its record was better in terms of actual accom-
plishment and long-range effect than that of any Congress in which I have ever served.

That trail blazing, sometimes stubborn, always controversial Republican-controlled Congress had faced the
problem of reversing government machinery to make
peace instead of war. Housing, living costs, and efficiency
in government became prime campaign issues. To a public
fed up with wartime controls, sky-high taxes, massive
spending and a "mess" in Washington, the Republicans
raised the sensitive question: "Had enough?"

That Congress acted responsibly in foreign policy,
where its far-reaching decisions strengthened the nation's
security. In domestic matters, although there was some ac-
commodation to the standpat "conservative coalition" of
senior Republicans and Southern Democrats, the record

was still constructive. There was a pragmatic acceptance of many of the New Deal's uses of Federal power, despite a tendency among some Republicans to attack the philosophy of some of the very programs they supported. Action and ideology do not always coincide.

Another Truman stratagem trapped Republican leaders with the abortive "Turnip Day" [2] session that convened July 26, 1948, and was to last only twelve days. With the campaign already geared up, the Democratic President confronted the Republican Congress with bills from its own platform. In effect he was saying, "You're for these programs, now put up or shut up!"

The request was outlandish, and it infuriated the majority leadership. In two weeks Truman wanted Congress to enact a two-year legislative agenda. Convinced that the public would see through the transparently political motivations of "Turnip Day," the impatient Congress did little except fulminate against Truman. Then it went home to campaign.

By doing nothing, Republicans abetted Truman's charges that they were too insincere to enact their own platform pledges. This got them into a backstage row with Dewey who was anxious for a record of selective action. The only first-rank Congressional leader who supported Dewey on this was Arthur H. Vandenberg of Michigan, then the Senate's farsighted President pro tempore. He was one of a group of senior Senate Republicans who met with me as National Chairman when the Turnip Day session was about to begin. Senator Lodge of Massachusetts joined Vandenberg in backing Dewey's position. Blunt Bob Taft decried Truman's political motivation, said it was obvious the whole program could not be passed even if it merited approval, and urged, in effect, that Congress go on strike.

"Bob, we ought to do whatever we can to show that we

are trying to use the two weeks as best we can," said Vandenberg. "Then we have a better case to take before the public."

"No," Taft said at length, "we're just not going to give that fellow anything." To anyone familiar with Taft's terse conversational style, that was the end of it.

Brilliant Bob Taft was not above such Olympian perversity, even as he threw his logical mind and considerable influence behind genuinely progressive housing, education and health bills.

Truman had a plan to siphon away the support among Midwestern farmers which the G.O.P. had taken for granted. He and his allies waited until the campaign's strenuous final fortnight to make a serious issue of a sudden shortage of bins for storage of price-supported surplus grain in the historically Republican farm belt. Truman pinned the blame in the usual place—the Eightieth Congress, which used its economy ax to slash funds for the Federal grain-storage program. Of the Republican majority whose votes helped pass the Marshall Plan and the Greek-Turkish aid program, Truman chose to remember that they "stuck a pitchfork in the farmer's back." [3]

Republicans had a good case and should have made the most of it. Dewey could have pointed out that leading Democrats in the Congressional farm bloc had failed to foresee the need to provide grain storage space when the farm bill was being drafted. Republican farm leaders could have nailed the point down with a pledge that the Dewey Administration would promptly correct the oversight. All this, of course is 20/20 hindsight.

Two weeks before the election, I joined Democratic National Chairman J. Howard McGrath on a pre-election radio program with the late Edward R. Murrow. I offered to bet a new Stetson hat (a Philadelphia product) on the outcome of the Presidential race. On the air, McGrath

said it was all right with him. Then, as we were leaving the
studio, he gave me the tip-off on his real mood. He would
send me the hat, he said, grimly, the next Wednesday or
Thursday. When the implications of his words sank in,
he added a qualification: ". . . assuming you win."
McGrath later told me he was not convinced Truman
could make it until he witnessed the fervent response to a
speech Truman gave in Brooklyn at the windup of his
"give-'em-hell" campaign.

As National Chairman, I hit the Truman Administration as hard as I could. My attacks were pretty harsh and
Truman fired back at me just as harshly. This made me a
kind of lightning rod, but I had no reason to resent the
role. I suspected it was just what Dewey's advisers had
anticipated.

In 1963, Truman came to Philadelphia to attend a
nonpolitical celebration and I was invited by the Mayor to
be there. I found myself standing immediately behind Mr.
Truman at the Liberty Bell, and I said over his shoulder,
"Mr. President, I particularly want to shake hands with
you because I feel I am one who contributed substantially
to your victory."

Mr. Truman turned around and didn't recognize me. I
thought he would know me and accept my joke about being Tom Dewey's National Chairman, but he didn't. He
said, "Well, God bless you for that."

At a luncheon following the ceremony, he asked the
man next to him who I was. After he found out, he very
pointedly talked to the other ten people at the table, addressing them one by one. He did not say a word to me or
as much as look at me.

One day in 1966, however, the former President slipped
into his old seat in the Senate, and Democratic and Republican leaders promptly got up to take notice of the
presence of former Senator Truman. I asked for recog-

nition and opened with mention of my service as Republican National Chairman during the Dewey-Truman campaign. I went on to say that it was a pleasure to pay tribute to the former Senator, and I brought in my little joke about contributing to his election in 1948.

Then I went further and said I felt that as the history of his period was written, he would loom larger and larger. I never would have thought this in 1948, but I believe it now. And this time, he favored me with a smile and a courteous bow, and I think he has forgiven me for the 1963 incident when I sneaked up on his blind side.

Many Republican insiders under-estimated Truman as a campaigner and as a man. In the course of four successive defeats, Republicans had built Roosevelt into a political superman. There was contempt for the very human Missourian who seemed so uncomfortable in F.D.R.'s mantle. The courage and fundamental patriotism that assure Harry Truman's place in history were shrouded in the smoke of political battle.

My first inkling of how the campaign was to end came when the early returns from the Connecticut towns were relayed to the National Committee's "victory" headquarters at the Statler Hotel in Washington. They were the same Connecticut towns I had watched for as the returns were tallied at Willkie Headquarters in 1940. An optimistic crowd was gathering as I combed the ticker for word from the towns I had learned to consider barometers of national election trends. The barometer was falling.

The returns from New Haven, Bridgeport and Stamford, Hartford, New Britain and Norwalk were steadily and distressingly worse for the Republicans than the equivalent figures from 1944.

Here I was, less than an hour after the Eastern polls closed, uncomfortably aware that I might be National Chairman of a losing campaign. The big Statler ballroom

was primed for a night of celebration. I kept my doubts
from the party workers, whose hopes soared when Mary-
land and Pennsylvania came in dependably for Dewey.
But the word from the Middle West was bad. Historically
Republican Iowa was going to Truman, as was Wisconsin.
The candidates were neck and neck in Illinois and Ohio.
California's late returns were close—too close.

It was half past four when I talked to Brownell in New
York on the expensive $1,500 "hot line" we used but twice
that night. He reported matter-of-factly that he and the
candidate were going home soon. Whether we had won or
lost depended on Ohio and Illinois and California, and we
wouldn't know for sure until morning. I left the Statler
ballroom at 5:10 A.M. to spend a few restless hours in one
of the hotel's bedrooms. The next morning, groggy with
loss of sleep, I telephoned Howard McGrath and told him,
"You win the hat."

Columnist Joseph C. Harsch recalls as "one of my most
poignant memories" the frustrated morning-after reaction of the party's National Chairman:

> It's a good thing. Those mastodons wouldn't listen to
> me. They had to learn their lesson. Now, maybe,
> they'll go out and [back] some social legislation.[4]

Brownell called back the next day to discuss the advisability of fighting for re-counts in some of the maddeningly close contests. The margin in Ohio was 7,107 votes;
in California it was 17,865; in Illinois, 33,612. A swing of
less than 30,000 votes out of nearly eleven million just in
those big states alone would have given Dewey 267 electoral votes, one more than the required majority. Instead,
the count was 303 for Truman, 189 for Dewey and 39 for
Strom Thurmond and his States Rights Democrats. It
was a cliffhanger, but it was still defeat. We decided after
a series of calls to let the record stand. The odds against

an overturn on re-count in all three states were simply too long.

Dewey called, too, on that gray morning after. He had missed the hope of his life, but his iron self-control was unswerving. The Governor said he wanted to thank me for what I had done on his behalf, and generously let me know he felt himself responsible for the outcome; it wasn't anyone's fault but his. He named no specific causes for his defeat, and I have never since heard him voice an opinion in this area, other than to wonder why no one in his camp ever recounted to him a single report of the growing farmer disaffection.

While Dewey kept silence, the Republican factionalism that had been held below the surface during the campaign erupted into open, bitter recrimination. Party regulars of the Taft school denounced Dewey and all the "Eastern" influences associated with his "unity" campaign. Republican progressives returned the fire with pointed suggestions that the outcome would have been different had "unity" been a fact, as well as a slogan.

Brownell warned me right after the defeat to secure for squalls in the National Chairmanship. "You're in for a rough time," he predicted. "I feel sorry for what they'll be doing to you." He said the party should understand that he, as campaign manager, had made the tactical decisions. He said he expected me to say so whenever I felt I should in the inevitably stormy months that lay ahead. I said I was no cry baby. I had to live with the fact that we had lost. I would do the best I could and see what happened next.

I did not have long to wait.

IV

THE BATTLE OF OMAHA

*"Those mastodons . . . had to learn their les-
son. Now maybe they'll go out and back some
good social legislation."*

HUGH SCOTT

As the hand-picked National Chairman of a defeated
Presidential candidate, I became the public custodian of a
bitter feud that had been dampened, but hardly quenched,
during the campaign. My one personal consolation was
that the 1948 election had returned me to the House for a
fourth term even though the Democrats had regained
Congressional control.

At the same time, National Headquarters was deluged
with Republican self-criticism. Swarming in also came the
non mea culpa types, the vindictive blame-throwers who
had themselves snafued matters but who now were hunting
for alibis and scapegoats. We were told that we needed
something more than negatives. There were demands for
party leadership capable of conceiving a positive program
and stating it in terms the people could understand.

In a letter to the New York *Herald Tribune* dated December 10, 1948 the Young Republican Clubs of Harvard, M.I.T., Wellesley and Radcliffe urged the Republican Party to "decide now in 1948 what kind of candidate it must run for President in 1952, and then develop a consistent Congressional record which that candidate can support and which will support the candidate." This sober criticism was aimed at the 1948 campaign so far as "the record of a Republican Congress spoke louder than the promises of the Republican platform and Presidential candidate." I welcomed this student demand for it, which echoed the dissatisfaction I had felt throughout the campaign. Like other students and center line Republicans, they voiced their hopes when they wrote that "a generation brought up under twenty years of the New Deal expect a forward-looking, progressive, internationalist policy as the basic doctrine of the party administering our national government . . . ."

In words that remain valid after nearly two decades, Kentucky's independently progressive Republican Senator, John Sherman Cooper, said, "The Party must be essentially a middle of the road party. It must recognize change, the need for continued programs and an obligation to meet the needs of the people. It must say plainly that it is the party of all the people and not the party of any particular group—labor, industry or the farmer." [1]

Soon after the election I asserted my belief that constant, hard-hitting criticism of the party in power, soundly based on fact, is the duty of the minority under our political system.

Dewey's unexpected refusal of this role and his deliberately low-keyed campaign had contributed to the defeat that postponed once again the victory needed to cement a fragmented party. This fifth successive Republican loss in the Big Race agitated conservative frustrations and deferred progressive goals. From November 1948 until the next August, I was at the swirling center of a fight for control of the party machinery. The climactic showdown was deferred until the 1952 convention.

As long as I was Chairman, I strove for a formula to bridge the factional gap. Without it, I could not get the Republican house in order. As the party's chief house-keeper I was too busy even to sweep dirt under the rug; I was doing my best to keep it from wafting in through the doors and windows.

In mid-December, I took a step tried by other Republican Chairmen: I proposed a G.O.P. policy conference. There were good precedents. In 1943, the Mackinac Island conference had cleared the way for the party's break with isolationism by endorsing the principle of American participation in a postwar world organization. As a preliminary to the highly successful 1946 campaign that swept the Eightieth Congress into power, Congressional Republicans had conferred and agreed to a persuasive declaration of principles. I floated trial balloons in the press proposing that the National Committee organize a conference that would take in Congressional and state leaders, Republican governors, former presidential candidates and members of the National Committee. The concept was shot down ten days later by Senator Taft, then the influential leader of the 6-member Senate Republican Policy Committee. The Old Guard feared limitations on the party leadership in Congress—even though the most constructive leadership at the Mackinac Island conference had come from Congress.

There were already rumblings for a "new face" in the Chairmanship. I retorted that mine was newer than any on the National Committee.

As it became obvious that I should call an early meeting of the National Committee, I conferred with Dewey about the site. After the campaign, Dewey had urged me to keep in touch with him and with Representative Joseph W. Martin of Massachusetts, whom the election had demoted from Speaker of the House back to leader of the Republican minority.

Dewey and Martin agreed with my plan to send out a call for a 2-day meeting in Omaha, Nebraska, starting January 26, 1949.

Anxious to get on with the party replastering job, I used the interval to send a form letter to our mailing list of 22,000 asking suggestions on how to improve the G.O.P. We got back over six hundred replies and we stirred a lot of pungent advice, especially with one question: "Where did our party fail?"

For a Chairman seeking guidance, the experiment was at once rewarding and disconcerting. Our correspondents tended to start off with some form of the statement, "I am a loyal Republican, but . . . ." —and then they split along the same old cleavage lines.

About half wanted the party to appear progressive in its responses to Democratic reform proposals. The other half held out for the brand of "real Republicanism" that gives the voters a black-and-white choice on every issue. For the letter that bade us stop being "the party of big business and anti-labor" there was another that berated the G.O.P. for failure to "condemn the labor racketeers."

We were advised on the one hand to "get back the confidence of the people" and admonished on the other to become a "militant, fighting, conservative body." We were upbraided for running a "me-too" campaign, for losing the confidence of the farmers and the interest of the younger generation. I gulped at a terse note from Brooklyn: "Dear Mr. Chairman: Drop dead!"

Among my conclusions on these thousands of letters was this one: "The Republican party must get down to grass roots and brass tacks."

Before leaving for the party meeting at Omaha, I sketched the framework for a Republican program for the people in these terms:

Assuming a better and more secure life is the American goal, the people should decide what they can justly expect of government and what they should be free to do for themselves. Where there is a role for government in the attainment of aspirations, determinations should be made whether the job can best be done at the local, state or national level. Where government has a responsibility, my party has an obligation and an opportunity to offer workable programs. Where the responsibility rests with the individual, my party has a duty to shield him from government interference.

These guides, I felt, left ample room for a program that was both Republican and acceptable.

Jack Bell of the Associated Press reported an interview with me on January 19, 1949: "What he had in mind, Scott said, is to weld together a party that has its conservatives and its liberals but is made up mostly of the middle-of-the-road folk he thinks can cast a lot of votes if they are stirred up." [2]

On the eve of the Omaha meeting, Senator Taft announced that Congressional Republicans expected to have a voice in the National Committee session. At the same time, he objected to a member of Congress serving as Chairman and demanded that I resign either the Chairmanship or my seat in Congress.

A few days before, I had called at Taft's house in Georgetown to tell him I intended so long as I was National Chairman to remain neutral toward any and all possible candidates for the Presidency. Taft was eating orange slices from "my good friend John Jackson" (Republican National Committeeman of Louisiana). He reacted coldly, making it clear that he never expected me, as a Dewey man, to be for him.

"Don't you think the Chairman should be neutral?" I asked.

"Yes, he should be *neutral*," Taft replied, bearing down so hard on the last word that it was clear he disqualified me.

Taft was circumspect through most of a radio interview with Bert Andrews, of the old New York *Herald Tribune*, that focused on the Omaha meeting. In the closing minute, Andrews threw in an afterthought question: Did Taft think there should be a change in the National Chairmanship?

"Yes, I think so," Taft replied without elaboration.

He threw away the line, as he almost always did. But those four little words from the conservative champion were soon to make big medicine in Omaha, where standpatters on the National Committee construed Taft's casual words as an open invitation to unseat the Chairman.

I found myself confronted at Omaha with an improbable Midwestern coalition that proved once again that politics does indeed make strange bedfellows. The Taft forces were lining up with supporters of ever-hopeful Harold E. Stassen.

The Taft-Stassen combine aimed to build a counterforce to repel any move to use the effective Dewey organization to support another candidate. The new champion of the Dewey people appeared even then to be Eisenhower.

The "Battle of Omaha" appeared to press and public as a brawl among defeated politicians. But underneath the wrangling and the hunt for a scapegoat was a crucially important contest for the future direction of the party.

I was fighting from and for the middle position. I was beleaguered, but fortunately not alone. In Republican politics, the men of the center are at a disadvantage in

such skirmishes. Zeal seems to come more readily to
protagonists of outward positions—sometimes way out—
than to believers in the median approach. Loaded catch-
words and inflammatory adjectives are better suited to
mission-conscious zealots of the left and right than to
sober-minded adherents of the center. The Aristotelian
mean often lacks political sex appeal and the political
power of the blast.

One embarrassment muted the fervor of those who had
hoped to turn the Omaha meeting into a political lynch-
ing. Most of them were irretrievably on the record in support of the conduct of the Dewey campaign. It was a confidential record, but all present knew of its existence.

The evidence consisted of a series of recorded talks between Brownell and Republican National Committee
members and state chairmen all over the country. Mindful
of post-election recriminations in 1944, the campaign
manager had closed the 1948 campaign by placing conference calls to Republican leaders in all forty-eight
states. Virtually all the leaders praised the campaign, and
outside the South and a few border states, they predicted
that Dewey would carry their states. The one notable exception was big, affable cattleman Harry Darby, the
Kansas Committeeman and a staunch friend of Dewey's,
who warned the Chairman of a dangerous slippage of Republican strength in the corn belt.

"We should carry Kansas, but I don't like the way
things are going. We've been losing ground out here
lately," Darby reported with prophetic candor.

All at Omaha knew that the tapes of those incrim-
inating revelations had been turned over to me after the
election. Word spread that I had brought them with me,
and reporters began to barrage me with questions. I said I
had "no intention of using the recordings to the disadvantage of any National Committeeman." I suggested that

"If there was any challenge by people inclined to say 'I told you so' after the election, then the recordings would indicate that memory can be a very faulty thing."

Then there was a public demand for my resignation. Anonymous letters circulated, and the rough tactics grew rougher. I was portrayed as the advance man for a third Dewey candidacy in 1952. After consultation with Darby, Owlett and Leonard W. Hall, I said that I put face value on Dewey's announcement that he had foresworn any ambitions for the Presidency.

The Senate Republican Policy Committee forwarded a restrictive request that a decision on my plan to call a Republican Policy Conference be held up pending study by a special committee of the National Committee.

From another part of the Republican forest, that outspoken Yankee loner, Senator Charlie Tobey of New Hampshire, urged the party to stop "yelling 'socialism' at every proposal that is made for social welfare" and to ". . . develop a heart as well as a head." [3]

Taft presented a compromise proposal that the National Committee choose a special subcommittee to try for agreement on the Chairmanship. I agreed, but insisted on remaining Chairman. I pointed out once again that I had been elected for a 4-year term.

The 7-member subcommittee gave up after I rejected a proposal that I withdraw from contention. I felt I could not surrender without letting down my friends, particularly those in the Western states. Some had cheerfully risked home state problems to stand with their beleaguered Chairman.

I said that the coalition lacked enough votes to unseat me, but it had enough to be embarrassing and to insist on a larger voice in Committee affairs.

As the various coalition groups tried to work out solutions, I flatly refused to resign under fire, whatever the circumstances. At the same time, I was fed up with the controversy that seemed built into the job, and with the continuing deliberate sabotage of my work.

I said to Owlett: "Mason, the only future in this job is a resort to tranquilizers or isolation beyond telephones. Let's hunt for a man all can trust freely, unscarred by 1948 and unbranded by any candidate, but I won't quit until we find him."

Harry Darby averred: "We'll stick with you. A man's entitled to a run for his marbles."

It was agreed that we would fight next day's ouster move.

The expected motion to declare the National Chairmanship vacant was filed at the National Committee's opening session on January 27. Its sponsor was Maryland's National Committeeman Jacob France, an accomplished and persuasive speaker. Unlike others among my critics, France also came from a state which had gone for Dewey.

The burden of Jake France's argument was that Governor Dewey wanted a third try at the White House. In a voice hoarsened by oratory, he demanded: "Hugh, are you staying here to help Tom Dewey?" [4]

As he reached for the water pitcher, I poured a glassful for him as he remarked: "Hugh, I'm still dry."

"Help yourself, Jake," I said with a grin. "I wouldn't want to dry you up. You're doing fine."

Not doing quite as fine was the noted author, Clarence Budington Kelland, National Committeeman from Arizona. His charge: "I spent much time back at national headquarters during the campaign and I had a feeling Mr. Scott was only a ghost wandering around looking for a campaign to haunt." [5]

Bud Kelland, an excitable, wizened, monkey-on-a-stick

sort of a person, did not confide that in all the time he had
spent around headquarters, he had voiced only loud admiration for the way the campaign was going, plus pleas
for more funds for Arizona. More money went to Arizona,
but Bud didn't. He spent the greater part of the time at
his home in New York City.

Spangler of Iowa and Hallanan of West Virginia
warmed to the attack as they seconded France's motion.
Spangler said the committee ought not to "endorse our ig-
nominious defeat" by keeping me as chairman. This was
too much for my friend Harry Sommers who was aware of
Spangler's praise of the Dewey strategy in the last week
of the campaign.

The Omaha *World-Herald* of January 27, 1949, carried this blow-by-blow account:

> Angrily Harry Sommers of Georgia jumped to his
> feet.
>
> "This atmosphere of recrimination and revenge
> makes me feel there is no hope for the future," he
> asserted.
>
> He deplored enemies of Mr. Scott "who express
> great regard for the Chairman while knifing him in
> the back."
>
> "My experience with Mr. Spangler causes me to
> feel that he utterly lacks principle."
>
> The room hummed.
>
> Up popped Mr. Scott to say: "I'm sure you would
> like to withdraw that last remark."
>
> "No," said Mr. Sommers. "I would not like to with-
> draw it."
>
> Nevertheless the National Chairman directed it be
> stricken from the record.

George L. Hart, proxy for the D.C. National Committeeman (now a Federal Judge) said: "We say to Hugh

Scott, 'Hugh, you are a lovely fellow; you are really an awfully nice fellow. We have to cut your throat. We love you but we are going to cut your throat.' "

Said Ezra Whitla of Idaho, regarding the election results: "If we made a mistake, let us as men and women of honor stand up and say the mistake was ours." [6]

Mason Owlett of Pennsylvania made the point that he had no apology for supporting Governor Dewey—"just as most of you did."

I made no personal defense of myself before Mac Faries of California forced the vote. The tense roll call bore out my overnight tally; the motion to unseat me was tabled fifty-four to fifty. I could complete my unsalaried 4-year penalty tour if I wanted to. In my own mind I was already sure that I should not stay on beyond the 1950 midterm elections.

Meanwhile, I believed the Omaha vote brought time to find a successor who might stand a better chance than I of uniting the party. Resignation under fire in January, 1949, would have amounted to surrender of a strategic beachhead for constructive Republicanism. It was a viewpoint stronger in the country than in the Congressional leadership.

Those were the factors behind my decision to stand and fight to hold the Chairmanship of a party whose recent stunning defeat widened and deepened the old cleavages between its warring wings.

I did not make the decision without legal advice that a Chairman's election by the National Convention was a 4-year term that could not be truncated by the National Committee without a change in the party rules. But I still believed that I was morally subject to a no-confidence vote, and so stated before the decision on the France motion.

I felt I had set a useful precedent. Its usefulness was

affirmed twelve years later when Dean Burch resigned the Chairmanship he had held through the disastrous 1964 campaign after it became clear that he lacked clear majority support on the National Committee.

The Omaha meeting staved off a showdown, but certainly contributed nothing to the party's forward motion. The machinery was still cracked; the gears were still clanking. The bickering Republican leaders at Omaha reached no agreement on clear directions for their party. There was no sign that they could get together on a program that would appeal to the voters.

The National Committee had barely adjourned before Representative Clarence Brown of Ohio hoisted the first storm signal. He suggested for publication that "it might be no more than six months before Scott's hard-won retention of his office is challenged again." [7]

I had escaped the fire, but the frying pan was still sizzling. The conditions were hardly conducive to orderly development of constructive long-term policy. But I had signed on to do a job, to the extent that it was possible under the unremitting harassment of the anti-Dewey forces.

In this spirit, I resumed the more normal role of a spokesman for the minority by presenting the case against the party in power. When I addressed the Convention of the California Republican Assembly on February 5, 1949, I plugged anew for a national Republican policy conference to give our forces badly-needed direction. Through the Californians, I was hoping to sell the conference concept to the newly-appointed strategy committee.

Mindful of Senate sensitivity, I was careful to add that "during the next two years national policies can be implemented only by Republican members of the Senate and House." [8]

I twitted the Truman Administration for its seeming indifference to early action in the Eighty-first Congress on the Twenty Point Program which Truman had demanded that the Eightieth Congress pass at its special 15-day session. I dared the Administration to finance new proposals by repealing the Republican income tax reduction bill. Senator Karl Mundt of South Dakota mentioned that it was the kind of fighting speech we needed during the campaign.

At the request of newly-elected State Chairman Ray Bliss of Ohio, whose calm friendship I had long valued, I made the Lincoln Day speech at Columbus the following night. In an overture to Taft supporters, I said the loss of Senator Taft in the 1950 election would be "an inconceivable thing which must not happen."

My new book, *How to Go into Politics*, was announced at this time. One commentator suggested that it be sold together with a bound copy of Truman's campaign speeches as a set to be called: *How to Do It* and *How I Did It*.

Congressional leaders frown jealously on a National Chairman who "makes policy." I felt the Chairman had a responsibility for offering guidelines for action that could aid the party's return to power. I said publicly that the duty of the opposition was to do more than oppose. There was obvious advantage, I argued, in an affirmative program that offered more than sullen obstruction.

For these comments, I was haled to the woodshed by Republican leaders of the Senate and put on painful notice that "policy" was a Congressional prerogative. It was perhaps an oversight that Joe Martin's minority leadership of the House was unrepresented at this "blast" meeting. Nor was there any consultation with Republican governors; none of the Senate's high command wanted to reopen any doors for Dewey. It may be remembered that Dewey later led the Republican governors who helped the

Eisenhower cause in 1952 by opposing procedure allowing delegates whose seats were in dispute to vote on the seating of other delegates.

Unchastened by the "conscript fathers" of the Senate, I kept searching for a common denominator of Republican purpose, an affirmative commitment more stimulating than drearily limited preachments about "the duty of the opposition." Too many people were inclined to take Republicans at their word and keep them the permanent opposition.

My public relations adviser, Bill Murphy, Sr., and I paraded phrases, seeking the right one to convey the affirmative role I had in mind for the party. Our final choice was "constructive alternative." Programs offered in this context would be consistent with the best of the Republican past and with the hope of future progress.

Once the idea was hatched, we set about nourishing it. In subsequent speeches, I praised the party's "constructive alternatives" to past Democratic proposals and suggested the need for more. Murphy began dropping it into press releases and radio scripts.

And so it was that Republican "constructive alternatives" came under discussion in print and on the air. The term is now part of the language of government and politics. I like to feel that I helped give impetus to a concept most Republican leaders now support through conviction.

In the spring of 1949, the main concern of national headquarters was the 1950 Congressional elections, just a year and a half away. I became a traveling salesman on a nationwide circuit, appealing for progressive party policies and an intelligently aggressive assault on the Truman Administration.

On February 20, 1949, Minority Leader Joe Martin set up a new House Republican Policy Committee which

he chaired. Now, after a number of ups and downs, it is
operating well with excellent research assistance—and
steadily turning out "constructive alternatives!"

It soon became apparent that the fragile Omaha armistice was falling apart. Both progressives and standpatters
were speaking their minds in patterns that prevailed before the National Committee meeting.

To my distress, but hardly to my surprise, assurances
of harmony from the standpat South barely lasted
through the month of March.

There were other storm signals along the Old Guard
horizon. I still can savor the late spring evening of 1949
when I dined at the posh Links Club in New York with a
party of bull elephants from industry's inner sanctums,
including the oldest living Du Pont and Colonel Robert R.
McCormick, the British-educated Anglophobe who was
the Chicago *Tribune*. Most of them were Taft-oriented,
and they were in an I-told-you-so mood. Our host, Harold
E. Talbott, the Republican National Finance Chairman,
was my friend—but was understandably reluctant to rub
the party's donors hard enough to start sparks.

Talbott stressed the Finance Committee's need for
friends and introduced Taft, who reported on the views
and hopes of Republican Senators.

The oldest living Du Pont turned on the Ohioan, quite
as much in anger as in sorrow, and upbraided him for "me-
tooing" the Democrats with health care and education
bills. Taft's reply was mild but bluntly to the point: "We
Republicans have a responsibility," he said. "I think my
bills met that responsibility."

"In my opinion, you've been acting like a damned so-
cialist," growled the elder Mr. du Pont.

At that point, I undertook my assignment—to tell
these manifestly moved, badly shaken movers and shakers
of industry about the state of their minority party.

The cumulative fatigue of months of travel, hundreds of speeches and endless hours of mediating in-party squabbles welled up in anger. I could feel my blood pressure surge and I decided to go for broke. With considerable passion, I started talking my way around the table, addressing each of that powerful, well-tailored company by name.

In sum: "I am not here to save the Republican Party for you. I'm not worried about you at all. You have your resources, your talents and your lawyers to help you keep what you have. You've had your opportunities and you've made the best of them.

"I am not interested in you, Charlie White, but I do want other boys to grow up free to become presidents of steel companies.

"I am not interested in you, Mr. O'Neil, but I am anxious that some young man shall have the same chance you had to become president of a rubber company.

"I am not interested in you, Colonel McCormick, but I do think of the Republican Party as the vehicle to keep enterprise free so that other young men will have their chance some day to run great newspapers like your Chicago *Tribune*."

There was a spatter of handclapping, backed by smiles from the two persons I knew I could count on. Then, taut silence.

My breathing was slowing down when Colonel McCormick's well-upholstered frame loomed by my chair. I tensed.

"Young man, you're all right," he said in his clipped, near-British tones. "I like you. But look at these sissy English hunting scenes on the wall. This is an English-aping club—typical of what's wrong with these damn Easterners."

He cleared his throat, sounding the ruffles and flour-

ishes of a big decision coming up. "They make me sick,"
the Colonel snorted. "I'm going to the bathroom."

It was apparent in the spring of 1949 that the party's
progressive wing was forming to resist the Old Guard.
The battle plan was the one I had privately hoped would
guide the Dewey campaign: the enlightened, construc-
tively affirmative 1948 platform.

Wherever occasion offered, I suggested that Congressional Republicans were basing their view of legislation
not on the past, but on a pragmatic 3-point test which
asked: 1) Is it good? 2) Will it work? 3) Can we afford
it?

The party was full of feuds, but I still continued to
stress my beliefs that there could be no future for the Republican Party in outpromising the opposition; that the
function of the G.O.P. was to try to find what the people
really want in their Federal Government and, if compat-
ible with the framework of a federated Republic, to develop effective ways to provide it. I emphasized the vital responsibility of local and state organizations to choose
good candidates who will help the party put its best foot
forward.

Around mid-July *The Philadelphia Inquirer* splashed
the news that Dewey's foes on the Committee were renew-
ing their battle against the Governor's "hand-picked"
Chairman, and were promoting a National Committee
meeting at which I was to be served with "something like
an ultimatum" to resign or fight it out in open meeting.[9]
The report was painfully accurate. Worse yet, it came at
a time when squabbling threatened to derail the 1950
Congressional campaign.

Senator Taft disclaimed any knowledge of the cabal.
Ken Wherry, the Senate minority leader, praised me with
the faintest of damns: "My theory is that they haven't
got anybody to beat him."

It was not, in fact, a question of beating me, but of finding a generally acceptable replacement. I was still sure I had enough of my old backing to win a showdown. At the same time, I felt there would be continued civil war if I simply turned the machinery over to a clique best known for its long record of obstruction and intransigence.

There was another, more personal consideration: my chairmanship was becoming a political burden to Senators and Representatives who stood by me. Understandable uneasiness beset popular Senator Edward Martin, Mason Owlett and other Pennsylvanians who wanted to be free to side with Senator Taft.

Also, I was yearning to assert the right to take sides. Dewey had withdrawn himself from the 1952 race and had personally urged General Eisenhower to be the candidate. While I had, up to this point, abstained from backing any candidate publicly or privately, I wanted more and more to come out for Ike. This I could not do as National Chairman. My friends had their imperatives. I had mine: I wanted out. But I wanted out with honor.

On July 17, I learned from a reporter that Pennsylvania's leaders, Senator Martin, Owlett and Bloom had agreed to persuade me to resign.

On July 18 I met with Bloom and Len Hall, Chairman of the Congressional Campaign Committee. I told them I would step aside if they would support a neutral successor, rather than a designee of the Coleman-Brewster-Gabrielson forces. They agreed.

After a talk with Joe Martin later the same day, I called a meeting of the National Committee for August 4. At the same time, I announced my decision to resign when the Committee convened. I urged selection of a man "who can bring the desired harmony and cohesiveness to the party organization."

President Truman peered over the party fence and

commented that the less harmony there was among Republicans, the better he liked it.

At this point, at the urging of the National Committeewomen from California and Washington, all Western members of the National Committee, except, as I recall, the mettlesome Bud Kelland of Arizona and one other, initiated a drive to urge me not to resign as Chairman. A number of these members had not voted for me at Omaha.

Meanwhile, a group of House Republicans set a day on the House Floor to speak in my favor. I again indicated that my intention to resign was final.

The day before the August 4 meeting of the National Committee, twenty National Committeewomen adopted a resolution asking me to reconsider. A vote check showed that the outcome would have been a fifty-eight to forty-two vote of confidence.

I then suggested Harry Darby as my successor. Harry withstood twelve hours of pressure (he was assured of sixty-six out of one hundred votes) and my supporters then agreed to support National Committeeman Axel Beck of South Dakota, an outstanding Swedish-American. Some of the former Stassen supporters came over to Beck. A few of the party's Neanderthals snickered that Beck had an accent.

I retorted: "I can't think of anything the Republican Party needs more than an accent."

The eager, Taft-toted Gabrielson slipped in by the landslide plurality of two votes.

My last public appearance as Chairman of the National Committee was described in *The Philadelphia Inquirer* on August 8, 1949:

> The blithe spirit of Representative Hugh Scott stood him in good stead the other evening when he made his valedictory at a dinner of the Republican National Committee following the election of Guy

George Gabrielson, of New Jersey, as chairman.
Although Gabrielson's victory was a defeat for
Scott, the retiring chairman bowed out with a gay,
humorous speech and a generous pledge of co-operation to his successor which won him a standing round
of applause.

Scott . . . said his situation reminded him of the
epitaph on the tombstone of an infant who had died at
the age of one:

"If I was to be so soon done for. What on earth was
I begun for?"

Chairman Gabrielson soon turned the National Committee into a virtual Taft-for-President campaign committee. Efforts to heal the party split were junked. Gabrielson's reception by Congressional leaders was cool. Senate Minority Leader Wherry of Nebraska called his selection "one of the worst mistakes the party has made." [10]

I knew from my months in the Chairmanship how much
ammunition could be accumulated and used by alert Republicans. And I knew how wasted it would be without a
leader competent to deploy our forces into an effective line
of battle. I felt sure General Eisenhower was such a
leader. Once out of the Chairmanship, I was at liberty to
do what I could to help install him at the head of our
troops.

Now that I was a free man at last, I also knew what I
was going to do.

V

PORTLAND TO PORTLAND

"I'm going to roar out across the country for a clean, decent operation."

DWIGHT D. EISENHOWER

ANYONE who has organized a grassroots political movement knows with Shakespeare's Brutus that there is indeed ". . . a tide in the affairs of men, which, taken at the flood, leads on to fortune; omitted, all the voyage of their life is bound in shallows. . . ."[1] A political tide may run strong, but if it is not caught before the ebb, it will not float a campaign to the landfall of success.

Before the troops can be moved there must be commitments from the leaders and opinion makers all the way down the line. Nowhere in politics is the art of timing more highly developed than among the professionals—candidates and state and county chairmen—whose political futures are at stake. For them, a commitment made too late can be worse than useless; one made too early can be an invitation to unnecessary trouble.

The politician making his jump to support a candidate or a cause is like an acrobat landing on a teeterboard: his

66

leap is sure to project an opposition group into orbit from the other end of the board. Under such circumstances, a professional may be forgiven if he looks before he leaps. He needs to make reasonably certain that he has enough weight and muscle on his side to balance the opposition that his move and others like it are sure to stir up. The man who times it wrong puts his career on the line.

There was, in the pre-Presidential year of 1951, another consideration: no careers would be left for many Republicans if 1952 should add another defeat to the long roll of Republican misadventure.

There did not appear to be a Republican Presidential candidate with overwhelming national appeal in the United States—a dark prospect. Yet there was light eastward beyond the darkness. If there were no sureshot standard bearers in the United States, there certainly was in France. If he could be persuaded, there could be no more popular candidate than the victorious General of the Army, Dwight D. Eisenhower, returned to Europe by President Truman's order as Supreme Commander, North Atlantic Treaty Organization, Paris.

Was the road to Paris open?

Reece, Gabrielson, Spangler, Clarence Brown, Tom Coleman, Creager and Taft's cousin, David S. Ingalls, were already polishing their abundant contacts with party leaders in the South and Midwest. By the time I gave up the Party chairmanship, the Taft organization was already grinding away for his nomination.

These were the G.O.P. Bourbons, more dedicated to the past than was the distinguished Senator in whose cause they labored. Sons of rural America, uniformly well-to-do, they had prospered in the *laissez-faire* economy of their salad days. They were not so much indifferent to change as impervious to it; the status quo had done well by them. Compulsive negativism had become a way of life.

The New Deal's "revolution of rising expectations" (in the late Adlai Stevenson's phrase) had, in distributing largesse to the many, distressed these stalwarts deeply. They could envision no safe future for those who shared their fears other than a return to the happy hunting grounds of the early 1920's.

There was no guarantee that a Taft Administration could turn the clock back to their complete satisfaction. Still they believed that Taft could be persuaded to abandon such heresies as the education and health proposals which he had, to their horror, espoused.

In any event, they were ruled by the conviction that if Taft couldn't "hold the line" against the pressures of what they regarded as socialism, nobody could. They were certain their guidance could shield him against future error, and they intended to surround him with their full devotion.

Much as I disagreed with them, I knew these competent political professionals were quite capable of capturing the 1952 convention if they maneuvered without effective opposition. I also knew the weapons at their disposal. As National Chairman, I had learned more about the machinery of the Republican Party than anybody else— including Taft—because I had been tinkering with the machinery. I knew the men who made it go in all of the then forty-eight states. I knew the Indian trails.

From the moment I relinquished the chairmanship, I knew that those who had captured the party machinery could also control the next national convention. Or would, unless demand for a more engaging candidate prevented them.

I believed Eisenhower was the man to do this. By his record in peace as well as war, Eisenhower had already earned national respect. He had no past history in the party, which left him untainted by the old bitter factionalism. On this basis alone, he was in a position to unite the fragmented party. Professional politicians of both parties rated him topflight candidate material.

Even though he scrupulously observed the military ban on political involvement, I was personally convinced that he was a Republican. He had gone to the Military Academy as the appointee of a Republican Congressman; the Republican tradition was strong in his Kansas homeland, and all his brothers were Republicans. I knew his record as a soldier-diplomat and the burden of his speeches as President of Columbia University; it was a constructive, moderate record, in the pattern of middle-road Republicanism.

Then, hardly less significant, was Ike's appeal. As the victorious General of the Army, the popular hero with the warm and ready smile, the Kansas farm boy, he generated enormous national goodwill. Ike was the public's favorite among the war's commanders.

So far my enthusiasm for Eisenhower was based entirely on personal conjecture. I had no assurance that he would be a candidate. He was then in his second year as President of Columbia University and thoroughly immersed in the job. I suspected that he would be willing to talk politics, but I decided on an oblique approach.

I wrote to him as a member of the Subcommittee on Public Health of the House Commerce Committee. In that capacity, I asked for an interview on the application of the Hill-Burton Hospital Construction Act to university medical schools. Eisenhower agreed to meet to "discuss the various provisions of the bill affecting scholarships and other types of educational aid."

My first meeting with Ike was all I could have asked for. After a forty-five minute discussion of health legislation with the General and the Dean of the Medical School, who was an authority on the subject, I indicated

that I would like to discuss some other things. The Dean
excused himself.

General Eisenhower listened attentively as I told him of
the interest I had found in his candidacy and predicted
his nomination and election. I sketched for him what I had
learned of the "Indian trails" during my year in the
chairmanship. I told him I was ready and anxious to follow those trails from state to state to work with the many
others I knew who already "liked Ike" to organize an
effective political striking force.

Eisenhower made no commitments during our friendly
talk, but he did startle me a bit when he observed that
both parties had asked him to be their candidate in
1948. I was already aware that he had turned down the
suggestion that he be the Democratic candidate when it
was tendered by Harry Truman in a burst of Missouri
exuberance. What I did not know was that Ike had also
turned down prominent Republicans who had the same
idea. (Before Governor Dewey moved in 1948, I later
learned, he visited General Eisenhower to report his intention of seeking the G.O.P. nomination—if the General
didn't want it for himself. I also learned that Dewey,
early in 1949, was the first highly-placed Republican to
urge the General to make the 1952 race.)

I was not sure what to expect from the Columbia meeting, but I did seek some indication of the General's interest. It was not volunteered during our pleasant hour of
talk, so I tried a low-keyed squeeze play as I was leaving.
Our exchange, as I recall it, went something like this:

"General," I said, "unless you tell me I cannot do so, I
am going to work from now on for your nomination as the
Republican candidate for the Presidency."

"I don't know about the future," Eisenhower replied,
"but I will say this—I wouldn't be interested in the sort of

thing like a fight at the convention where X gets 385 votes and Y gets 495 votes, something like that."

The qualification was ironic, for it came close to forecasting the first-ballot outcome at Chicago in 1952, which showed 595 votes for Eisenhower and 500 for Taft with another 111 scattered. But I had my answer, incomplete though it was: Eisenhower was interested enough not to countermand my decision to work for his candidacy.

"You'll get all the votes you need," I said as we shook hands. Ike smiled a noncommittal farewell.

My determination to begin effective missionary work on Eisenhower's behalf was aimed at three goals: to show Eisenhower himself that there were Republican troops awaiting his leadership; to arouse the interest of the noncommitted party members and to focus public enthusiasm. So I recruited wherever I went.

In February 1950, my sense of urgency was intensified when the National Committee came out with a declaration of principles that so faithfully reflected the conservatism of Chairman Gabrielson that it went considerably beyond the view of Senator Taft, whose election was Gabrielson's reason for being. I joined Senators Lodge and Margaret Chase Smith and others in an effort to raise the declaration's sights at least to the minimums set in Taft's announced views. I was especially disappointed, though, that the Declaration skirted any specific endorsement of bipartisan foreign policy actions. This kind of inflexibility of the men then at the helm in the G.O.P. led me to declare at a meeting in Bluefield, West Virginia, that my party needed "to improve its circulatory system by getting rid of some of the blood clots." [2]

I knew where some of the clots were, and I began in the spring of 1950 to try to dislodge them. My targets were the "post office Republican" leaders who held unchal-

lenged sway over the paper organizations in some of the
Southern states. Generals without troops and without
honor in their own country, they hoped to be conduits for
patronage if Republicans ever recaptured Washington,
and they lived meanwhile by back-room deals. They dealt
in delegates in Presidential years, and in between they
trafficked for peanuts with the dominant Dixiecrats.

I knew the Taft people were counting on the post office
factions to hold Southern delegate strength virtually solid
for their man. I also knew there was dissatisfaction, not to
mention disgust, among many Southerners who wanted a
vigorous two-party system in their region.

Illustrative of these disillusioned Republican insurgents, themselves respected civic personalities, was Louisiana's Ike man, John Minor Wisdom, an internationally-
minded lawyer with a social conscience. He eventually
ousted the National Committeeman, took over his job, and
turned the party from rabble to rallying post.

I was ready when my friend Bert Andrews interviewed
me as a kind of consolation prize for the broadcast of January 1949 in which Taft tersely blessed the move to evict
me from the chairmanship. I advised Bert in the studio
that he might be interested in my views on the one-party
South. He obliged.

Naming names as I went, I told his national radio audience there was no two-party system in too many Southern
states because the state parties were closed organizations,
and paper ones at that, so disinterested in victory that
they neither encouraged electable candidates nor developed effective machinery.

I suggested that there was an alliance between Tennessee's Republican committeeman—a former National
Chairman—Carroll Reece, and the malodorous Crump
machine in Memphis. I mentioned John Jackson in New
Orleans, who kept control of Louisiana's paper organi-

zation by voting an ever-flowing pocketful of proxies. And then there was Mississippi's Committeeman Perry Howard, who had no trouble manipulating his state's special G.O.P., although he was a year-round resident of the District of Columbia. I suggested that some of the Southern organizations collected "hush money" from Democrats who were interested in keeping the Republicans as silent as they were impotent. I cited proxy shenanigans in South Carolina, and "vest pocket" Republicanism in Alabama.

I found some signs of hope in Jack Porter's successful drive to make bipartisanship a reality in Texas and in genuinely hard-working, respectable organizations that had shown some muscle in Arkansas, Georgia, Virginia and Florida.

"The South can have a two-party system," I told Andrews, "if enough people will band together in a state to battle it through as a prime objective, keep their organization intact and growing, learn the devious details of state party control, fight to select their delegations and name the state party officers and national committeeman and committeewoman. And keep a sharp eye out for skullduggery."

Even if Andrews had wanted to, which he didn't, he could hardly have avoided one more topic: Did I think General Eisenhower would seek the Republican Presidential nomination—or even accept it if it were tendered? My answer reflected hopes borne out by subsequent events.

"He won't seek it. I'm sure of that," I said. "I think it is up to the people to seek him. He is the kind of great, selfless American who would, in my opinion, find it impossible to resist a draft by a majority of the American people. It would have to be a real demand. But I have traveled all over this country and I am absolutely certain that the demand is there."

As a realist, Andrews questioned whether the General could overcome the aversion of political professionals to allowing "another amateur to come along and steal the show, as Wendell Willkie did." Wouldn't Eisenhower "have to make himself available before long?"

I replied with a prediction: after the 1950 elections "draft Eisenhower organizations will come into being all over the country." Meanwhile, I said, the job with first priority was the election of a Republican Congress this fall, including the return of Bob Taft to the Senate.

I meant to stir things up with the Andrews broadcast and it created quite a furor. I was speaking with malice aforethought to jab a will to act into the South's decent Republicans and those Democrats who were ready to make the big switch to a live second party. I was trying to tell them the G.O.P. was a hollow shell in most states of the old Confederacy. But it could become a vehicle for victory with a compelling candidate. Pick your state and get something going for Eisenhower, I was telling them, and if you want any advice, here I am.

There was top-heavy opinion that Taft was the man to beat for the nomination. But some of his supporters were jolted by the hard reassertion of the isolationist line in his recent foreign policy pronouncements.

The Republican National Committee, meeting at Tulsa, Oklahoma, went out of its way to ignore the declaration of twenty-one Republican Congressmen who urged the party leadership to take a more affirmative and constructive approach to the tremendously intricate problems facing the nation.

Other than Taft, the only candidate attracting any attention was General Dwight Eisenhower, then in Paris as NATO's Supreme Commander. I told his story wherever I could find listeners. I was interested, in the light of my talk with the General at Columbia University, to find considerable concern that if the Republicans didn't choose Ike, the Democrats would. To the extent that it suggested new arguments against picking Taft, this talk had its advantages. Far less publicly, I was involved in a diplomatic venture of strategic importance to the Eisenhower cause: the installation of Senator Duff, who was a power in Pennsylvania, as an active leader of the developing Eisenhower team.

"You cannot beat somebody with nobody" is the way the old political maxim goes. Even more to the point, you cannot beat an organization with no organization.

The likeliest machinery for the Ike team in the preconvention battle was, I decided, the still-viable interstate network of connections and friendships that helped Tom Dewey win the 1948 nomination. It was an organization without a candidate and Eisenhower was a potential candidate without an organization.

Duff was not enthusiastic over the Dewey campaign but after a number of discussions with me and with Herbert Brownell, Duff indicated in April 1951 that he was ready to work for Eisenhower and ready to talk it over with Dewey. I immediately relayed the word to the New York Governor.

The formative conference of the Eisenhower campaign took place in Dewey's suite at the Roosevelt Hotel in New York on June 1. I went there with Duff. Dewey, tanned and chipper after a Bermuda vacation, was joined by Brownell and James C. Hagerty, the knowledgeable and seemingly indestructible press secretary to Dewey (and later to President Eisenhower). The session went well. We had another meeting ten days later which was also attended by former Senator Harry Darby of Kansas.

The upshot was an agreement under which Darby was to act as unofficial co-ordinator of our enterprise: Thomas E. Stephens, a resourceful political professional on Dewey's staff who later was White House appointments secretary, was to join me in working out first-phase details of a national preconvention campaign. To the extent that the Eisenhower movement had a front man at that time, it was Darby, working out of his Topeka office. He was soon swamped by visitors, phone calls, letters and wires from Eisenhower enthusiasts.

We therefore were authorized to set up the first official Eisenhower headquarters anywhere—a quiet one—two offices in the Dupont Circle Building in Washington. The entire organization consisted of Tom Stephens, activist, myself as chief prowler-around and a secretary we borrowed from Senator Alexander Smith of New Jersey.

In June 1952 I found myself among a number of Republican leaders who felt so concerned about the possibility of Senator Taft's nomination that they journeyed to Paris to try to assess General Eisenhower's availability. At separate, thoughtfully spaced times, Senator Cabot Lodge, Paul Hoffman, Ed Bermingham and I all pried at the General's thoughts.

We did not look for final answers, but wanted some assurance that the General's personal political beliefs would not stand in the way of his candidacy. As expected, the results were not conclusive. But we felt we had enough to go on so that I would publicly assert my belief that the General could be a candidate and that he would return to the United States at what he felt was the proper time.

We began to shape a skeleton organization headed by Darby. My assignment was the South, together with unfinished business elsewhere in the country.

In early September, after a second trip to Paris, I told a meeting of Republican Senators and Representatives I was convinced we had the "green light" from Eisenhower.

Although I had again failed to receive a hard commitment from the General, I felt safe in reporting to my colleagues and to the press a significant exchange that took place near the end of our long, thoughtful talk. It went approximately like this:

Scott: "Since there are so many people advocating your nomination . . . they have a right to expect something in return . . . an assurance that the rug won't be pulled out from under their activities by any contrary statement from overseas."

Eisenhower: "I'm engaged in a terribly important job to myself and the free world.

"I took that job at considerable personal risk. If there are people at home who think that a cause is worth pursuing, then they ought to be willing to accept whatever risk is incident to making that fight for that cause." [3]

Before I posed my question, I pointed out to the General that a good many Republicans working for him without hope of patronage or reward were looking for encouragement. I said they were in a contest with "engine room" professionals who were dangling promises of high Federal posts before those with power to swing blocs of delegates to Taft.

Earlier in the interview, I had put the General on notice that I would have to say something when politicians and reporters in the United States questioned me about his availability. General Eisenhower referred me without comment to a newspaper article on his desk which said he would of course accept the nomination if a majority of the delegates were lined up for him in advance of the convention.

At the same time, the General voiced concern about the possibility of a 1952 Taft-Truman contest that would utterly exclude his viewpoint. He said he personally would prefer to return to Columbia University after the end of his NATO tour, but realized that his hopes of getting back to private life were dwindling.

I asked for confirmation of my belief that Eisenhower subscribed generally to progressive Republican views. His reply was again oblique, but hardly disappointing: he suggested that I read his recent speeches, the same speeches on which I based my understanding of his philosophy.

The General's statement that his adherents should be willing to accept "whatever risk" the fight entailed seemed to me to pretty well end the interview.

"I assume by that that I am free to do what I've been doing for so long a time," I said, rising to go.

He did not challenge my assumption, and I left SHAPE impatient to spread the word. The convention was less than ten months away.

The unwillingness of General Eisenhower to give his supporters an unmistakably green light was, of course, maddening. His reservations were honorable, but crippling to a struggle to sway public opinion and to win delegates. We would continue to battle this handicap until the New Hampshire primary.

During the summer of the preconvention campaign, I was made chairman of regional organizations, to coordinate the work of groups already in being and encourage formation of new ones. We dipped our toes gingerly into the Sea of Delegates and set our course for two states.

We believed we could rack up an early score for Ike in Rhode Island with a modest expenditure of effort and money (both of which were limited). Then we could hail the victory as we campaigned in more difficult states.

Conversely, we felt we could shrug off a possible setback in faraway Washington State. Seattle and Spokane were remote enough from the main tent on the banks of the Potomac for distance to dim the impact of events. The experience could help us gauge Eisenhower's appeal in the Northwest. And Washington *did* have eighteen delegate votes (later increased to twenty-four).

In Seattle, I took a room at the Olympic Hotel and advised the press I was available (the word was eager) for interviews. There was already a Taft-for-President headquarters in the hotel, and all the visible motion in the state had been on the Taft side. Press reports about Eisenhower had dealt with negative questions, like: "Where does Ike stand?" or—worse yet—"Is Ike REALLY a candidate?"

So, when I was asked by a reporter how I expected to form a "Washington for Eisenhower" organization, I tried the affirmative approach.

"I'll be at home in Room 560 of the Olympic Hotel to any Republicans who may want to join the Eisenhower movement," I replied. "If you publish the room number, I predict that I'll have plenty of visitors."

He did—and I did. The eventual result was "Washington for Eisenhower," headed by Owen Clarke of Yakima. Clarke's group went on to capture the King County (Seattle) delegates, which nailed down our eventual twenty-to-four control of the state delegation. From Washington came investment banker Walter Williams, onetime national head of the C.E.D. who later was National Chairman of "Citizens for Eisenhower and Nixon" and eventually Ike's Under Secretary of Commerce.

The Rhode Island operation was a pushover. The state shared New England's pro-Eisenhower leanings before we started. We began with a stronger base than the Taft people and we ended up on schedule with six of the state's eight delegates.

Back at the Capitol, one of those partial surveys that suggest so much and prove so little uncovered seventy-one of the 190 Republican Representatives for Taft, and only fifty-four for Eisenhower. The Taft wing at the controls of the National Committee passed the word that Taft could already count on four hundred of the 603 delegates needed for the nomination.

The Eisenhower headquarters had reason to feel sure of better than three hundred delegates.

The pace quickened as the contest moved into November 1951. Taft's cousin Dave Ingalls was named as the Ohioan's campaign manager. The choice of Senator Lodge as the Eisenhower campaign chairman was announced.

When Ike came to the States to consult with President Truman about his work as NATO's Supreme Commander, he responded to the clamor for a press conference just before he left. He pointedly avoided partisanship as long as he was in uniform, but he promised that "if the time ever comes" for him to speak out on politics, he would do so "positively and definitely."

As for the actions of his friends, the General told a questioner he would not interfere "so long as they believe they know how I would act and react under given situations." [4]

This was certainly an invitation to push ahead. I made a public statement to that effect.

Newspaper editorials and political commitments showed that the political Promised Land was in sight. We had yet to cross Jordan, however, for in spite of all the evidence that Ike could win, we had as yet no solid proof that he was a candidate. His would-be followers were growing restless. On the basis of our talks in Paris in June and September, I personally felt that he could not fail to heed the unmistakable evidence of wide support. But I knew better than most how important it was that he say so before the political calendar advanced too far.

Our doubts reached a gloomy nadir in December 1951. Partly to escape the bleak necessity of providing reassurance when we really had nothing new to offer, I took a year-end vacation at the Kawama Beach Club in Cuba. The Caribbean sun did not dispel the gloom of cables and telephone calls from my friends at home. They carried one monotonous message: If Ike doesn't announce something pretty soon, the nomination will go to Taft by default. For the first time since the "We want Ike" calls first sounded, the campaign for him was really hurting from the enforced limitations which muffled the music of his would-be drumbeaters.

To change the metaphor, the movement was still airborne, but the balloon was clearly drifting down as priceless time ebbed away. The man closest to the General who was directly accessible to me was his brother, Dr. Milton S. Eisenhower, then President of Pennsylvania State University. I placed a telephone call direct from Kawama Beach.

"Milt," I said in sum, "General Eisenhower will just have to say something. I don't think his friends can hold this thing together as much as a month more. Nothing any of us can say is going to come home to the people we are trying to persuade unless we can back it up with a statement. We've got to be able to say authoritatively that Ike will, at the proper time, come home from Europe; that he will permit his name to be entered in the New Hampshire primaries and will, if he's nominated, actually campaign for the Presidency."

I recalled to Milton Eisenhower my conversation with the General in 1949 in his office at Columbia and how he had professed disinterest in a tough, close convention floor fight. This was just the kind of fight that was developing, I said, and the General would have to be prepared for it. But he could win the nomination if he would make clear his acquiescence, if not his approval, to his supporters before Taft's people sewed up a winning majority of stampede-proof delegates.

Milton reassured me. As opposed as I was to excess caution, he fully understood the problem. He predicted that it would be solved very quickly by a visit of Senator Lodge to SHAPE. But much as he sympathized with our impatience, Milton scrupulously refused to speak for his brother or to do anything to hasten the General's decision.

Lodge came back from Paris and in a press conference on January 6 voiced confidence that Eisenhower was in the race to the finish. He accordingly entered the General's name in the Republican primary in New Hampshire.

A day later, the General himself said in Paris that he would under no circumstances seek the nomination personally or campaign for convention delegates. But he added that he would accept a "clear-cut call to political duty," which some construed to mean he would insist on a genuine draft. Strictly speaking, there is no such thing, because even the most massive latent support means little in a preconvention campaign unless it is organized to win delegates—or at least to keep them uncommitted.

We had known for months that the political hills were alive with Eisenhower enthusiasts. But they could not be recruited or organized into effective troops for the preconvention wars without firm word from the General that he was ready to go all the way. We now had that word. We could unmuffle the drums.

There was electricity in the air when Henry Cabot Lodge, Jr., took the floor to tell the Eisenhower story to one hundred members of the Republican National Committee who had assembled in San Francisco on January 17, 1952, for what was to be a showcase meeting heavily covered by the press. The tall, articulate Massachusetts

Senator was still charged with the enthusiasm he had brought with him from Paris. His impassioned persuasive talk was clearly the day's best. It set the teeterboard tipping our way.

Taft's spokesman was his Ohio kinsman, Dave Ingalls, a courtly lawyer who flew over France in the First World War with the famed Yale squadron. His presentation was sincere and colorless and a mite defensive, plainly aimed at the "Taft-can't-win" talk that dogged the Senator's efforts to broaden his support.

California's rugged Senator William F. Knowland presented the case for his Governor, Earl Warren, whose record in three campaigns for the Sacramento Statehouse showed a healthy ability to attract votes of Democrats along with Republicans. Knowland had a good man to talk about and he made a good case.

All three camps followed up the public presentations with personal persuasion around the clock, in corridor talks or in separate hospitality suites which offered propaganda of all kinds, along with a mite to drink. It didn't escape notice that almost everybody wanted to get into the back room with Lodge. I spent most of my time in a room adjoining Lodge's suite sifting and sorting the likeliest prospects to meet with Lodge.

The San Francisco meeting helped us nail down people who were already half-converted to the Eisenhower cause. It encouraged quite a few contributors at a time when money was badly needed. Where we tapped normal sources of Republican funds, we snapped some purses shut in the faces of the Taft people. That was the name of the game.

By the time of the San Francisco conference, we were already well launched on our effort to turn the New Hampshire primary into a psychological springboard for the entire preconvention campaign. Victory in the nation's first primary on March 11 would give Eisenhower's cause an incalculable lift in the primaries and state conventions that lay ahead. It could prove our thesis that "Ike can win"—but only if Ike won, and won convincingly.

It took persuasion to convince Eisenhower that primaries were important; that he could not afford to oppose entry of his name in New Hampshire. I became aware that this could become a problem during my September visit to Paris when the General said he had heard a lot about the New Hampshire primary, but failed to see what it proved. He said he would like to know more.

Immediately on my return to Washington, I drew up a digest of state laws governing all Presidential preference primaries, forwarded it to the General at Paris with a covering letter that stressed the open opportunity in New Hampshire. I further pointed out that he would be a candidate if friends filed his name for him, so long as he did not affirmatively order it withdrawn. If it seems odd that a major Presidential prospect required instruction in the importance of primaries, one must remember the unique circumstances.

Like most career officers, Ike had shunned politics. When politics, in effect, came to him, I think he reasoned that the politically-minded people who were urging him to run for the Presidency must know how to go about winning a nomination. I suspect that he reasoned further that there was no need for him to be burdened with decisions on detail that he did not have to make. The obvious fallacy was that there *were* decisions which only he could make— if only to decide to say nothing at the right time.

The General's silence at this stage was golden for our cause because of the quirk in the New Hampshire law that in effect allowed his friends to make him a primary candidate unless he publicly said no. So long as Ike said nothing, this in itself constituted a decision.

Eisenhower supporters in New Hampshire began working in the late summer of 1951 with quiet help from our Washington headquarters and the blessing of Governor Sherman Adams. On January 6 when Lodge flatly predicted that the General would run as a Republican, he made a point of noting that he had "assured Governor Adams that 'General Eisenhower is in to the finish.' " [5] By that time, Adams had already announced his intention to run in the primary as a delegate.

Lodge's announcement that Ike's name would be entered in the New Hampshire primary was crucial to the plans of the Eisenhower leaders. Unless we won there, the ball game might well be over in a very early inning.

In February, before I addressed a Republican dinner in Hanover, I told the press that Ike was indeed in the primary to stay and, I predicted, to win.

A month later, after Eisenhower had swept the preference contest by a four-to-three margin over Taft and won all of the first fourteen delegates picked by primary in 1952, I sent Adams a jubilant telegram: "The whole Ike and nothing but the Ike, so help me Bob." In a warm answering letter, Adams termed the results better than he had "dared hope" and added: "You helped."

Of special significance was an exchange of correspondence between Washington and Paris. It began on February 22 when nineteen House Republicans, among them Christian Herter, Thruston Morton, Gerald Ford of Michigan and myself, drafted an appeal to General Eisenhower to return to the United States and campaign actively. The General's reply, dated the day before the New Hampshire primary, set the political drums beating.[6]

Ike left the door open wide enough to fan the draft. While he could not leave Europe "during the immediate future," he promised his supporters he would "regularly re-examine my position, bearing in mind your message."

At the same time, the General used the letter to block out the vital issues of the time as he saw them—and as he would presumably approach them when and if he went through that half-open door.

"World peace and human freedom, American solvency, prosperity and unity," he wrote, ". . . dwarf every American citizen's personal preferences and his personal decisions on his duty as an individual." [7]

Having sounded the challenge, the General gave the response we awaited in the next paragraph:

"There is no question in my mind concerning the propriety of answering a clear-cut call to another and higher duty, a call that is traditionally and universally recognized as the voice of the American people speaking through a national convention." [8]

But even as he conceded that "such a call imposes an obligation of citizenship" and agreed that there was "complete validity" in our arguments that he should return, the General weighed the urgency of his current mission against the political summons and found reason to wait.

"But in the absence of a compelling call or relief by higher authority, I cannot see in any personal or political circumstances a sufficient warrant for me to leave this assignment during the immediate future," he wrote.[9] The "higher authority," of course, was President Truman, who had said he would not interfere if the General wishes to come home and campaign, but he hoped Eisenhower would stay on. The President did not withdraw as a candidate himself until late March.

The letter, clearly presaging the General's return to campaign in late May, was the final signal to go all out.

Following President Eisenhower's election, the nineteen Congressmen to whom he wrote the March 10 letter presented him with a silver-bordered desk blotter engraved with the seals of the United States and of SHAPE and the autographs of the letter writers. The General still uses the blotter at his Gettysburg office.

Early in the campaign we dusted off an old super-weapon of the Willkie era: the grass-roots citizens' clubs which can, under proper direction, stir up enough fuss to make even the toughest pro sit up and listen.

The club organizations were ideal instruments to show reluctant G.O.P. leaders that General Eisenhower had a live following in their states, and they had better get with it. Our weapon here was the petition. We had them printed by the thousands, pledging the signers to support Ike and urging the state leadership to do the same. The results were living proof of what we knew: that in almost every state except Ohio, there was far more rank and file sentiment for Eisenhower than for Taft.

Work on the Eisenhower clubs was begun late in 1951 to achieve some kind of co-ordination among the wide variety of Eisenhower organizations that were mushrooming all over the country.

The effort really began when two young executives, Charlie Willis and Stanley Rumbough, dined with me in Washington to discuss practical ways to get the idea on the rails. My informed guess was that a minimum of $6,000 could start a state-by-state club system.

I told my visitors if they organized the clubs properly, contributions would cover costs. They were out of the red within weeks. The system was organized under a set of by-laws adapted from a model in my book, *How To Go Into Politics*.

We ended up with some sort of official Eisenhower organization in every state except California where all Republicans respected Warren's "favorite son" bid. We had a one-man Eisenhower organization in the Virgin Islands.

The hundreds which had sprung up by convention time later became the nucleus for the Citizens for Eisenhower and Youth for Eisenhower organizations which helped greatly to spread our message beyond the party fold.

Thus, by early 1952 I found myself traveling for Eisenhower with my office in my hat. My beat extended wherever I had contacts, from Maine to Washington State, with way stations in the Midwest and Border States and outposts throughout the South.

Selected as campaign chairman at the suggestion of Dewey, Duff and Darby, Lodge had taken on a tremendous obligation and was finding it impossible to cover all the bases. He was an articulate and impressive advocate and an able strategist, but the campaign also needed a top co-ordinator who had tactical contacts with the states and the authority to put them to work. The old Dewey machine had developed a network of such contacts and Herb Brownell knew how to plug in the connections. In early February, Brownell took over as our chief tactician after some persuasion by retired General Lucius D. Clay, Ike's old deputy in Europe, who was acting as his chief personal representative in this country.

Brownell found a setup with three directing centers: the New York operation at the Commodore Hotel, where Clay and Brownell were in charge; our Washington headquarters at the Shoreham, which was home base for our Congressional leaders, Senators Lodge, Duff and Carlson and for Wesley Roberts of Kansas, soon to become National Chairman, and the Topeka office, which had been set up as the National Headquarters, but was actually so out of the way that the campaign flowed past it.

It was decided in January to subdivide the campaign into four regional efforts. In the South, John Minor Wisdom of New Orleans, Elbert Tuttle of Georgia and I were the men responsible. In the West, we had three governors, Douglas McKay of Oregon, Dan Thornton of Colorado, and Arthur B. Langlie of Washington. In the Midwest, those in charge were ex-Senator Harry Darby and Howard Bentley of Kansas.

We had problems in the early days with such questions as: Is Ike a Republican? and Where does Eisenhower stand on this or that issue? Ike's rather Delphic stance continued to be a problem. We had to grin and bear it, while putting together appropriate folders and pamphlets and pumping them out to the state Eisenhower chairmen for distribution through the clubs and frequently through cooperating Young Republican organizations.

Like others who were making the same restless rounds, I was impressed by the zeal and caliber of Ike's supporters, but depressed by difficulties we encountered in getting a go-ahead from headquarters to move on with organization plans.

Then the tide changed.

Success in the New Hampshire primary and the clear promise (at last!) of the General's latest letter from Paris made the enthusiasm really boil at an eleven-state Atlanta meeting called by Lodge on March 22. I was sufficiently encouraged after the all-day session to approve an optimistic statement predicting that the strong Southern delegate bloc theoretically committed to Taft would fly apart "like a covey of quail" under convention pressure.

The conference drew extensive press coverage and we did our best to take advantage of it, praising Southern newspapers for exposing "a very ugly pattern" of attempts by Taft supporters to gobble up entire state delegations. I documented a list of abuses: county and precinct convention halls so packed with Taft people that Eisenhower backers could not get in; unscheduled precinct

meetings held in private homes; county conventions for
invited ticket holders only—an ingenious series of devices
to circumvent primaries.

One of the problems that faced the professionals as they
were forced to lead regular party workers outside the
standard organization track was: Would General Eisenhower, if elected, work through the G.O.P. organization in
distributing patronage? The assumption, of course, was
that the Eisenhower men would, by election day, have
turned the Old Guard out and that today's insurgents
would thereby become a strong part of tomorrow's organization.

His foes charged that Ike said, "If given the opportunity, I would completely ignore organization and loyal
workers in order to be a wild maverick." This idea was
damaging so I went promptly through indirect channels
to get the truth from Ike. And his response nailed the dis-
tortion and made him sound at last like a candidate.

Terming the idea "a little incomprehensible" to one
whose life had been passed "in activities in which strong
organization is the requisite," Eisenhower went on to say
what his workers wanted to hear:

> I, therefore, would not hesitate to let it be known in
> some proper manner that I would never ignore the
> rank and file of any organization. I think my record
> will show that I never have lacked faith in those with
> whom I have been associated.[10]

The communication was handily timed, for it undercut
an argument by the Taft people that they alone could be
depended upon to remember the faithful in the orthodox
way.

The record of the primaries rather tarnished the victorious illusion the Taft camp sought to nurture. After
the shutout in New Hampshire and a pasting in Min-

nesota, they won an inconclusive plurality in Wisconsin, and a narrow victory in a write-in test against Eisenhower in Nebraska.

Taft did win three fourths of the vote in an Illinois primary where Ike's name was not entered. But the next week, Ike swept New Jersey's preference primary three-to-one.

As expected, Eisenhower outran Taft in Pennsylvania, New York, Massachusetts and Oregon. There were predicted Taft sweeps in Ohio and West Virginia, then a draw in South Dakota. The season ended June 3 when California loyally elected a 70-delegate slate pledged to Warren.

Overall, Ike was doing magnificently in the East, more than holding his own in the Far West and making inroads in the Midwest. In the South, where delegates were chosen by county and state conventions, we picked off our delegates a few at a time.

As the state convention was beginning in Birmingham, I was notified that delegates were being browbeaten into supporting Taft.

I exploded as I watched the proceedings from the gallery. My shocked reaction was loud enough to attract the attention of a woman in a red dress who was sitting beside me. When she said it "wasn't very fair," I protested: "It's totally wrong and the presiding officer knows it."

"I agree," she said. "My husband's a delegate for Taft and I'm going to make him vote for Eisenhower to even this up, because I don't like people being unfair."

I checked up later and her husband voted with us. We also ended up with one of Alabama's four at-large delegates, a triumph of sorts in a state that had once been written off as unassailably for Taft.

Nowhere did we have to fight harder than in Texas, where the old-line organization led by National Commit-

teeman Henry Zweifel, was besieged by zealous Eisen-
hower forces organized by Houston oil man Jack Porter.
A war raged between Zweifel's concept of the Texas
G.O.P. as a private club and Porter's hopes of making
Texas into a genuine two-party state.

Zweifel and his state committee excluded all but thirty
of the challenged Eisenhower delegates. The pro-Taft
credentials committee pitched in and barred another
twenty-one. The contested Taft delegates were permitted to vote to seat themselves and—presto—the convention was cocked and loaded to fire a Taft delegation to
Chicago. The disgusted Eisenhower delegation marched
out of the hall in a body, leaving Zweifel and his crew free
to name an "uninstructed" delegation—with thirty delegates "uninstructed" for Taft, four leaning to MacArthur and a token four all-out for Eisenhower.

The Eisenhower forces gathered in a hall across the
street, boiling mad, and named their own delegation—
thirty-three for the General and five for the Senator,
which they insisted was all Taft had won in the district
races.

I was not at Mineral Wells; Brownell handled the
Texas convention for us. But I had kept in close touch
with Porter. I recite the record of the so-called "Texas
steal" because it became in due time the *cause célèbre*
around which our forces rallied for the first great morale-
building victory at Chicago.

Within a fortnight of the Mineral Wells convention, I
was telling friendly mountain state delegates in Denver:
"If the Texas fight goes to the convention floor, and Taft
wins it, the Republican nomination won't be worth a
plugged nickel."

This "Texas pitch" was a potent weapon forged out of
outraged virtue and practical politics and it went like
this: Be ready to fight the issue of the Texas delegates all

the way to the convention floor and put everything you
have into winning it, because if Taft's people get away
with this "steal," they may get Taft the nomination, but
they will rob the party of its chances for victory in
November. If the Democrats are able to link the G.O.P.
Presidential candidate with such tactics, I told the visit-
ing delegates, the Republicans can forget about using the
"corruption" issue in the fall campaign.

"Corruption by administration officials is one thing," I
said in a talk to delegates quoted by Philip Geyelin of *The
Wall Street Journal*, "but corruption of the electoral system is quite another, and by far the greater of the two." [11]

Taft argued that his Texas backers were just trying to
protect the state party from the Democratic invaders. But
we won the first round when the National Committee left
the issue for decision by the convention. It put us in a
position to go for broke at Chicago.

The Texas experience was paralleled in other states.
Disputes led to selection of rival Taft and Eisenhower delegations in Georgia, Louisiana and Mississippi. At stake
in these three states and in Texas were potentially crucial
votes.

We eventually wrote off the five Mississippi delegates,
but we carried our fight for the seventy others to the
convention floor and won it. The manner of our victory
was quite as important to the final outcome as was the not
inconsiderable arithmetic.

A month before the convention opened with 137 delegates still to be chosen in state conventions, the score on
known commitments among the 1,206 delegates stood:
Taft 399, Eisenhower 380. The other 290 seats were contested, uncommitted and scattered.

As the primary season headed toward its finale in California, General of the Army Dwight D. Eisenhower flew
from Paris to Washington to make his last report to Pres-

ident Truman on his tour as NATO's Supreme Commander. The country knew much of what he had done, but little of what he was like. It was tied to Truman's Fair Deal
and the abuses that went with twenty years of one-party
government in Washington. It was dubious about Taft's
isolationist leanings, but it hated the Korean War. It
wanted very much to "like Ike."

The General had barely hung up his uniform on June 3
to become the candidate the whole country called Ike when
he met his first tests. In a grueling round of press conferences, his knowledge of world affairs and his engaging
frankness overshadowed his understandable vagueness
about some domestic details. He was feted at Abilene,
Kansas, his boyhood home, and braved a drenching thun-
derstorm to make a nationally-televised speech that was a
near disaster. While he firmly asserted his Republicanism,
the Chicago *Tribune* was not alone in gibing at his "five
star generalities." He met with batches of delegates in
Abilene, New York and Detroit before he finally moved on
to his Denver field headquarters.

Denver was picked for personal, political and logistical
reasons. Mrs. Eisenhower's mother lived in Denver and
the city had many pleasant associations for the family. It
was far enough from either coast so Ike could not be accused of falling under "internationalist" influence, yet it
was well out of the Chicago *Tribune*'s isolationist orbit.
Colorado's Governor, Dan Thornton, was an Eisenhower
enthusiast, the mountain states were friendly and Ike
could also find some respite in the golf and fishing. Finally, Denver was a transfer point for transcontinental air-
lines.

During the Denver campaign, I came up with a punch
line that helped to distil Ike's feelings about the honor of
the party. Out popped the phrase which has served me as
campaign guide in many a party gathering: "For a Re-

publican to win, he must *deserve* to win." The General used it in Denison, Texas, often repeated it later and it still appears in his philosophy.

Meanwhile, the Taft-dominated convention arrangements committee predictably picked Taft men to run the convention. Its selections of officials were so one-sided that Oregon's National Committeeman Ralph H. Cake, one of the outnumbered Eisenhower men, stamped out of the Chicago meeting declaring: "They've rigged us, but good!"

No Eisenhower man won a key post. General Douglas MacArthur, the choice of some conservatives, was named keynoter. Perhaps the unkindest cut was the selection of the temporary chairman, Walter S. Hallanan, belligerent manager of Taft's successful primary campaign in West Virginia.

As Republican delegates swarmed toward their July 7 appointment at Chicago, the National Governors' Conference was meeting in Houston, directly exposed to all the shock waves stirred by the "Texas steal." Tom Dewey, drawing on his experience and skill as a District Attorney, used this ready-made opportunity to mobilize his Republican colleagues to take a stand on the issue of contested delegations. They did, and hit Taft where it hurt. Twenty-three of the twenty-five G.O.P. governors signed a manifesto urging that the sixty-eight challenged Southern delegates be barred from voting at the convention until their seating contests were resolved.

Otherwise, the manifesto said, "the Republican Party, no matter who ultimately may become the Republican nominee, will enter a vital and difficult campaign under a serious moral cloud." [12]

Prospective Republican voters heard the same message from Eisenhower as he barnstormed East from Denver, riding with Mamie to Chicago aboard a special train. People seemed to sprout from the Colorado and Nebraska wheatlands and the Iowa and Illinois cornfields, swarming by thousands to depots and sidings, craning off platforms, climbing up telegraph poles to hear the candidate pledge:

> I'm going to roar out across the country for a clean, decent operation. The American people deserve it . . . I'm going to fight for decency and clean operation in every aspect of government, including the election machinery.[13]

The conqueror of Europe was clearly in the mood to join the battle of Chicago.

VI

THE CHICAGO COUP

"We like Ike!"

THE conqueror of Europe was clearly in a mood to join the Battle of Chicago. And what a battle it was!

It began with a ham-handed attempt to railroad the convention for Taft. His friends insisted on Chicago, his midwestern citadel, as the convention site. They drilled in secret for the showdown there. The National Chairman, Guy Gabrielson, was a Taft man to the core. Taft stalwarts dominated the key Committees on Rules and Credentials. Above all, the National Committee, weighted 3 to 2 for Taft, manipulated every decision on contested delegations to the Senator's advantage.

Thus prepared, Taft's backers won the preliminary rounds. But they paid a price for every technical point they steamrollered through. They overplayed every hand, and their lack of subtlety was apparent to the public and to the uncommitted delegates whose votes they had to have. Once they lost the initiative, they lacked the trumps they needed to recapture it.

The first generally televised convention fascinated the

nation. Reporters swarmed over the National Committee sessions in the Conrad Hilton Hotel ballroom. Only closed doors could bar television's blinding lights and the cold, unblinking cameras.

The dispassionate lens zoomed in when the un-neutral Chairman Gabrielson and Representative Clarence Brown of Ohio made their first mistake. These two gentlemen, suddenly publicity-shy, decreed that the National Committee should meet in closed session to sift the conflicting claims for challenged delegate seats.

Impartial cameras focused upon the huge brass knobs on the twelve-foot black doors masking the committee's deliberations. It was a sterile picture, but it told the story. The nation was quick to get the point.

As I stood before those symbolic doors, I was asked to speak for the Eisenhower forces. The issue: why a closed meeting? With considerable passion, I exclaimed to the TV viewers: "Those doors are locked and they are being kept locked. Why? Because inside are people who are trying to do in secret what they don't dare do in public. What is that? They do not want you to see them deny the rightful claims of delegates to sit in this Convention and vote for Eisenhower. These doors are not closed against the press. They are closed against *you*, the people who want Eisenhower for President.

"Wire in!" I exhorted. "Write in! Phone in! Tell your delegates, tell your newspapers, you want open decisions in an open convention!"

General Julius Klein of Chicago, a staunch Taft man, pointed out in the strongest terms that the National Committee had met at other conventions in executive session, that the rights of all to full debate would be preserved and that the result would be subject to ratification by the convention in any event. It was the most impassioned impromptu debate I had ever enjoyed.

A few hours later, a flustered Chairman Gabrielson announced that final sessions of the committee would be reopened. But it became obvious that he had lost the strategic initiative when public and press responded thunderously in favor of the Eisenhower position.

The committee reversed precedent to replace a seventeen member delegation of Georgia "regulars" that favored Eisenhower 14 to 3 with a rival bloc that was solid for Taft. With plenty of help from Gabrielson, the bitter dispute over thirteen Louisiana seats was resolved 11 to 2 in Taft's favor.

Thunder rolled and lightning flashed across the G.O.P. horizon. Pundits recalled the 1912 debacle in which Teddy Roosevelt led his Bull Moosers out of another Chicago convention where the victorious party regulars rammed through the nomination of Bob Taft's father —and then went down to predictable defeat in the national election.

Overtones of 1912 haunted the Hilton ballroom as the committee prepared to deal with the "Texas Steal" which was the most notorious of the three contests. Gabrielson read a telegram from former President Herbert Hoover at the meeting urging "an amicable and equitable settlement." The chairman strove to glue a veneer of sweet reasonableness over the arbitrary record: a letter from Bob Taft proposing an "extremely generous" compromise on Texas.

The Eisenhower people said: Not generous, no compromise.

The battle was joined by white-haired, ruddy Senator John W. Bricker of Ohio, Taft's loyal colleague, with a motion for temporary adoption of the 1946 rules. Those rules would have permitted the sixty-eight challenged delegates cleared by the National Committee to vote on the question of their own eligibility.

The future of Taft—and Eisenhower—depended upon the outcome of this issue. If the Bricker motion were to carry, control of the convention would rest decisively with the Taft forces and the sixty-eight challenged delegates would be seated permanently.

Governor Langlie of Washington moved an amendment to require two-thirds approval by the Credentials Committee before anyone could fill any of the challenged seats.

It was an either-or situation. Gabrielson, whose office would go on the line if Taft lost, was ready with a counterploy. He recognized big Clarence Brown, a Taft man to his dying day. The Ohioan was expected to raise a point of order that would have the effect of requiring a two-thirds vote for adoption of the amendment.

"Point of order!" bellowed Brown.* His answer was a chorus of boos that rose to an angry crescendo. Brown had the hide of an elephant, but he was too experienced a professional not to react to the convention's hostility. He switched signals and extemporized a milder compromise. Brown proposed that the convention accept Langlie's amendment, but soften it by excluding seven of the challenged Louisiana Taft men from its coverage. This was a desperate attempt to save Bob Taft's friend, John Jackson, National Committeeman from Louisiana. If the Brown compromise succeeded, Jackson would not only control a majority of the Louisiana delegation but the Louisiana Republican organization. Moreover, Ike's key Southern leader, John Wisdom, would be put to rout.

Shouts of "No!" thundered through the flag-draped arena. Gabrielson gaveled down the protests and decreed

---

* This was, of course, before the late Senator Joe McCarthy made "Point of order, Mr. Chairman!" a famous—or infamous—phrase in Senate Committee hearings. Currently legislators eschew the remark, with its macabre reminders, in favor of "Parliamentary inquiry!"

two hours of debate on Brown's motion. The debate was a dubious asset, for Taft was the butt of the emotion-charged argument.

When the roll call came, Brown's amendment was beaten 658 to 548. It was a crucial milestone involving the good name of the party along with the fortunes of the candidates. I was heartened to note that the side we favored had support in forty of the forty-eight states, and that forty-nine Southerners voted with us. Langlie's motion then carried by voice vote. The breadth of our support was revealed as clearly national in scope.

Three days later, the issue was back before the convention in more direct terms: reports by the Credentials Committee on the contested delegations. The delegates dealt first with a minority report recommending that Georgia be represented by seventeen Eisenhower men. Its adoption would automatically nullify the contrary recommendation of the Credentials Committee's Taft-oriented majority.

In a decision crucial to the Eisenhower cause, the convention adopted the minority report 607 to 531. As the steam went out of their drive, the Taft men waived on Louisiana and agreed to seat our thirteen delegates. John Jackson's pocket Republican Party was out. A second minority report, upholding a Texas delegation split 33 to 5 for Eisenhower, was accepted on a voice vote. To political historians, the decision to seat the Georgia delegation was the turning point of the convention.

The still-new medium of television produced unpredictable results. There was such a happening when my own Pennsylvania delegation voted on the minority report.

Pennsylvania's Governor John S. Fine was one of the most-courted men at the convention, since our delegation was officially uninstructed, and the Governor controlled 30 of its 70 votes. A rockbottom 23 others supported Ike,

Taft had fifteen and two were for MacArthur. Nearly all of Fine's thirty friends were straining to be freed for Ike.

Fine and his state organization stood to benefit if Pennsylvania helped to nominate a winning candidate—and to suffer if he threw his strategic bloc of votes behind a loser. Before the delegation voted on the minority report, Fine wanted a Pennsylvania caucus. He obtained an oral agreement on a 45-minute recess from Walter S. Hallanan, the temporary chairman. Hallanan gave similar commitments to the Michigan and Wisconsin delegations.

Arthur Summerfield, the Michigan chairman, moved the recess from the convention floor, but delegates shouted it down. Hallanan then ruled out Fine's request on the basis of the Michigan decision. Fine, convinced of betrayal, tried to insist in a nose-to-nose shouting match at the rostrum. Hallanan gaveled him down.

It would have been just another convention flurry if television had not portrayed an indignant Pennsylvanian who seemed to be slowing down the dramatic push toward an Ike victory.

Pennsylvania's television viewers denounced their determined Governor for interrupting an absorbing drama. Editorial writers who weren't there took it out on Fine.

More immediately, our Pennsylvanians voted without benefit of caucus. Lacking instructions, most of Fine's platoon of delegates used their temporary freedom to back the Eisenhower cause. The Pennsylvanians supported the minority report 52 votes to 18. Bulldog Hallanan had outsmarted himself.

Our confidence surged with the seating of the Georgia delegation. The problem now was to hold what we evidently had against last-minute Taft pressure while the convention ambled through its elephantine minuet. On the fourth day, the rules were changed to bar challenged dele-

gates from voting before their seating contests were resolved. This was a breakthrough, crucial to Ike's supporters.

A platform acceptable to the party's internationalists
was adopted without difficulty. Most of the speeches that
day dealt with the need to end the war in Korea. Vivid in
my memory is a snatch from a talk by the Rev. W. H.
Alexander, Pastor of the First Christian Church of Oklahoma City:

"I asked Dr. Albert Einstein just the other day . . .
'What kind of weapons will we use in World War III?'
He said, 'I don't know, but I can tell you what kind of
weapons we will use in World War IV.' I said, 'Well, what
are they?' And he said, 'Stone clubs.' "

I was on the busy platform as an Eisenhower liaison
man when Senator Everett McKinley Dirksen of Illinois
offered Taft's name, jabbing at Dewey as the alleged mas-
termind behind Ike even as he hailed Taft's midwestern
virtues. Dewey's friends and foes launched fervent demonstrations. An eloquent affirmative case for Eisenhower was
offered by Maryland's Governor Theodore Roosevelt
McKeldin. Senator William F. Knowland of California
carried Earl Warren's flickering torch. A lonesome loyal-
ist pleaded MacArthur's hopeless cause. Finally on the
fifth day, July 11, the decision came.

At every contested convention, there comes a decisive
turn in the sonorous roll call of the States: the moment of
political truth when, from many contenders, one is called
to lead the party up or down the quadrennial hill. I shall
never outlive a sense of fresh excitement from the slow re-
cital of historic state names and the regionally accented
responses that build the cumulative total.

On that hot July day in 1952, the drama was height-
ened by a sense of exalted expectation absent from more
recent Republican experience. Changed fortunes and new

responsibilities await my party when it rediscovers that spirit.

At Chicago, my concern for a candidate involved me with the decisions of delegations from the four corners of the Union. Time crawled during the long, maddeningly close roll call. As the clerk intoned the roster, I tried to ease my tension by scrawling a tally of the states where we were doing better—or worse—than we had expected. I jotted down these shifts:

ALABAMA: Out of fourteen, five for Ike. We had picked up one (the delegate's wife in the red dress!).

COLORADO: Fifteen out of eighteen. Good! The lines were holding.

IOWA: Sixteen out of twenty-six. Good for Senator Hickenlooper.

MAINE: Brewster's folly. Promised twelve to Taft, delivered five.

MARYLAND: Sixteen for Eisenhower, eight for Taft; a loss of one, which I had expected.

MICHIGAN: Thirty-five out of forty-six, a big pickup. The Postmaster-Generalship looked safe for Summerfield.

MINNESOTA: Nineteen for Stassen, nine for Ike. A gain of five and more coming.

PENNSYLVANIA: Two for MacArthur, fifteen for Taft, fifty-three for Eisenhower. Walter Hallanan had shoved Governor Fine too hard!

VIRGINIA: Fourteen for Taft, nine for Eisenhower. Hard work and personal friendships gained us five.

WASHINGTON: Twenty for Eisenhower, four for Taft. We had refused a Taft offer of four and fought in every district. Our biggest turnover in any state—from two to twenty.

ALASKA: Two for Taft, one for Ike. Al White had kept his promise.

HAWAII: Hurrah for one switching Japanese-American! But who converted him?

The roll call ended with 595 official votes for Eisenhower, an even 500 for Taft, 81 for Warren, 20 for Stassen and a token 10 for MacArthur. Ike was nine votes short of pay dirt. A bandwagon rush was on; State banners waved frantically. Minnesota's standard caught the Chairman's eye. Stassen's 19-vote nest egg was switched to Eisenhower. Forty delegations rejiggered their lines. Some delegates were honoring second ballot commitments; some just saw an opportunity to "get right" and took it. At the actual end of the first ballot, Ike had it with 845 votes to 280 for Taft. The decision was made unanimous.

During the pandemonium that followed, two Senators who were candidates for re-election separately pulled me aside to confide gloomily: "I don't know how I'll ever carry Eisenhower in my state." In November, Ike's coat-tails lugged both of them over the line.

The General viewed it on television from his suite at the Blackstone Hotel with his brother Milton, General Clay and Herb Brownell. Ike later said he was trying to fathom a commotion during the first roll call when he was nearly pitched backward by the embraces of his three companions. They were shouting like fight fans:

"It's all over!"

"Minnesota's switched!"

"You're nominated!"

Not long thereafter, the new candidate left his headquarters to visit Taft in his rooms at the Hilton across the street. His courtesy later paid incalculable dividends.

Soon after Ike returned to his suite, Harold Stassen appeared. What Stassen said I don't know, but I do know that the General believed two years later that it was Stassen who engineered the "Minnesota switch."

I knew personally how little Stassen had to do with "the

switch." The day before the nomination, three Pennsylvanians had called on Stassen to urge him to release his
Minnesota delegates. Stassen refused to admit that he
hadn't a chance. He rejected our advice that seven Min-
nesotans were already backing Ike (nine actually supported the General on the first go-round).

Stassen was still standing on his burning deck when all
his delegates jumped overboard. While the tally was still
under way, the switch was arranged without the favorite
son's approval.

The only favorite son delegation that stood firm to the
end was Warren's bloc of seventy Californians. I think
Warren's determination to hold them on the leash was
double-locked by a belief that young Senator Richard M.
Nixon, the most promising of California's rising Republicans, was privately strong for Ike.

I reached the same opinion when I talked with Nixon
while flying to the convention. He was expertly informed
on details of Ike's campaign and left me with no doubt
that his sympathies were with Eisenhower in the struggle
with Taft. He clearly expected Ike to win the nomination,
but he honored his instruction to support Warren and
never said in so many words that he was for Eisenhower.

Nothing in Nixon's manner suggested any expectation
that he would even be considered as Eisenhower's running
mate. I think of the future Vice President on that flight to
Chicago much as I recall myself on the way to the 1948
Convention. I had no idea that I would leave Philadelphia
to barnstorm as National Chairman, so there was nothing
in my manner to indicate any speculations. Nixon, similarly, did not act like a man waiting for something to happen to him.

Eisenhower's choice of Nixon followed a logical pattern. The General, if he won, would be sixty-two years
old upon his inauguration, and Nixon would only turn

forty on January 9, 1953. His selection would give the ticket an age balance and also recognize the growing electoral power of the West.

The afternoon of Ike's nomination, Nixon was cleared by state delegation leaders, and the convention promptly nominated him by acclamation. That night, the representatives of a party that had lost five successive Presidential elections cheered with a zeal that seemed to submerge factionalism, as their jubilant nominee recruited them in his "great crusade" to return their Republican Party to power.

At its post-convention meeting, the National Committee installed Ike's nominee, Arthur Summerfield, to replace the unlamented Guy Gabrielson as National Chairman.

The 1952 Convention did much to advance the G.O.P. as a truly national party. By its recognition of vigorous new elements in the south, it ended the sway of Dixie's "post office" Republicans.

In some states, respectability has admittedly been a long time coming. But 1952 opened the door, and now there are many more dwellers in the house of Southern Republicanism. There are, moreover, many more moderate Republicans in Dixie than some Republicans in a few southern states are prepared to concede. Their day has not yet fully arrived; but I am satisfied that every year is bringing and will bring new gains to moderate Republicanism—South and North.

In early August, 1952, I was named Eisenhower's regional co-ordinator for the South, faced with the job of assessing how far we should go to invade a region that was dissatisfied with its Democratic inheritance, but still mesmerized by racism. The portents were mixed, except in Texas, where Governor Allan Shivers was in the process of leading his Democratic faction into the Eisenhower camp.

We reached a command decision that no one in our party would stay in a segregated hotel—and no hotels in the South were then integrated.

Where possible, we arranged to fly the candidate in and out of Southern cities in a single day. Where the need for more exposure made this impractical, he traveled on the "Eisenhower Special," a designedly nonsegregated campaign train which the candidate could use as living quarters and as the base for whistle stop talks.

Ike tried an airborne reconnaissance in force into the South in the first week in September. The results of six appearances in four states were promising enough to justify plans for a larger effort.

The South had been at outs with the national Democrats since the New Deal years, but never before had it showered rebel yells on a Republican. In the spirit of the tour, I wired home:

"Ike drawing tremendous enthusiastic crowds. Had bigger audience in Miami than Stevenson had in Detroit. Hard-shell reporters have admitted to me they never expected anything like it. The Southern friends you and I know have been jumping up and down, saying 'Didn't we tell you it would be like this?' Miami show biggest day for the South since the War between the States."

The South was but one speculative segment in a national campaign which depended for overall success on recapturing the farm vote we lost in 1948 and on breaking the Democratic hold on the cities.

Basic to these goals was a peace pact between the Taft Republicans of the Midwest and the still-dominant internationalist wing, whose new leader was General Eisenhower. To his credit, Senator Taft led his midwesterners into the battle after his now-celebrated September 12 breakfast with Ike at Columbia University produced the "Treaty of Morningside Heights."

Against this promising background, General and Mrs. Eisenhower set out during the third week of September for an intensive round of whistle-stopping through Bob Taft's Midwest.

In mid-September, flying back from one of Ike's quick forays into the South, Governor Adams talked of an unforeseen difficulty aboard the campaign train: there was no one to deal with the local leaders and candidates who swarmed aboard at almost every stop. Confusingly, but not surprisingly, everybody who got on the train insisted upon a brief visit with General Eisenhower. Of the technicians aboard, only Len Hall and Fred Seaton seemed to know the practicing politicians from the amateur enthusiasts.

Adams said: "You know some of these folks in every state. So get yourself out to that train and make those people as happy as you can." *

Aboard the train, I did whatever seemed most useful at the time. I hobnobbed daily with state and local politicos, ranking their demands according to their standing on the G.O.P. totem pole. As Chairman, I had learned enough of internal party politics in most states to evaluate what I heard and saw. I constantly phoned my gleanings back from train stops to Brownell or Adams. Where appropriate, I relayed reactions direct to the General or to Senator Fred Seaton, or occasionally, to Mamie. I was at times called on by Gabriel Hauge, the candidate's principal speech drafter on the train, to help with the local allusions, historical, personal, or topical, designed to warm up an audience by tickling community pride.

As a member of Congress, I knew most of the press

---

* I made Adams happy, too, when I recruited FDR's son, John, as an effective speaker for Ike's cause. He elected to speak in the big city areas where the name of Eleanor Roosevelt was magic. His reason: "We Roosevelts don't have to agree on everything and I'd like to counter my mother's campaigning for the other candidate."

aboard. Late hours with the reporters helped test reactions and, when fortune smiled, stimulated some favorable ones, for the love of Ike.

My life with the mobile part of the campaign began when my wife and I left to join the Eisenhower train at Kansas City on September 19. The auspices seemed superb. Reports stacking up from all hands told of real rapport between Ike and large, enthusiastic crowds at every stop while his train chugged across Minnesota, Iowa, Nebraska and Missouri.

Our first clue that the picture was shifting, and fast, came from a bulletin in a morning paper I scanned during the flight to Kansas City. I fuzzily recall reading that someone in California had linked Dick Nixon with some kind of slush fund. We dismissed it as campaign nonsense and began fretting because our plane was late and we feared we would miss Ike's speech. We decided to skip the auditorium and watch it on television at our temporary headquarters at the Muehlebach Hotel. We found a solemn group before a TV set in Arthur Summerfield's room.

"This looks like a wake," I cracked. "Why the gloom?"

Silently I was handed one of the afternoon papers that were strewn around the room. It reported the basic elements of the "Nixon fund" allegation which all but derailed the most promising Republican campaign in a generation.

The "Nixon fund" leaped full-blown from an exclusive story published the afternoon of Thursday, September 18, by the New York *Post*, Manhattan's only Democratic daily, under the headline: "SECRET RICH MEN'S TRUST FUND KEEPS NIXON IN STYLE FAR BEYOND HIS SALARY." The story quoted Dana C. Smith, a Pasadena attorney who said he was one of a number of well-to-do Californians who had contributed upward of $17,000 toward Nixon's expenses since he entered the Senate in 1951. It left the plain inference that Nixon was beholden to a California "millionaire's club."

I was filled in rapidly on details: How cautious rewrites of the story, spread nationwide by the wire services, had hit the Eisenhower train as it crossed Nebraska Thursday night; how the staff on the train had let the candidate go to bed uninformed about it after he addressed a tremendously successful rally that night in Omaha; how correspondents overheard an all-night staff debate on a demand—fired from the hip by Democratic National Chairman Stephen Mitchell—that Nixon be dropped from the G.O.P. ticket; how sensational stories that Nixon might be dumped had been filed from the train, and how Eisenhower on Friday morning had finally issued a formal statement that he believed Nixon "an honest man" and planned "to talk with him at the earliest time we can reach each other by telephone."

Nixon, then whistle-stopping in California, had been reached by Senator Seaton from a telephone booth at Auburn, Nebraska. Nixon had promptly issued a statement saying he had accepted the money for political expenses which he believed should not be charged to the Federal government—mostly clerk-hire, postage, printing and travel.[1] He had later exploded at a heckler that he was the target of "smears" by "the Alger Hiss crowd." Nixon then rejected Seaton's suggestion that he fly East and give a personal accounting to Eisenhower. Instead, he proposed to dictate a statement which the General could issue on his behalf.

Nixon's statement promised that Smith would issue a "full report" on the fund and predicted it would show the contributors to be public spirited citizens who received no "special favors, consideration or treatment" in return.

Ike read this unusual message from his running mate to
the audience at Kansas City's Municipal Auditorium and
to millions of television viewers. Then he added an impromptu personal postscript:

"Knowing Dick Nixon as I do, I believe that when all of
the facts are known to all of us, they will show that Dick
Nixon would not compromise with what is right. Both he
and I believe in a single standard of morality in public
life." [2]

The General's plea that the nation withhold its verdict
until it heard all the evidence was in accord with justice,
but not, I fear, with human nature. The press reaction
was overwhelmingly hostile, not only in the editorial
offices, but among the correspondents riding with us on
the train eastward toward St. Louis. The "dump Nixon"
crowd was led by Bert Andrews, the keen, forceful Washington Bureau Chief of the old New York *Herald Tribune*, who was at once a long-time friend of Nixon's and an
ardent Eisenhower supporter to whose advice the General
listened. Andrews argued that the ticket could be freed of
any taint of unethical conduct only if Nixon were replaced.

This view was wired to the world in one form or another
by most of the correspondents. It was espoused by many
in the official party, principally the enthusiastic non-
professionals. The professional politicians—Summerfield,
Seaton, Representative Leslie Arends of Illinois, and myself—argued against any precipitate action, at least until
all the facts were in. We warned that a substitution on a
national ticket under fire in mid-campaign was novel and
difficult and potentially disastrous.

Our position was urgently supported by Bob Taft when
he boarded the train at Cincinnati to whistle-stop north-
ward through Ohio and show his home state by his presence that "Mr. Republican" did indeed support the ticket.

The rear-platform crowds were big and responsive, and I congratulated Taft on them when we met in a Pullman corridor.

"I've always done pretty well in Ohio," was his characteristically diffident reply.

Not doing so well were the candidate and his advisers and the increasingly critical press. The "dump Nixon" speculation grew so intense that Ike walked back to the crowded press car on Monday night, September 22, to make it clear to the reporters that he still had an open mind on the affair. Sitting on the floor while the train lurched north toward Cleveland, the Republican Presidential candidate had it out with fifty skeptical newsmen in a long, frank dialogue.

"Let's be fair about this," Ike said as he began the off-the-record huddle. He seemed to be talking indirectly to his supporters around the country who had reached him by telephone at whistle stops, mostly to urge that Nixon be made to walk the plank. Eisenhower laid strong stress on statements by Dana Smith, Nixon's lawyer-friend, that the fund had been used not for Nixon's personal benefit, but rather for the heavy overhead that besets any Senator from a large, faraway state—return trips to keep speaking engagements in California, political mailings to constituents, clerical hire and the like.

Long after Ike had left the press car, Les Arends and I stayed there, doing our best to dissuade the newsmen from pushing ahead any further with their "Nixon-must-go" campaign. Tuesday's dispatches reflected Eisenhower's dual determination: that he would neither tolerate an associate who was not "clean as a hound's tooth," nor take part in destroying a man's career before the full story was known.

Ike was reserving judgement until Nixon could have his day in court—which in modern campaigning means a half hour on national television. A crash plan for such a program had already been developed in the wee hours of Monday morning at a meeting in a St. Louis hotel room of four acutely concerned officials of the Republican National Committee. By 2 A.M. Monday the time was reserved and $80,000 was earmarked to pay for it. Later in the morning, Eisenhower reached Nixon by telephone in Portland, Oregon, and counseled him to "put the whole works on the record."

As plans for Nixon's speech gathered momentum, the fickle winds that had blown so benignly for the Democrats veered abruptly and caved in a fragile glass house at Springfield, Illinois. It came to light that Governor Stevenson had, since 1949, accepted private contributions for an unpublicized fund to augment the patently modest salaries of key officials in his administration. The amount so disbursed: $18,744 contributed by 1,000 donors—just a shade more than the $18,235 certified by Dana Smith as the final total of gifts made by 76 contributors to the "Nixon fund."

The parallel was too close. Aboard the train on Monday night, September 22, I commented that "if Nixon is guilty of anything, then Stevenson is guilty."

"You can draw the line right down the middle and the funds are exactly alike," I told reporters. "In this case, Stevenson's friends were acting in the same role as Dana Smith, who contributed to the Nixon fund and helped manage it. They were contributing to a fund to help these men do a better job."

It should be noted that Stevenson never joined the Democratic claque that clamored for Nixon's head. Why should he when his fund was just as big and several times as busy?

The drama's great second act reached its climax at 6:30 P.M. Pacific Time, Tuesday, in a Los Angeles studio where Richard Nixon, accompanied only by his wife, Pat, looked into television cameras and put his defense before a jury of 155 million Americans.

In Cleveland, two hours before the start of Nixon's decisive talk, seven Republican strategists gathered in a room in the Carter Hotel to weigh the crucial next step. In addition to the foursome who arranged the broadcast— Summerfield, Bob Humphreys, Publicity Director of the Republican National Committee, Senator Carl Mundt of South Dakota and Len Hall—the participants were Senator Knowland, Representative Arends and myself.

Knowland, direct as always, urged that Ike clear Nixon in his speech that night. Mundt and I both contended that Eisenhower's expected endorsement of Nixon should wait a day, to avoid any suggestion that Ike responded emotionally to a telecast. We felt that since the incident had grown into a major campaign issue, its resolution should be considered in terms of maximum political impact. Summerfield put the question before Ike, who agreed.

I watched Nixon's astoundingly effective solo performance on TV from Ike's hotel room with Summerfield, Knowland and Mundt. We were four case-hardened professionals, keyed up to the breaking point by days of crisis. Tears were streaming unchecked down our cheeks before Nixon had completed his earnest presentation of his modest financial circumstances. He fully accounted for the fund and its use entirely for political expenses he could not hope to meet on his $15,000 yearly Senate salary. Although he owed $38,000 in mortgages and other debts, he said, he had accepted but one gift: "a little cocker spaniel dog . . . and our little girl—Trisha, the six-year-old—named it Checkers." [3]

My wife saw Nixon's fight for his political life on a television set in the press dining car on the campaign train. She heard one of the reporters gibe at it as "corny."

"If it's corn," Marian blazed back, "it's the kind that grows in green pastures." To her pleased surprise, she saw Bert Andrews, so recently a ringleader of the "dump Nixon" writers, nodding gravely at her from a table across the aisle.

Ike viewed the "Checkers" speech with Mrs. Eisenhower on a television set in the office of the manager of the Cleveland Public Auditorium while the words were piped to a capacity audience of 17,000 waiting in the hall. The talk set Mamie weeping, but it fired up the General. As soon as it ended, he seized a yellow pad and summoned staff members for a hasty rewrite of his prepared speech on inflation.

In the jammed auditorium, the crowd waited half an hour, alternately chanting "We want Nixon" and cheering mentions of the young Senator's name by warmup speakers.

The building rocked at Ike's opening: "Tonight I saw an example of courage. I have seen many brave men in tough situations. I have never seen any come through in better fashion than Senator Nixon did tonight." [4]

Yet the audience did not get all it sought; even as Ike extended the accolade, he withheld full clearance. He had to base his final opinion on something "more than a single presentation," he said. Hence, he was wiring Nixon to ask him to "fly to see me at once" [5] for a face-to-face talk Wednesday night when the General was to appear at Wheeling, West Virginia.

Ike previewed the Wheeling appointment at every whistle stop as his train huffed across Ohio toward West Virginia. At Portsmouth, Ohio, the General had an opportunity to reach Nixon by telephone while the Senator was changing planes out West. There were two telephone booths back to back on the platform, and dozens of keyed-up reporters competing for every crumb from the most sensational news story of the campaign. Ike and Adams headed for one of the booths and both of them, the broad-shouldered General and the wiry Governor, jammed themselves inside.

The adjoining booth could have been a sounding box for any reporter who could reach it. To maintain Ike's privacy, I charged into the empty booth and lifted the receiver in a businesslike sort of way. I had no one to call at the moment, but I managed to look busy for the benefit of the press by explaining to the operator the delicate nature of the emergency.* I said, "If you like Ike, just hang on. I can't explain why." "O.K., you said it," replied the lady. Ike's call stayed confidential.[6]

My wife and Rachel Adams were among those pressed into service at the business end of the train to handle a blizzard of telegrams and special delivery letters that poured aboard at every stop. There was time only to tally them. The first wave was 4 to 1 for Nixon, but the ratio after the first 10,000 messages was a resounding 10 to 1. A similar lopsided verdict for Nixon was reported by the Republican National Committee, which estimated that it received two million messages of all kinds by the end of the week. Another blizzard of telegrams so deluged Ike Headquarters in New York that Western Union recruited dozens of the Bowery's sidewalk habitués to man an all night delivery service.

The Eisenhower Special clacked on to Wheeling to meet Nixon. The location was hardly ideal. West Virginia had a Democratic administration and a Republican organization headed by Taft man Walter Hallanan, notably slow in warming up to Ike and ostentatiously absent from Wheeling.

It was a crisp, footballish evening as our motorcade

* This call, showing the two phone booths, is illustrated between pages 172 and 173, in *First Hand Report* by Sherman Adams.

sped to meet Nixon's plane at Wheeling's airport. The chill didn't deter a crowd which grew to thousands during the 50-minute wait. West Virginians surged in the starlit dark around Ike's car. Bill Knowland and I stationed ourselves on either side of the hood and were almost pushed down by the crush. When Nixon's plane landed, tall, handsome Pat came down the gangplank with the staff, but the Vice Presidential nominee was still aboard, groping for his topcoat. Ike hesitated just a moment on the apron, then ran up the steps and into the plane.

"Why, General, you shouldn't have come here," someone heard Nixon say.

"Dick, you're my boy," was Eisenhower's much-quoted reply. After a private talk in the plane, he came down the steps with his arm over Nixon's shoulder in the glare of spotlights and a volley of flash bulbs.

In my years as a politician, I have come to accept confusion as part of the drama, but that chilly night in Wheeling was a case apart. The crowd, officially estimated at 8,000, had dutifully shivered there for four hours with little entertainment and no information from the reception committee, which had collectively disappeared under the stands for a wee drappie to keep the cold out.

As we stepped out of our car in the gloom behind the platform, we made out Ike and Adams right beside us. The General seemed pretty worked up.

"Where the hell is Mamie?" he demanded. Nobody knew, so he ordered: "All you fellows go out and find Mamie."

We scattered to our cars and went careening back to Wheeling, where someone finally sighted the black car carrying the wives of the candidates. When they reached the stadium, we began the business the crowd had waited four hours to hear.

Ike raced through part of a prepared speech on Republican unity, then ad libbed:

"Ladies and gentlemen, my colleague in this political campaign has been subject to a very unfair and vicious attack. So far as I am concerned, he has not only vindicated himself, but I feel that he has acted as a man of courage and honor and . . . stands higher than ever before." [7]

It was the answer to the "Checkers" speech that most Republicans had hoped for. It brought the Wheeling crowd to its feet, applauding and cheering. Nixon looked tense through it all, but when Ike presented him, he responded with an emotional tribute to the General. At its end, he turned back toward his seat, then surrendered to the nightmarish week. With the crowd still cheering, he dropped his head on Bill Knowland's square shoulder and gave way to racking sobs.

The official party made the return trip minus an escort, for the two motorcycle men had apparently gone off duty. The caravan wormed over the bridge back to Wheeling and into an unpoliced jam. Sturdy Bill Knowland leaped out of our car, strode to a corner and began directing traffic. Mostly by the considerable force of his personality, he extricated the little motorcade, and Ike returned to the train.

The Eisenhower Special rumbled on into a campaign that had actually been strengthened by the Nixon fund incident. It would have been impossible to contrive circumstances which better displayed Ike's fair-mindedness and good judgment in the face of pressures from one side to dump Nixon and, from the other, to keep the ticket intact at all costs. Nixon came out of the ordeal a far stronger candidate, one whose qualifications triumphantly survived far more public scrutiny than they received at the time of his nomination. The young junior Senator from California developed an ardent personal following which supplied many volunteers for him in the 1960 campaign.

Ike's campaign sustained its first physical accident after a Richmond speech when enthusiastic Virginians
swarmed on the platform to try to shake the candidate's
hand. With Knowland running interference on one side
and me on the other, Ike tried to edge into the Capitol to
greet local notables. All at once, the wooden platform gave
way with a crack like overloaded ice on a skating pond.
Arm in arm, we fell bolt upright to the steps four feet
below. Startled but unhurt, we somehow helped one another out. Ike, quite himself, moved swiftly through the
doors of the old Capitol exchanging an affable handshake
with a lady in a wheelchair.

We were too busy to give the incident much thought.
Not so Richmond's Republican City Committee and the
Republican State Committee of Virginia. Both groups
leaped to their typewriters to point out to General Eisenhower that they had nothing to do with construction of
the offending platform. The arrangements, they noted
darkly, were entrusted to the Virginia Citizens for Eisenhower, and they wanted an apology from Eisenhower himself, for letting "a bunch of Democrats take over." A few
days later, the letters were bucked over to me by Sherman
Adams.

"I didn't build the platform," I remonstrated.

"You'd better build one now," barked my brusque
boss.

"With what?"

"Use your ingenuity."

In the first week of October, Ike dipped South again,*
and I spent some time with a special task force organized
to deal with a special problem: Harry Truman. The pep-
pery Democratic President let Stevenson wow the egg-
heads with his polished Princetonian periods, but Truman

---

* A souvenir cigarette lighter bearing Ike's signature records his travels, between nomination and election, on a map of the United States:
Rail miles 20,871, Air miles, 30,505.

believed there still were votes along the same low road that
led him to victory in 1948. He hired a train and started to
whistle-stop. Our answer was the "Truth Squad," a crew
of Republican legislators—usually three at a time—
assigned to follow Truman's trail by chartered plane, to
field his multitudinous whoppers and then throw the facts
back in his face.

I served two week-long stints on the Truth Squad,
speaking in the Middle West and Far West at or near
points recently visited by Truman. We primed ourselves
for these affairs by listening in on the President by television or radio. Where possible, we would hold on-the-spot
press conferences right after Truman spoke.

He left us some magnificent openings. For example,
there was his statement that the Democratic Party had
"led the nation to victory in World War II, and is leading
the country now to victory in the struggle against communism." [8] We countercharged that "No leader contributed more to the victory in Europe than Dwight D. Eisenhower . . . but the Truman Administration lost the
peace." [9]

Truman tried to lug General Eisenhower, as former
Chief of Staff, into Administration decisions that left
South Korea exposed to Communist attack. The Truth
Squad retorted that it was Truman who "gave Russia an
open door to Korea over Eisenhower's protests." [10]

When Truman declared that General Eisenhower was
"deeply involved" [11] in political decisions that permitted
the Red Army to surround Berlin in 1945, the Truth
Squad showed by the record that Ike "protested the political decisions by Mr. Truman that led to the Berlin mess."

We felt we had fulfilled our mission when Truman began fighting with the Truth Squad instead of with Ike.
What Ike himself refrained from saying aloud is better
left still unsaid.

When Ike flew into New Orleans, he started a 16-hour

Mardi Gras of his own. With a bow to the Creole tradition, Canal Street sprouted buttons reading *"J'aime
Ike."* *

Mindful that Stevenson had been widely criticized in
the North for staying in a segregated hotel there, we had
a special train waiting for Ike. We were still most anxious
to avoid friction involving any of our Negro staff members. Among them was Fred Morrow, a successful former
CBS official who later became a White House personnel
advisor to President Eisenhower.

As the Canal Street parade was forming, Governor
Adams gave me my order of the day: "No matter what car
you're supposed to be in, you ride with Fred Morrow and
if anyone lays a hand on him, I want you to hit him, whoever he is, with all you've got."

I looked up Morrow, half a head taller than I, nine
years younger, maybe twenty pounds heavier and all muscle (which I wasn't). As we set out together, I wondered
who would protect whom if need arose. I never found out.
If there were any incidents that day, they were remote
from Morrow and me.

Truman, who did not hesitate to pin a wholly unjus-
tified charge of race bigotry on Dwight Eisenhower,
screamed foul when Ike questioned the Administration's
capacity to bring an honorable end to the Korean War.
Truman could rail at Ike and his "snollygoster advisers,"
but the remote, deadly conflict had resulted in 150,000
casualties in two years. It had become far and away the
least popular war in our history up to that time. Republicans could hardly be blamed if they drew an ironic
contrast between Truman's "you never had it so good"
claims and the grim realities facing the troops in Korea.

In September, Ike dwelt on the failure of truce negotia-

---

* I conceived another button, which sprouted everywhere: "Ike and
Dick, They're for You."

tions, then fourteen months old, and strongly helped his candidacy when he promised that he, as President, would actively explore avenues to peace.

"I will meet anybody anywhere in the world any time I believe there is a worthwhile result to be accomplished," he told a group of Republican Congressional candidates in Cleveland. "But . . . I would first inform the United States exactly what I was trying to do." [12]

He pursued this idea to its devastatingly effective conclusion on October 24 when he pledged in Detroit's Masonic Auditorium: "I shall go to Korea." Ike promised, if elected, to "concentrate on the job of ending the Korean War." [13] Stevenson denounced the speech as "slick," [14] Truman called it a "fraud," [15] but the peace-hungry nation responded. Ike renewed his pledge on October 27 in Pittsburgh. Less than five weeks later, nearly two months before his inauguration, President-elect Eisenhower was off on a fact-finding tour of the war front. Six months after he took office, the Korean Armistice was signed. Thereafter during the entire Eisenhower Administration, the American people had lasting peace.

As November 4 drew close, the polls and the experts were all counting Ike in. I had vivid memories of my experience as National Chairman four years before. As a candidate for re-election to Congress, I was not putting out victory press releases in spite of a gut feeling the self-ordained prophets were right. The field reports were so favorable and Ike's crowds were so big and so enthusiastic that it had to mean something.

On the morning of Election Day, Governor Adams handed the presidential candidate a prayer I had written for him alone.[16] Ike read it as he stood by the mantel in his Morningside Heights living room. Perhaps this incident inspired his decision to open his First Inaugural Address with a prayer of his own.

I was working in our Commodore Hotel Headquarters on the night of November 3—election eve—when one of my better-known (and better-heeled) friends telephoned. Some might have considered his query unsettling in view of his substantial contributions to the Citizens for Eisenhower.

"Is Ike going to win tomorrow?" he asked. "I've been offered an $8,000 bet on Stevenson at even money. I want to take it, but I'd like to be right. Shall I grab it?"

I had never made a cash election bet in my life (although I had delivered a new Stetson to Truman's National Chairman when Dewey lost in 1948), but I knew the bookmaker's odds against Stevenson were a good bit longer than even money.

"You'd better take it," I said, and promptly got carried away. "And you'd better put me down for $300."

And so it was that very early Wednesday morning I received a $300 check from a prominent Democratic department store owner. At a more appropriate hour the same Wednesday, I basked in my favorite indulgence at Yamanaka's lovely Oriental art shop on Park Avenue.

The check just covered an early Chinese painting which had most fittingly belonged to the estate of Mrs. McCormick Blair, a relative of Adlai Stevenson's. The painting has worn well and the irony improves with age.

I bought my Chinese trophy in a mood of triumph. I had passed election night at the Commodore, shuttling between our headquarters, where the increasingly favorable returns were piling up, and Eisenhower's third floor suite, where Republican leaders from all over the Nation waited expectantly. Mrs. Scott and I joined Senator Jim Duff there as Pennsylvania's representatives. "Come on in," said Mamie Eisenhower, using the old Army post greeting style, "there's food to eat and folks you know."

I chatted briefly with Helen Geis, one of my secretaries

on the campaign staff and later the bride of Representative Jack Westland of Washington. It came out that I was in a close re-election fight.

"I didn't know *you* were running for anything," said Helen. She had never seen me involved with any campaign but Eisenhower's.

Although I managed to make only a very few speeches on my own behalf in 1952, I eventually pulled through my Congressional race by a respectable 6,200-vote margin. I was more fortunate than Cabot Lodge, whose preoccupation with the Eisenhower campaign gave John F. Kennedy the opportunity he sought to step up from the House of Representatives to the Senate.

In Ike's suite, I watched on television as Stevenson conceded defeat with a wry epigram: "It hurts too much to laugh and I'm too old to cry." [17]

I stepped into Ike's bedroom with the news, which had been anticipated for a couple of hours. The General was in high good humor as he reached for his black tie to finish dressing for the formal reception downstairs in the ballroom.

The candidate had become the President-elect when he strode into his sitting room. The assembled Republican bigwigs were jubilant, but a trifle tonguetied. There was a quizzical set to Ike's grin.

"I guess what I like best is that I carried Illinois and Missouri," said the President-elect.

The thought of tripping Stevenson and Truman on their home grounds seemed the most soul-satisfying thing in the world to that roomful of keyed-up Republicans. As laughter banished the tension, a Senator ventured to suggest to Ike that he would "bear an awesome responsibility."

"Well, Senator," replied the grinning old Supreme Commander, "I've had responsibilities before."

In the ballroom, 2,000 party workers were cheering returns that brought Ike 442 electoral votes from thirty-nine states and a 6,600,000-vote plurality over Stevenson. It was the widest margin, popular and electoral, since Roosevelt flattened Landon in 1936.

The picture in Congress was somewhat different; we held the Senate by one thin vote, 48 to 47, after Wayne Morse of Oregon stopped being a maverick Republican and declared himself an Independent. We were in shape to organize the House by the uncomfortably narrow margin of 221 to 213.

The Congressional returns were still coming in when Ike entered the Commodore ballroom, already shadowed by three men from the Secret Service. Many of the exuberant party workers were too young to have worked before in a victorious national Republican campaign. Joyful pandemonium greeted the President-elect. But triumphant partisanship was not Ike's dominant mood. His opening words dwelt on the importance of national unity.

The next morning, I paid my ceremonial call at Yamanaka's and stopped at the Commodore Headquarters just long enough to leave a letter of resignation on Sherman Adams' desk. Then I took a cab to Pennsylvania Station and the next train to Philadelphia. By midafternoon, I was slumped in a chair in my old stone house overlooking the gardens of the Morris Arboretum, luxuriating in a stack of congratulatory telegrams. I was far from bashful about them, for I was the only one of six Republican House candidates from Philadelphia who had made it. One of the wires was a message from Dick Nixon asking me to meet with him in Washington a week later. Well, I thought, I may be in shape to talk politics after a week's rest.

The rest lasted less than twenty-four hours. The next

morning there was Sherman Adams' commanding twang on the telephone.

"Why aren't you at your desk?"

Appalled silence.

"Get in here by 8 A.M. tomorrow."

I pleaded lack of sleep, the party's over, you'll be smothered in volunteers now that you've won, et cetera; every et cetera I could think of. I ran out. At the other end of the line, an impatient intake of breath.

"O.K., get in here Monday," said Adams. He topped the concession with a mite of largesse: "Eight-THIRTY o'clock."

"At the same pay?"

The attempted wisecrack was an unsalaried volunteer's way of saying yes, I get the message.

The staff of a President-elect is, as we lawyers say, both *ad hoc* and *de facto*. Its members cannot expect pay and their voluntary service can raise no obligation.

On Monday, November 10, I was back at the Commodore as Chairman of the Eisenhower Headquarters Committee. My job was to do whatever was necessary to establish and operate a command post for a President-elect who then held no public office and hence lacked any appropriate headquarters. It was imperative that he have proper facilities in which to discuss and consider appointments, to plan for the Inauguration, to see essential visitors—and to be securely screened from a horde of other, not-so-essential callers.

I rapidly discovered one acute and basic shortage: money. We could count on only limited assistance from the Republican Campaign Committees, which had spent close to the legal limits to promote Ike's election. Ahead of us lay a two-month operation which I (optimistically) estimated would cost $20,000 a week. Even with Adams' talent for dragooning executive-level volunteers, we still faced heavy overhead expenses.

We searched the precedents and there were none, for all modern Presidents had gone from another public office to the White House.

To help run the office and deal with a steady stream of V.I.P.s, I called on Representative (now Senator) Clifford P. Case of New Jersey for willing help. We made up the rules as we went along. First, I drew up guidelines designed to shield Ike from questionable demands and still meet our needs for money. No laws governing elections or campaign financing were relevant to our unique situation.

Late in November, we organized the "Eisenhower Headquarters Committee" as a "voluntary association" chartered under New York law to assume the financial obligations of the President-elect. We were set up as a "nonpolitical" committee, and we urgently wanted to cut loose from official G.O.P. support. We had designs on a surplus amassed by the National Citizens for Eisenhower.

Governor Adams referred Sidney Weinberg, Treasurer of the Citizens and one of Ike's best friends, to me with the observation, "Sidney giveth, Scottie taketh away."

We recaptured some $200,000 in Citizens' funds for a kitty, then raised a public cry for help. We faced one nice problem in propriety: since there was no applicable law, there was nothing to bar large gifts from corporations or unions. We felt there could be no harm in token-size donations, provided we took no money in such an amount or under such circumstances that the donor could believe it had bought special favors.

I decided that, except for the "Citizens" refund, we would accept no contribution in excess of $1,000. To head off any illusions about special favors, I ruled that the first contribution we received from any business or labor group would set the ceiling for all others in the same category. For example, if our first gift from a civic group was $600, we would take no more from any other unit of the same kind. As it worked out, with a little guidance, there was a remarkable uniformity in the contributions received from each group. Thus nourished, the headquarters operation ran with a staff of about 90 until Inauguration Day.

The procedure was hand-to-mouth and I don't recommend it to any future incoming Administration that finds itself in the same predicament. I have several times urged Congressional Committees to amend the election laws to assure a more satisfactory arrangement when and if another President-elect lacks an official base.

My work with V.I.P.s included preparations to receive Prime Minister Winston Churchill, who came over in early January to visit with the President-elect. Discussing the forthcoming visit by his old wartime associate, Ike said to me, "As great as Churchill is, these deathless phrases don't just pop out, you know. As he makes brief remarks in a general conversation, you can almost feel his mind at work preparing and shaping some great thundering comment, while the front part of his mind is making ordinary talk. After a while, out comes the Churchillian sentence." Ike added: "I used to work with him. I still can." A mischievous grin suggested to me the thought that there had been some changes made since the wartime days.

In policy planning for the new Administration, the basic conflicts of the preconvention campaign began to reappear. The aboriginal Republicans, who had backed Taft to a man but were actually more conservative than the Senator, construed the election as a mandate to liquidate all traces of the New Deal. Opposed were many original Eisenhower supporters, including myself, who main-

tained that we could not bury twenty years of history,
even if we would. We urged that the President begin his
administration with a legislative program that would
prove that Republicans stood for intelligent progress, not
blind reaction. We held that social legislation embedded in
our government by ratification in many past elections
should be kept and improved and made more workable
where possible.

Previewing the Eighty-third Congress for the Poor
Richard Club of Philadelphia in mid-November of 1952, I
accurately predicted that Eisenhower would receive considerable co-operation from minority Democrats.

"Basically we are all the same kind of people," I said
hopefully. "Nine times out of ten, they will work with us
for the good of the country." [17]

VII

THE WHITE HOUSE

"A people that values its privileges above its principles soon loses both."
DWIGHT D. EISENHOWER

WHEN the Eighty-third Congress ended its first session in 1953, it seemed time to blow the whistle on a vocal but stubborn minority of the President's party. The bulk of Eisenhower's program had squeaked through the closely-divided Congress—but only with the help of Democratic votes. I was one of four Republicans who backed the President 97 percent of the time. But forty-odd Republican back benchers, whose reflexes were apparently set during their years of fighting Democratic Presidents, voted against every Twentieth-Century proposal of the Eisenhower Administration.

After private persuasion failed, I decided to give this grotesque situation a public airing, and let fly with an article for the September 1953 issue of the *American Magazine*. It was strong stuff and it drew as much attention from the press as from the G.O.P. foot draggers in both Chambers who were my targets.

I classified my backward-peering colleagues variously as "noisy obstructionists" and "free-wheeling grandstanders." The Eighty-third Congress, I wrote, featured "the spectacle of G.O.P. players clipping their own teammates, making grandstand plays and running for the wrong goal line."

Of those who from force of habit continued "sniping at the Administration, even though it is now headed by their own leader," I wrote: "Sometimes the noisy obstructionists in our party make us sound like a bunch of quarreling old women . . . They sometimes act as if it were the president who is on probation, whereas, in the eyes of press and public, it is more apt to be the Congress."

I topped the indictment with bills of particulars against six of the most unreconstructed Republicans, Senators Joseph McCarthy of Wisconsin, Herman Welker of Idaho and George Malone of Nevada, and Representatives Noah Mason of Illinois, and Clare Hoffman of Michigan.

My attack was predictably denounced by my old antagonists on the Chicago *Tribune*—but it was commended by most of the American press. My unrepentant targets returned the fire. Perhaps the most revealing report came from Joe McCarthy, who suggested that I was "probably wanting to get a headline"—which I was, but not for the reasons that occurred to him.

Then, with the sarcasm that helped make him the bad boy of the G.O.P., McCarthy added: "I am very happy to receive advice from such a real authority as Hugh Scott, who was in charge of and brilliantly managed the 1948 campaign which bankrupt [*sic*] and nearly wrecked the Republican party." [1]

The crisis that led me to write the article was deepened by the tragedy of Taft's death on July 31, 1953, from a voracious cancer of the hip. Not until the Adams affair five years later did the fate of a single individual affect so profoundly the relations between Eisenhower's White House and Capitol Hill.

I am convinced that the Republican Party would be stronger and more effective today if the first—and only— Republican Administration in a generation had been allowed the services of the blunt, honorable Taft as Senate Leader and if Sherman Adams had fulfilled his promise as the Assistant to the President.

Although he remained the hero of Republican "regulars," Taft shelved his blighted hopes, worked hard in the Eisenhower campaign and, after the election, made his unique experience available to the President-elect. A relationship that was tentative at first grew close with time. Taft became the President's most valued adviser on Congressional affairs, magnanimously sharing his knowledge and his skill with the Chief Executive. On the floor of his Senate citadel, he was as formidable as he was dependable.

Taft knew in his bones the compound of pressures and sensibilities that turns the wheels in Congress. He knew the reflexes and prejudices that could block Administration programs unless key Senators were conditioned to go along. He knew the thresholds of Congressional acceptance, the points where a drafting modification would save a programmed bill from grief. He helped shape measures that could be passed, then rounded up the votes— Republican where possible, Democrat where necessary— to push them through.

When Taft limped off the Senate stage, his intimate relationship with the President was serving both the Nation and the Party. I firmly believe both would have fared better had he lived. He was a true conservative, dedicated to preserving that which is good, as opposed to reactionaries who want to turn the clock back on everything. Taft

worked for legislation which broad segments of his party
and the nation could approve. He discouraged extremes,
on the right as well as the left.

Continued association with Taft's forceful leadership
would have strengthened the President's position on Capitol Hill. More than that, it would have increased the President's awareness of the importance of the Party structure
as a means to legislative ends. Taft knew the value of good
working relationships with Republican State Chairmen
and appreciated the proper use of patronage as a per-
suader. Ike and those around him often seemed to draw no
clear distinction between the majority of appointments
that properly belong in the career and civil service cate-
gories and the sensitive minority called "political." These
appointments are relatively few in number, but they help
sustain the party structure. They are tangible recogni-
tions of creditable work for a party, thus strengthening
its leadership and building morale in its ranks.

Taft's death left Eisenhower insulated from these
cogent practicalities. No successor in the Congressional
leadership equaled him in judgment or stature or closeness
to the President. Lack of such intimate, expert counsel
explains in part Eisenhower's failure to leave a stronger,
more viable party to his political heirs. Instead, by a process that was avoidable but unhappily not avoided, the
Great Crusade gradually disintegrated and supporting
groups fell away.

Some of the responsibility belongs to Sherman Adams,
the tireless, self-effacing New Englander who had such a
major share in Ike's primary victories and Presidential
elections and who served nearly six years as Ike's eyes and
ears and good right arm. The former Governor of New
Hampshire was curt, sometimes abrasive. His manner
seemed to many as harsh as the climate of his native state.

But screened behind it—almost as if Adams were ashamed of it—was a deeply emotional personality, capable of strong attachments to people deemed worthy of confidence.

As the Assistant to the President, Adams made it his mission to protect the President from embarrassment and from the ways of error as defined in the stiff standards he set for executive personnel. His favorite phrase as he winnowed proposals involving the President was: "We cannot permit this man to be hurt." He spoke constantly and affectionately of Eisenhower as "this man."

Adams considered it a part of his job to be accessible to people who felt their ideas could benefit the Nation, the Administration or the Republican Party. Many never got to see the President, but the Governor's concurrence in a proposal carried great weight with Eisenhower. He was perhaps one or two points to the left of center on the Republican ideological scale, and he was a relaxed and pleasant listener when moderate Republicans came down to the White House with ideas. (To his everlasting credit, he never affected the alarm clock wrist watch, a device some lesser White House staffers somewhat cravenly used to speed the parting guest.)

In his zeal to conserve the President's time and strength, Adams tended to shield Ike from the discord that is built into the policy-making process. Sometimes he was over-protective, so insulating Ike from the clash of ideas that final Presidential decisions may have been made without consideration of all viewpoints.

Appointees who turned out, after inspection, to be not quite "as clean as a hound's tooth" were quietly but effectively eased out by Adams. Republicans in Congress and party moguls in the states found him impervious to requests for the slightly rancid favors that grease so many political wheels. Inside the White House, he was known to all as "the Governor," but Washington wags dubbed him "the Abominable No-man."

Now and again, associates glimpsed the shyness that underlay the Governor's sandpaper mannerisms. More than once during my meetings with him he went out of his way to discuss some individual with whom he was at odds. A typical exchange would begin with an Adams question:

"Why do you suppose that fellow is mad with me?"

"Because you chewed him out."

"I didn't chew him out; I just gave him the facts."

"You gave him the facts in rather strong language, Governor."

"Well, that's the only way I can get them to understand," was Adams' weary, half-defensive explanation. As often as not, he would let the subject lapse, then worry it some more: "I wonder why that fellow was hurt; I didn't mean to hurt him."

This attitude may help explain the equivocal relationship between Adams and Bernard Goldfine. No substantial reason save misplaced friendship has yet emerged to account for the Governor's acceptance of Goldfine's hospitality and gifts that included a celebrated vicuna coat. It may be that the complex Governor went along with his aggressive benefactor out of unwillingness to hurt the feelings of a man he first knew as the rescuer of the dying textile industry in his home state.

It should be noted that the practice of using the hotel suites of friendly constituents neither began nor ended with Adams. This does not justify a course the Governor himself conceded was "unwise." But it does suggest that his actions might have been judged on a different scale if anyone but Adams had been involved.

It is an irony of history that Adams was the principal target of the rigid standards he had done so much to set for the Eisenhower Administration. "The Abominable No-man" had crossed too many Republicans on matters rang-ing from petty patronage to highest policy to find many in his own party to stand by his side when his personal cri-sis struck. Influential Democrats felt he had made their roads more difficult—and 1956 was a Presidential election year. Short of issues, many an officeholder of less stern stuff was privately gleeful though publicly saddened at being handed a chance to hack at a fallen oak.

Washington is a town where half the people are waiting to be discovered and the other half are afraid they will be. When discovery comes, Washington follows a curious double standard. It deals quite as harshly with a single misstep by an upright man as it does with the manifold transgressions of the most brazen operator.

To suggest that Adams' forced resignation was a pun-ishment that dwarfed his "crime" is not to defend the propriety of accepting favors from one who clearly sought to trade on the influence of the Assistant to the President. But it should be noted that more profound abuses are still tolerated every day in Washington.

Congress continues to countenance brazen lobbying by pressure groups that pay off in campaign contributions for concessions received from those close to the seats of power at both ends of Pennsylvania Avenue. Reform of the time-honored system of campaign financing, with its curious quids paying for dubious quos, is long overdue. There is obvious need for a realistic financial disclosure law and for reasonable—and workable—codes of ethics for the legislative and executive branches.

I have digressed into the Adams case because the Gover-nor, like Taft, could be and was replaced, but actually was irreplaceable. To rank-and-filers on the Hill who were battling for Eisenhower programs, and anxious for the President to know it, he was a reliable avenue to the President. The avenue closed with his departure. A growing conservatism permeated Administration programs in Eisenhower's last two years and did much to chill young people and loyal progressives.

There was no such prospect in December 1953, when a dozen Eisenhower Republicans from the House called on the President. Our avowed purpose was twofold; to assure Ike of support for his progressive programs, both domestic and foreign, and to promote the newly-formed Citizens for Eisenhower Congressional Committee. The Committee was assembled to foster re-election of modern Republican Members of Congress, and we all shared a special stake in its success, for we represented a dozen urban and suburban districts where Republican candidates started with a handicap. Our constituencies insisted on more than the standpat Republicanism so dear to the "old fuds." And, happily, so did Ike.

When the Eighty-third Congress reconvened for its election-year second session in 1954, the political war drums were already thumping. Some Democrats, following Harry Truman's lead, saw a business recession around the corner and sought to brand as a "rich man's" measure the Administration's record tax cut bill, which in fact brought $1.4 billion in reductions to millions of taxpayers. Some Republicans were more preoccupied with Joe McCarthy's indiscriminate hunt for Communists, first in the Truman Administration, and eventually under Eisenhower, than they were with current business. Some days it just seemed easier to them to hunt for Communists than for solutions.

The situation prompted me on February 16, 1954, to propose a fair swap to both parties. "I suggest," I told my colleagues in one of those one-minute speeches that speed business in the House, "that Republicans agree that Democrats generally are loyal Americans, that subversion and treason are personal to the offenders and that these offenders are no longer in the Government.

"I suggest that Democrats, in grateful return, stop trying to scare people into reducing employment by cutting out accusations against Republicans as alleged promoters of hard times.

"Suppose Democrats stopped running against Hoover and Republicans stopped running against Truman? Could we not just get on with mutually constructive efforts on behalf of all the people?" [2] I suppose we could have. But we didn't.

Two weeks later, I unwittingly missed my chance at a player's role in the event the press adjudged the most dramatic of the session: the March 1 round of gunplay in the House chamber that attended a demonstration by four heavily-armed Puerto Rican nationalists. I was walking back from my office and up the steps of the House wing when the unusual sight of Capitol policemen on the run gave me my first inkling of the outrage in which five of my colleagues were wounded. All the injured members recovered and won re-election. The most permanent result of the incident was a decision to make individual members responsible for the issuance of passes for admission to the public galleries in both House and Senate.

Election-year politics threatened to run as wild as the Puerto Ricans until Ike stepped in with a firmness he had not previously shown in dealings with Congress. The Democratic minority decided it had a sure-fire issue in a move to add $2.4 billion in election-year tax slashes to the Administration's carefully-tailored tax revision bill. Some panicky Republicans feared they would lose their seats if they failed to go along.

It looked like an Administration rout until Eisenhower took up the challenge. The President, who began his term declaring that Congress should dispose after he proposed,

reversed his field. He went on the air to appeal for public
support in heading off a cut that would have thrown his
budget seriously out of balance. The nation responded,
and so did many Republicans. The simple fact that the
popular President was fighting for his request brought
most of them back into line. Waverers heard from the
White House that they might lose patronage plums. Pressures were even brought to bear on Democrats from
Southern districts where the President was popular. On
the crucial 210-204 roll call that blocked the Democratic
amendment, nine Southern Democrats crossed over to tip
the balance for the Administration.

Eisenhower's Great Crusade of 1952 had given Congressional Republicans their second chance at leadership
in twenty years, and the judgment of history will have to
be that they muffed it. Their 1952 lead failed to survive
the 1954 mid-term elections, and the two elections that
followed opened new gaps in the ranks of the G.O.P. Republicans were hurt in part by blind fortune: the death of
Robert Taft just as he reached full stature as the priceless link between the Capitol and the White House; and
the controversial liquidation of Sherman Adams by the
wretched Goldfine affair on the eve of the 1958 elections.
But in many other ways, the party hurt itself by failure
to build a record that held voter support.

Many of the Administration measures were hemmed in
with restrictions, often zealously backed by the standpat
fringe of the President's party.

Many Republicans of this same breed were supporters,
overt or covert, of Senator Joe McCarthy's free-style in-
vestigatory techniques, and instances of unproved charges
were spreading to House investigations. The power to in-
vestigate can mean the power to reveal, educate, and point
the way toward needed legislation. It can also operate to
demolish character, especially when a trophy-hunting

committee is working a field as emotionally charged as was the issue of Communist subversion in that era. There was a call for guidelines to safeguard both the Congressional right to know and the rights of witnesses.

I found myself in the middle of this one by virtue of my promotion to the House Rules Committee, the immensely powerful group of senior members whose prime function was to decide when—and whether—bills reported by committees were to reach the House floor. As the Committee's name implies, it also has initial jurisdiction over changes in the rules of the House. It was in this capacity that I was named Chairman of a special subcommittee instructed to develop a code of fair play for committee hearings.

I believed workable rules could do a lot to allay the almost hysterical fear which Congressional subpoenas aroused in witnesses during the McCarthy era. And I believed passage of such a code would redound to the credit of Congress and the Republican Party. After hearings and deliberations, I offered a bill proposing a fair-play code which would, among other things, have insured the rights of witnesses to testify in their own behalf, to cross-examine their accusers and to refuse to have their testimony broadcast or telecast. For better or worse, principally for lack of Republican leadership support, the uniform code was not adopted, but several committees incorporated some of its recommendations in their own rules. In the following Democratic-controlled Congress, the Doyle Resolution, embodying some of my earlier suggestions, was adopted. Credit for a modest reform, which should have gone to the Republicans, went to the Democrats.

Like most House members I was free from entanglement in the year's stickiest issue, Joe McCarthy's mudslinging public brawl with Army Secretary Robert T. Stevens. It was the Senate's problem, but it was the Party's headache. It raged through thirty-six days of televised public hearings that brought the Wisconsin Senator into open war with the Administration and led eventually to a Senate vote of condemnation against McCarthy. That vote came after the November 1954 elections, in which the McCarthy issue did nothing to help Republicans fighting to hold their narrow control of both Houses.

Ike, privately sizzling mad at McCarthy, maintained his dignified aloofness as McCarthy ranted that his Administration, too, was coddling Communists. Democrats gleefully suggested it was time for formation of a McCarthyite third party.

"If people want to split off . . . that will have to be their business," Ike told a news conference in October. "The great mass of the people of the U.S. want . . . progressive moderates handling their business, and that is exactly what I am working for." [3]

Ike kept working toward this goal despite continuing objections from the party's Dinosaur wing. He never gave up in his efforts to convert those Congressmen who saw socialism in any Federal appropriation—except where the money went into their own districts. They appeared to define "socialism" as Federal money going somewhere else. As the 1954 session moved on, the Eisenhower program progressed, despite sniping by the old conservative coalition of right-wing Republicans and Southern Democrats.

The Administration's health bill was watered down, in spite of the fact that once its original imprimatur was from Bob Taft's hand. Ike had told Taft it was a liberal measure, adding jokingly, "Where did you get that conservative label?" Ike's proposals to revise the Taft-Hartley Act and grant statehood to Hawaii were shelved. There were basic improvements in tax, farm and social security programs, but the Republican Party was vulner-

able in the hard-fought "swing" districts it had to carry
to win Congress.

Ten days before the 1954 mid-term election, the President invited Pennsylvania's State and Congressional candidates to his still uncompleted Gettysburg farmhouse to
underscore his endorsement. Before the luncheon meeting,
Ike spoke feelingly of the new confidence he felt in the
signing of agreements making West Germany an equal
partner in NATO. With evident relief, he boxed the com-
pass of world trouble spots and found the outlook encouraging.

"We have seen the terrible threat in Iran disappear,"
said Ike. "That annoying situation in Suez has been composed. The sensitiveness of the Trieste question has been
removed. The first beachhead of Communism in the Western Hemisphere, at Guatemala, has been eliminated by the
Guatemalans themselves. . . ." [4]

But when the smoke cleared after the elections of November 2, 1954, Republicans had little to cheer about.
House Republicans lost eighteen precious seats—not bad
for an off-year election, but not good, by any means. We
were back in the minority, 203 to 232 in the House and 47
to 48 in the Senate.

In both Houses of the Eighty-fourth Congress, Ike's
Modern Republicans faced the double disadvantage of
minority status and Old Guard leadership in most important slots. It was an unpromising position from which to
write the record that would inescapably be the basis for
the 1956 Presidential campaign. Many assumed Ike
would run for re-election and almost certainly win; the
unsolved problem was the recapture of Congress. To some
of us, it appeared that closer cooperation with the eminently electable Ike could not help but build party
strength even as it advanced the Eisenhower program.

Out of this approach developed an informal organization of Eisenhower Republicans from Congress who met periodically with Administration officials. Vice President Nixon presided over the sessions. The aim of the meetings was to supplement the work of the President's regular weekly meetings with the titular Republican leaders of Congress, to multiply their effect in Congress, rather than dilute it. All Republican members ready to take the initiative for Ike were welcome, and many attended.

The "Ike Loyalists" were a factor in building a Republican *esprit de corps*, which held our ranks nearly solid on most important questions before the Eighty-fourth Congress outside the fields of farm price supports and reciprocal trade, "gut" issues on which both parties divided. Ike himself was an active and most effective missionary for his "progressive moderate" policies within the Republican Party and sometimes outside the fold. But you can't pass a bill without votes. The program bills that passed were generally those acceptable to the "Texas Twins," House Speaker Sam Rayburn and the Senate's dynamic eyeball-searching Majority Leader, Lyndon B. Johnson.

When the first session of the Eighty-fourth ended, Congress had gone all the way to back the President on foreign policy and had given him most of what he wanted in extensions of reciprocal trade and foreign aid programs. It had raised the minimum wage to $1.00 an hour and hiked government salaries, including its own. It had squelched the efforts of some Democrats to reinstate high, rigid farm price supports, but it notably failed to heed Ike's calls for action on important domestic fronts. School and highway construction, immigration reform, new public housing authorizations, reinsurance for private health insurance plans and statehood for Hawaii and Alaska were the most prominent casualties.

On September 24, 1955, came the dismaying word that

the President had suffered a heart attack while vacationing at Denver. He had carefully avoided any commitment on his candidacy for a second term, but most Republicans felt the party's chances for success depended on his running again. The party's long-run future depended quite as much on Ike's leadership in office as on his phenomenal success as a candidate.

Many members of Ike's party shared his concern that "Modern Republicanism" should be continued. It was much in his mind the previous March when a group of Republican Congressmen joined him at the White House for lunch.

"I don't know whether or not I am going to run," the President told us, "but this I do know—I will want to be damn sure that whoever does run will be a man whose views are consonant with the way I think about things." [5] "He'll run," said optimistic Chairman Len Hall.

As the President recovered, there was endless press speculation about his future, but lesser Republicans discreetly restrained any overt expression of Presidential ambitions, while Nixon and Adams ran an efficient caretaker government. I personally felt, and said, that the President should be allowed to make up his own mind, without pressure, when he saw fit.

Notwithstanding Len Hall's confident assurances, the big question of Ike's intentions was still unanswered as the Eighty-fourth Congress reconvened for its climactic, inevitably political second session in 1956. The Republicans were deployed all across the middle of the road, meeting conservative demands for a balanced budget and developing the sound social programs urged by party progressives. If our ranks could be held firm under the banner of Modern Republicanism, the Democrats could go along or make the unpleasant tactical choice between flanking us on the far left or risking the charge of obstructionism.

The state of Ike's health kept the question of his candidacy open, but his State of the Union Message offered an opportune launching platform for any Eisenhower Republican. It stressed government "response to human concerns" and it bade Congress to act in the fields of social security, school construction, housing and immigration. In a significant step forward, the President proposed creation of a new bipartisan commission to work for the protection of the civil rights of all Americans.

The civil rights issue was one in which I was already deeply involved. The first of a series of bipartisan meetings on tactics to set the stage for action on a civil rights bill in 1956 was held in my office early in January. I became co-chairman of a bipartisan group formed "to counteract the growing determination of the Southern block in its resistance to Constitutional guarantees." [6]

On April 9, the Administration submitted a three-part bill proposing creation of a new Civil Rights Commission backed up by a special Civil Rights Division in the Justice Department, and new authority for any citizen to sue in Federal courts to protect his right to vote.

It was a modest enough program—but it was a start, after more than a half century of callous inaction by the government. Even so, our first step put Southern backs up. In the Senate, the Dixiecrats promptly sounded a filibuster alarm. In the House, it stirred seventy-nine Democrats and four Republicans into the high-flying bluster of the "Southern Manifesto" which vowed an all-out battle to stall the bill. That mischievous paper became the symbolic charter for the organized white resistance to civil rights progress that kept the South in turmoil and built up demagogues like George Wallace.

Skilled Southern parliamentarians slowed action so long that it was late in the session's final week before the civil rights bill cleared the House by a 153-vote margin.

It was pointless at that date to try to blast it out of the Southern-dominated Senate Judiciary Committee.

The Administration had nothing to be ashamed of, I reminded 2,000 delegates from thirty-five states who gathered in Washington for an Assembly on Civil Rights. I recounted Eisenhower's moves to bring complete desegregation of the armed forces, the Administration's support of integration in Washington's public facilities, its enforcement of nondiscrimination clauses in government contracts, its advancement of Negroes to high government posts. Now, I said, after seventy-eight years of legislative neglect, Congress was being asked to advance Negro rights. As I pledged our bipartisan group to advance the fight, I made a pardonable political point: ". . . While both parties must share the blame for this inaction, the inescapable fact remains that the present control of Congress and of Congressional Committees is in the Democratic Party." [7]

The election-year Congress scrambled to break camp in time for the late summer Conventions. It had been a frustrating session that muddied more issues than it clarified. It was a great relief to get to San Francisco, particularly refreshing when one recalled the former sweltering Republican battles in Philadelphia and Chicago. One blessed the beautiful, breezy bay and hoped an inconspicuous hope that the storm-tossed G.O.P. would enter its second century as a Grand New Party in Eisenhower's image.

It was an undramatic convention in 1956. By the time Republicans had arrived, their only surprise was behind them. Harold Stassen had been dissuaded in time from his attempt to bump Nixon off the ticket and name Massachusetts Governor Christian A. Herter as Ike's new running mate. Herter hastily disavowed the oddly-timed maneuver, then agreed to put Nixon's name in nomination. Stassen abruptly decided to offer a second after a talk with Ike. The whole performance looked to me like an act of political loneliness.

Since there were no insoluble credential fights, I had the time I wanted to counsel with the Platform Committee to do what I could to insure that our civil rights plank did not echo the weasel-worded effort of the Democratic Convention. The Chicago platform drafters had approved a plank that tiptoed delicately around full endorsement of the Supreme Court's historic 1954 school integration decision. Our final product reasonably maintained that progress in carrying out the Supreme Court order must be encouraged " . . . in every legal manner by all branches of the Federal Government to the end that the constitutional ideal of equality before the law, regardless of race, creed or color, will be steadily achieved." [8]

I spoke for the rights plank before the unwontedly harmonious convention of 2,646 delegates and alternates massed before television cameras in the vast Cow Palace under banners proclaiming the campaign theme of "Peace, Prosperity, Progress." Like other speakers, I also carried the message: If you like Ike, give him a Republican Congress to carry out his program.

Certainly Americans showed that they liked Ike when they re-elected him with a record plurality. The Congressional vote was another matter. The Republican Party failed to regain its 1954 losses. One outstanding casualty was Pennsylvania's Senator Jim Duff who missed being elected by a hairline even though Ike carried the State and I ran 5,000 votes ahead of Ike himself in my own district.

As the Democratic dominated Eighty-fifth Congress buckled down to work, President Eisenhower pledged at a press conference, to work "industriously and incessantly" for Modern Republicanism.

The election returns, the President suggested, should

convince even the Party's foot-draggers that "some change in the understanding that the public has of the Republican party is necessary." [9]

But as Ike set out on a four-year effort to produce that change, there was recurring evidence that the Party's Bourbon wing had learned nothing from recent experience and forgotten nothing from its catalogue of past grievances. At the beginning of Eisenhower's second Administration, their hopes to repudiate "welfare statism" seemed mostly the stuff of troglodyte dreams, for the Administration, so recently and triumphantly returned to power, dominated the Party machinery outside Congress. The National Committee, which the Old Guard had controlled 60 to 40 in 1952, was now more than eighty percent on Ike's side.

The Democratic leaders, too, could read election returns, and they saw political peril in frontal attacks on a President so manifestly popular as Eisenhower. They knew his influence would wane with the progress of his second term, which was fixed as his last by the new Twenty-Second Amendment to the Constitution. So, they saved their ammunition, particularly in the Senate, for "the men around Eisenhower," sniping at individual targets of opportunity even as they supported many of Ike's programs.

I became more interested in seeing the Administration's Civil Rights package, basically unchanged from the 1956 proposal, clear the House. As a member of the Rules Committee who had the pivotal vote, I voted with the majority that cleared the right to vote bill for action. This was accomplished after a bitter Southern-led rear-guard effort to require a jury trial in cases involving violations of injunctions against interference with the right to vote.

It took twenty-five days of debate for Majority Leader Lyndon Johnson to head off any further Southern filibustering in the Senate. To avert Senate deadlock, the cutting edge of the bill was blunted. Use of injunctions to enforce all Constitutional rights was limited by the Senate to cover only voting rights. Then, with Johnson's blessing, the Senate compromisers threw in a revived jury-trial amendment. Gone was the bill's famed Title III, which would have permitted Federal intervention in court proceedings to enforce a broad range of constitutional rights.

The situation required judicious bargaining for the best compromise we could get before the session adjourned. The normal conference between the Houses was short-circuited because the Senate conferees would be headed by an arch-segregationist. The alternative was informal negotiations to develop a compromise amendment acceptable to the Senate that could be added from the House floor.

After two hectic weeks of seemingly endless bargaining, a hard-won formula brought a substantial concession to the Republican viewpoint: it allowed the presiding Federal judge to decide whether violators of injunctions against interference with voting rights should be tried before a jury.

The Senate version of the bill could not return to the House floor without clearance from the Rules Committee. The Committee's adroit segregationist chairman, Representative Howard W. Smith of Virginia, took Senate passage of the rights bill as a signal to stop holding Rules Committee meetings. The committee's six Democrats soon signed a petition calling for a meeting. They needed one more signature. I provided it when terms of the compromise were finally worked out.

The Bill finally passed the House in duly amended form and cleared the Senate two days later after exhaustion halted a dramatic solo filibuster by Senator Strom Thurmond that lasted a record twenty-four hours and eighteen minutes. All the opposition came from Southern Democrats.

Blunted though it was, the 1957 Civil Rights Act of the Eisenhower days divided two eras of Congressional thought; it signaled the nation that there would be no turning back to the hypocrisy of state-sanctioned inequality. The wedge broke through the cement that long had bound Dixiecrats and right-wing Republicans in the comfortable old conservative coalition against progress.

The immediate result was less progress than "prudence" cast in the image of Lyndon Johnson's astute leadership of the Senate majority. Democratic votes undercut Ike repeatedly, especially on the budget, which was slashed by more than $5 billion. In contrast to Republican support of Truman's Marshall Plan program, Democrats led assaults that hewed $2.4 billion out of Ike's defense request and $1 billion from his foreign aid program.

High-stakes politics saturated the election-year session of the Eighty-fifth Congress. Parties and factions within parties jockeyed for advantage first in the mid-term campaign, then in the 1960 elections which would, under the Constitution, signal the formal end of the Eisenhower Era.

New issues spawned since the first session's adjournment in August were paramount when work resumed in January. The Soviet launching of Sputnik I had raised a challenge that could be met only with a massive and costly effort. Arkansas Governor Orval Faubus posed a challenge of a different sort when he forced Ike to use troops to enforce court-ordered integration of Little Rock's schools, and a brief recession prompted demands for government spending which the imminent campaign did nothing to abate.

In March, I won the Pennsylvania Republican organization's endorsement for Duff's old Senate seat and nailed it down later in the May primaries. Overriding all other questions at the storm center of Pennsylvania's political winds was the issue of unemployment arising from the sudden, happily short recession that began late in 1957 and reached its peak in the election-year summer. It hit hard in the coal and iron industries that are the heart of the Pennsylvania economy, and it was a blow to the President's party.

The White House asked, and secured, legislation to extend the term of unemployment benefits. But Administration forces successfully resisted tax-cut proposals.

The acute problems of my own state helped bring passage (with my support) of a bill allocating $279 million for the relief of distressed industrial areas. It went far beyond guides set by the President, who eventually vetoed it.

I had fought a losing battle for a distressed area bill of my own (the Scott-Van Zandt Bill) which used the rifle shot rather than the scatter gun approach. My bill would have channelled larger sums to the limited areas of acute distress. I personally urged President Eisenhower to put his Administration behind a workable distressed area bill, but the President informed me that his economists had submitted unfavorable recommendations. The Administration was in a squeeze between raised spending and falling revenues, leading to a deficit.

Statehood bills had waited unhappily in the wings of Congress for years. Hawaii was then generally regarded as Republican in outlook and previous votes on Hawaiian statehood had included many Republican supporters. Conservative opposition, involving fear of a "Japanese Senator," long blocked final approval.*

---

* At a House Rules Committee hearing on statehood for Hawaii, Mississippi's Rep. William M. Colmer voiced this fear at a public hear-

The general expectation had been that Hawaii would become a state before Alaska. Speaker Rayburn, noting Democratic trends in Alaska, decided to reverse the process and gave Alaska the green light. Hawaiian statehood was not achieved until August 1959.

Ironically for both parties Hawaii has been largely Democratic in its voting pattern and Alaska presently sports a Republican Governor and a Republican Congressman-at-large. The best laid eggs sometimes end up in the wrong basket.

Well before the session adjourned on August 24, I was deeply involved in the Pennsylvania Senate campaign against Democratic Governor George Leader. It was becoming apparent that all Eisenhower Republicans shared a common problem: the Adams-Goldfine affair. The House inquiry dragged along all summer, piling mountains of innuendo on genuine evidence of damaging links between the hitherto untouchable Cerberus of the White House and the self-serving, pushing textile man.

Before adjournment, many Congressional Republicans (of whom I was not one) had passed the word to the President that a campaign with Adams as the Assistant to the President would be a disaster. Their true motive in seeking to dump Adams, in my opinion, was his lack of rapport with Republican Congressional leaders on both legislative and patronage matters. Nothing overt happened until Maine's early-season election brought defeat to Senator Frederick G. Payne, who had also been identified, with more political purpose than total accuracy, as a Goldfine associate. The White House was swamped with frantic demands for Adams' resignation. The President accepted it "with sadness" on September 22.[10] Then

ing. I interposed with some crispness: "If the first Japanese Senator served in that battle on the Rapido (Italian campaign), I'd go down to the airport to welcome him to the Capitol."

Sherman Adams went on national television to insist
again that he had "done no wrong" and to charge with
evident conviction that he was the victim of a "calculated,
contrived effort to destroy me." [11]

I was on the Hill when the news of the resignation
broke. I had been astounded and dismayed by the evidence
presented at the House hearings, but was never convinced
that the full story was told. I had known a great deal
about Adams, beginning with the early days before the
New Hampshire primary. It remained for me to be convinced that he was not one of the most honorable men in
Washington. And I knew in a thousand ways his tireless dedication to the kind of government in which I believed.

I knew, too, how unfashionable my view had become in
Congress. On an impulse born of sympathy, I had gone
down to the White House to call on him during his travail,
and shortly before the President's decision. I found the
Governor grimly composed, but his entire staff was in
tears and work in the once-bustling office was near a
standstill.

In the 1958 off-year balloting, I moved to the Senate as
the lone Republican to survive a Democratic sweep in
Pennsylvania's statewide elections.

There was personal triumph in the victory, for I had
weathered a national landslide—the Democratic majorities leaped to lopsided proportions.

While the Democrats knocked over thirteen Senate
seats that had formerly been held by the G.O.P., they
scored most of their gains against the Republican right.
Disturbed by the conflict between the Conservatives in
Congress and the moderates surrounding Eisenhower;
confronted with the problem of candidates running on a
pro-right-to-work platform and the recession issue, the
Republicans could have well used a more effective strategy.

The three G.O.P. newcomers who made it—Kenneth Keating of New York, Winston Prouty of Vermont, and I—all qualified as "Modern Republicans." Keating, incidentally, rode the tide that carried progressive Nelson Rockefeller into New York's Governorship. Only in Arizona, where personable Barry Goldwater won a second term, was a full-fledged right-winger re-elected to the Senate that year under the Republican label.

My own state-wide campaign had been waged initially against the traditional forces in Pennsylvania Republicanism whose sole criterion in a Senate candidate was that he be a "sound" man dependably steeped in their conservatism. I won the nomination against the opposition of those powerful forces, such as the followers of State Senate President M. Harvey Taylor and the Grundyite leaders of the Pennsylvania Manufacturers Association.

The typhoon that decimated the party also shifted its balance; the little knot of Republicans who had stood by Eisenhower policies while the party's right wing was selling them short had weathered the storm. The bulk of the casualties were on the party's right flank, and its proportionate strength was accordingly reduced.

The old New York *Herald Tribune*, the sorely-missed, often eloquent voice of progressive Republicanism, surveyed the wreckage and asked the more prominent survivors how they made it and what the G.O.P. should do to build for the 1960 campaign.

I told the *Tribune:* "I tried to make it plain that I oppose extremism, either of Right or Left. I think they accepted me as a man of moderation, but not as a man of inaction." [12]

Perhaps it was prescience, perhaps it was luck, but the *Tribune's* editors followed my views with those of Barry Goldwater. The conservative credited his re-election by

Arizona's frontier-minded voters to his opposition to "continued concentration of power in the Federal government, in big business and big unions" and his support of state's rights and individual freedom.

"The Republican party can win in 1960," Goldwater maintained, "if it is truly conservative and its candidates do not run on a 'me too' Democratic New Deal or Fair Deal line . . . ." [13]

In a powerful editorial that led off with my statement, the *Herald Tribune* rejected the Goldwater view and called attention instead to a comment by Vice President Nixon that the 1958 crop of Republican candidates had been "one of the poorest since I entered public life." [14]

As it urged Republicans to seek out top-drawer candidates, the editorial said the party had lost communication with the voters. It cited a general failure to develop adequate political capital from the Administration's successful use of "vigorous but sound and moderate" policies to speed the end of the 1957 recession. The editorial suggested, too, that the party could reach high ground again if it could rekindle the zealous support among young voters that made Youth for Eisenhower such an effective force in 1952.

In sum, the editorial said, the party needed candidates, solid issues and solid programs and a well-researched, positive approach to U.S. problems "which will create an image of the Republican party as a true party of all the people, genuinely responsive to their concerns, genuinely determined to meet them." To be a party of all the people, the editorial said, the G.O.P. should follow Nixon's advice and get out among the people to explain that radical programs are dangerous "not because they provide too much, but because they produce too little." [15]

To this I add a continuing loud amen that extends to

some of the less-considered aspects of the Great Society's
"War on Poverty."

Columnist Joseph Alsop sharply compared the old-line
G.O.P. organizations with horsemen who lose races because their entries are "spavined, string halted or afflicted
with glanders."

Alsop wrote: [16]

> It is perfect nonsense to talk of the 1958 results in
> terms of a gigantic, irresistible tidal wave. What
> looked like a tidal wave was first of all the sum of a
> long series of local Republican choices of candidates
> obviously likely to repel the maximum number of
> votes . . . [the old-line Republican organizations]
> surely deserve the fullest credit as sole architects of
> their own disaster.*

I was pleased to note that Alsop cited my victory as one
of the few cases available to prove his point.

I agreed with Joe Alsop that it wasn't the task of Republicans to repel voters. I thought Pennsylvanians would
welcome the opposite approach, if rapport could be established.

I therefore began my Senate career with a plan to encourage Pennsylvania's awareness of its Senators: a bi-
monthly television show featuring Joseph S. Clark, Democrat, and Hugh Scott, Republican, discussing any matter of current interest with any guest they could persuade
to join them. The program has become a fixture. If it benefits my Democratic colleague as much as it does me, let it
be remembered that our candor carries its own freight of
political risk as well. It gets our views and our differences

* "One [theory] holds . . . that the Republican 'Old Guard' which
dominated the Congressional campaign committees was disenchanted
with Eisenhower's relatively liberal policies and had no desire to defend
him or them." [17]

before the people we represent—and it is in large measure
responsible for the fact, established by polls, that three
quarters of Pennsylvanians know their Senators' names.
This is a claim which few rank-and-file Senators can
make.

The idea for the show came to me even before I had announced my candidacy. It was December 1957, and Clark
and I were seated side by side at dinner at the home of the
late Edward Hopkinson, a prominent Philadelphia attorney. Politics had never affected my friendship with
Clark, so I decided on the spur of the moment to disclose
to him the matter that was uppermost on my mind; after
all, I hoped to be his colleague.

"Joe," I said, "I'm going to run for the Senate and I'm
going to be nominated—even though the organization
people don't want me—and I am going to be elected."

"Well, I'll have to oppose you," my Democratic friend
replied. "But if you make it, I'll be glad to meet with you
behind the door and congratulate you."

The conversation went on in that vein, and before it
ended, I proposed that we flout tradition and make news
by collaborating on a bipartisan television program. He
called it a "great idea" and promised to take part if the
opportunity arose.

When I was sworn in, my senior colleague escorted me
while I took the oath. As we walked from the rostrum, I
said to Clark, "Now we'll get to work on the TV show."

We had it rolling on January 25, 1959, and have kept
it going ever since except during campaign seasons when
one of us is a candidate. (Federal law makes it impractical
for stations to give free air time to individual candidates,
and free time is essential to our venture.) Our producing
station charges only for the cost of our product, which
reaches fourteen television stations and forty radio stations every second week. We call it "award-winning" be-

cause some years ago we received the annual award of the
Pennsylvania Association of Broadcasters and we call it
"unique" because it is. Several bipartisan teams of Senators from other states have tried the same idea, but they
have never been able to make it work.

Clark and I appreciate the difference between fencing
and dueling; we go for points, not blood. For instance,
there was the time when we were talking of a bill on which
we agreed and Clark added: "Senator Scott wasn't in the
Senate when it was discussed, but I was happy to speak up
for him and state his position."

Score one for Clark, who knew I had been out of town
making a Lincoln's Birthday speech. The next week, I
showed up with an arsenal of official charts and graphs.
As the camera caught Clark's visible distress, I said help-
fully: "I know you haven't studied these charts, but I'll be
glad to explain them." We were back even.

Even is where we generally are in a program that veers
unpredictably from world affairs to national problems or
state issues and sometimes to the very personal rewards
and trials of two United States Senators. The program itself has become a trial of a kind for both of us. While it
has helped three fourths of our constituents to recognize
the Clark-Scott combination, nothing seems to help un-
scramble our monosyllabic names. When I am called "Senator Clark" in Pennsylvania, I respond first and correct
the error later if the chance arises. My Democratic colleague does the same when he is mistaken for his Republican associate.

Our guests in the early years included Senator John F.
Kennedy of Massachusetts and Vice President Richard
M. Nixon. If only we had billed them on the same
program—what a preview!

Nixon, who had worked hard in the mid-term campaign
(and had banked political credits across the nation in the

process), started, within the week after the 1958 election, to pick over the wreckage to find sound timbers on which to build for 1960. I accompanied the Vice President to the White House that week, seeking closer liaison between the White House and the Eisenhower Republicans in Congress. While Ike was forbidden by the Constitution to run again, his actions over the next two years could materially affect both the leadership and the posture of the party as it entered the 1960 campaign.

As Eisenhower's constitutional heir apparent, Nixon was working to build an organization which he might well lead in the 1960 campaign, and many Republicans were ready two years in advance to concede him the nomination. But there was no dismissing the spectacular 573,000-vote majority by which Rockefeller won New York when most other Republicans were doing well to hold their own. The returns were hardly counted before talk began of a Rockefeller-Nixon battle for the nomination. I thought it a bit early to choose up sides. Also, I did not want ever to see an East-West division disrupt the party.

But it wasn't long before the Republican schizophrenia against which I had warned immediately after the election began to reappear. Our troops were lining up into Nixon and Rockefeller contingents.

The conflict was boiling when the Republican National Committee met in Des Moines on January 24, nominally to plan for the 1960 convention, and actually to try to get a fix on our position in the wake of the typhoon that hit us in 1958. The same kind of troubles that beset me at Omaha in 1949 swirled around Eisenhower's hand-picked Chairman, Meade Alcorn, at Des Moines, but never quite reached the showdown stage. Alcorn proposed an ambitious program to strengthen the party for 1960, but I was not surprised when he tendered his resignation after an appropriate interval. I imagine he departed from this onerous job with as much relief at the prospect of normal living as I had in 1949.

The word was out in March that the President would support Senator Thruston B. Morton of Kentucky as Alcorn's successor. The party's Old Guard bridled against Morton, a middle-of-the-roader from a border state whose views represented the real Republican center. Senator Goldwater, then Chairman of the Senate Republican Campaign Committee, and Pennsylvania's popular Representative Richard M. Simpson, his House counterpart, led the assault.

I strongly recommended that the national chairmanship go to Morton (who was generally believed to be pro-Nixon). For the argument that it should be a full-time job, I noted that Goldwater and Simpson both headed campaign committees and suggested that their jobs, too, should be full-time if the same reasoning were followed.

When the National Committee met in Washington on April 10, Morton had no trouble winning the chairmanship.

Around this time, I endorsed Nixon. As much as I admired Rockefeller and his performance in New York, I felt and said that Nixon had both the qualifications and training. He had earned his right to make the race through seven years as Ike's loyal understudy and, on frequent occasions, as the President's competent deputy. I expressed my respect for Rockefeller without reservations, but I thought he could be a presidential nominee in four or eight years.

The skill and control Nixon demonstrated in the face of the cold war enemy were telling arguments as the new campaign neared, for until Rockefeller's election the New York Governor's principal achievements had been in the foreign policy field. The Rockefeller people were trying to portray the rivalry as another Ike-Taft collision, but the

parallel was invalid. Nixon and Rockefeller were just not
that far apart. Both fitted easily under Ike's "Modern
Republican umbrella," although Rockefeller stood to Nixon's left on some domestic issues.

While old Taft backers supported Nixon, so did a good
many of Ike's early supporters. Republicans all over the
country were indebted to Nixon for campaign help; Rockefeller had not held elective office long enough to build up
such credits. Rockefeller had the support of his party's
avant garde and some of its political "outs;" Nixon was
tolerated by the right, liked by the middle-roaders and
widely acceptable to the "ins." The Nixon position was
hard to assail, as Rockefeller reluctantly conceded when
he disbanded his campaign operations just as the political
year was about to start.

Soon I became publicly—and accurately—identified
with the "Nixon Team." In a roundup of the men close to
Nixon, Allen J. Otten of *The Wall Street Journal* observed that it was "obviously not by chance" that I was
emerging more and more as a Nixon spokesman.

". . . The 'liberal' and 'Eastern' Sen. Scott is a good
balance weight for Mr. Nixon of California, who could well
be cast in the convention as a 'conservative' against the
'liberal' Gov. Rockefeller . . . ." Otten wrote with considerable perception. His vision clouded, however, when he
added that I "undoubtedly" had Vice Presidential ambitions.[18] I had yet to finish my first year in the Senate seat
that had been my actual ambition for years. However, I
was mentioned as a possibility by several writers who were
dreaming up "geographical balance" for a prospective
G.O.P. ticket headed by Nixon.

The idea apparently haunted Barry Goldwater, who
told a Republican audience in Reno in December he would
accept the Vice Presidential nomination if it were offered,
but really thought it should go to a midwesterner because

"we need Midwestern influence in the Vice Presidency rather than New York influence." [19]

Rockefeller pulled the cork on his own candidacy at Christmas time with a statement of withdrawal that roused complete surprise and some dismay in the Nixon camp. The New Yorker suggested that his own ceaseless campaigning had convinced him the convention was already "controlled" for Nixon. He vowed that he would continue speaking out because of concern about "the future vigor and purpose of my party." [20] And he announced that he would not accept the Vice Presidential nomination if it were offered, thus demolishing a "dream ticket" that was being proposed by some Republicans, including me.

With the Presidential nomination pretty well staked out for Nixon, the Vice Presidential speculation continued. I was mentioned often enough so that I told a news conference in January I was not a candidate and voiced a hope that Rockefeller still "possibly could be persuaded" to take the Number 2 spot.

At the same Washington news conference, I felt it advisable to warn my fellow Republicans that I had been around in 1948 when the party "snatched defeat from the very jaws of victory"—and that they could do it again. But when a reporter asked who I thought the Democratic nominee would be, I couldn't resist the opening. It might, I suggested gravely, be "somebody not presently a candidate" like, for instance, Supreme Court Justice William O. Douglas or Mrs. Eleanor Roosevelt. The "alleged front runners" who abounded in the Senate (Kennedy, Johnson, Humphrey and Symington) were all "excellent candidates for Vice President."

The Scott-for-Vice-President boomlet never got far outside Pennsylvania, and there it became enmeshed in the political machinery. Our convention delegation held its or-

ganization meeting May 20. Nixon had won ninety-eight
per cent of the vote in the April 26 preference primary, so
there was no shadow of a question where the overwhelming
majority of our seventy delegates stood. But there was
considerable question as to who would lead them. I was
elected chairman, over State Senate President M. Harvey
Taylor, by a vote of 46 to 22.

On the question of endorsements, a Nixon-Scott slate
was approved with only one (highly predictable) dissent.
It came from Harold E. Stassen, who was one of the Philadelphia delegates and was still on the "dump Nixon"
trail he tried to blaze in 1956. He maintained the endorsement should be delayed until after California's June 7
primary so he might have a chance to "adjust" his convictions in the light of the vote in Nixon's home state. (In
that primary, 1.5 million Republicans voted for a slate
pledged to Nixon.)

"It's about time somebody clarified the situation," I
said with considerable understatement. "I am honored by
the resolution endorsing me for Vice President. But I
want to make it clear it will be received only as an
honor."

Turning directly to Stassen, I continued: "If you want
to repudiate the Vice President, this is the time to do it. I
suggest we endorse him now." We did, and Stassen stood,
as is his wont, entirely alone.

The meeting was barely over before Stassen made public a letter to the sixty-nine other Pennsylvania delegates
which declared that Nixon could not win as a Presidential
candidate and urged support for any one of four other
candidates: Rockefeller, United Nations Ambassador
Henry Cabot Lodge, Secretary of the Treasury Robert
B. Anderson, or Interior Secretary Fred Seaton. Stassen
released his letter the day after Rockefeller reversed his
course and told New York Republicans he would, as many

had suspected, be susceptible to a draft for the nomination. To start a draft in big time politics, someone has to hold the door open. At that late date in the political calendar, there were few door holders left.

The door was being firmly closed by professionals all along the line. One of the most skillful was the new Senate Minority Leader, Everett McKinley Dirksen of Illinois, who moved into the slot left vacant in 1958 when Bill Knowland resigned to run unsuccessfully for Governor of California. Dirksen, the minority whip under Knowland, was a forceful, eloquent Senator whose great talents had recently been recruited to serve the Eisenhower cause, a task which he performed energetically and ably.

Nearly a month before the 1959 session, a conference of ten modern Republicans was called by one who had worked hard and well for the President's policies, Vermont's Senator George D. Aiken. The meeting, which included the three still-unsworn Republican freshmen, was aimed primarily at trying to install party leadership that believed in the President's avowed purposes. Whether or not we succeeded, we hoped to show the nation that a segment of the party in the Senate could not accept more of the brand of Republicanism so vehemently repudiated at the polls.

We faced crucial handicaps. Even though the party was down to 34 Senators, we were still a minority within a minority; we needed at least eight more votes to prevail. Our chances of success depended very largely on support from the President, whose influence remained considerable with the moderates in the Republican center. I tried to generate White House interest and drew a blank. In the deficit-haunted atmosphere of 1958, Ike classed his party's moderates with the "spenders." He adhered to his policy of non-interference in Congressional affairs. But the simmering revolt attracted fourteen determined Senators

when the showdown caucus came at the opening of the
Eighty-sixth Congress. We lacked the votes to support an
entire new leadership slate, but we were too large a faction
to be disregarded. Under a settlement worked out by the
adroitly influential Styles Bridges of New Hampshire,
then the Republican Policy Chairman, Dirksen won the
leadership 20 to 14 over our candidate, John Sherman
Cooper of Kentucky. By the same vote, the whip's post
went to the moderates' choice, Senator Thomas H. Kuchel
of California. As matters evolved under Dirksen's deftly
tactful leadership, this combination brought a unity to
the Republican forces which in later Congresses made
them effective beyond their scanty numbers.

The session's most noticed achievement was enactment
of the landmark Landrum-Griffin labor reform bill, which
I supported after amendments to ease problems in the textile and construction industries. Less constructive, but
fully as controversial, was the Senate's bitterly political
49 to 46 vote early in the morning of June 16 to reject
Eisenhower's nomination of Lewis L. Strauss as Secretary
of Commerce.

The political flavor of the first session of the Eighty-
ninth Congress was just a curtain raiser for its second
climactic meeting. In those hectic months, the Senate
chamber was the one stage on which most of the leading
national candidates of both parties were in intimate and
repeated collision. While Democrats tried to cut one another up on the floor (with occasional impartial assistance
from Nixon-abetted Republicans calling themselves the
"Needlework Guild"), the all-but-nominated G.O.P. candidate was Vice President Nixon, the chamber's presiding
officer.

A complete catalogue of breakthrough achievements of
these eight Eisenhower years cannot be recounted here,

but some not previously elaborated at least deserve mention: With Congressional support the Administration rebuilt American defenses into the most powerful military force on earth; launched the first nuclear submarines and atomic missile programs; initiated space explorations; established the Health, Education and Welfare Department; started the 41,000 mile Interstate Highway System; and after stopping the Korean War, waged peace successfully for eight years.

Despite the political pressures—and partly because of them—the session produced the first substantial addition to the 1957 civil rights bill. The act made it a crime to obstruct integration in schools and created a system of Federal referees to deal with voter-registration disputes. It was achieved only after a determined Southern filibuster which the joint leadership wore down by holding the Senate in grueling round-the-clock sessions. To be on hand for off-beat quorum calls, the filibuster's foes had to sleep in shifts on cots beneath busts of long dead statesmen in the drafty old Supreme Court Chamber. Senators called it "the pajama game."

The record of party positions was of general interest to all, but was an acute concern for the Senate majority leader. Lyndon Johnson was among those Democrats who were privately amused when I wrote an ironic open letter to John Kennedy purporting to keep the Massachusetts Senator posted on events in the Senate during his hectic drive to take the Democratic nomination by storm.

"Well, we don't want to bore you, Jack," the letter said in a much-quoted final paragraph. "If you have time, drop in and if not, just send one of the other Kennedys down." [21]

Later, Senator John F. Kennedy privately inquired, off the Senate floor, of Senator Winston Prouty of Vermont, "Is Hugh mad at me?" "No indeed," said Prouty, "he just couldn't miss a chance for political humor." After that, good relations were restored.

When Congress stopped business on July 3 for the conventions, it did not adjourn, but recessed to August 8.

Before I left for the convention, I was a cosigner with fourteen other Republican Senators of a "Declaration of Purpose" circulated by independent-minded George Aiken of Vermont as a reminder to our Platform Committee that the "moderate Republicanism" Ike represented in two elections still had impressive support.

Some mistakenly viewed the declaration as a plug for Rockefeller's candidacy because it held that the economy "must be stimulated into an upsurge in economic growth" and urged that Republicans "place human values above material consideration." As a Nixon advocate, I signed the declaration because I believed in these principles and felt our stand would make it easier for Nixon to adapt Eisenhower Administration policies to the economic and political conditions facing the party and the nation in 1960.

The differences between the ebullient Rockefeller and the naturally reserved Nixon were more in personality than in basic policy, but Nixon, by eight years of active and effective service in the Eisenhower Administration, was inextricably linked with the record and the policies of "the team." One of our problems as we went into the convention was to dispense with the fiction that the Vice President was so inflexible that he could not work with the forward-looking New York Governor and, if he saw fit, incorporate Rockefeller proposals into national campaign strategy.

One means to this end could have been to put Rockefeller on the ticket as the Vice Presidential candidate. Many felt a Nixon-Rockefeller ticket, combining regional "balance" with vigor and experience and progressive Republican viewpoints, would be the most effective team we could field against the manifestly strong Kennedy-Johnson ticket nominated two weeks before by the Democrats in Los Angeles. Rockefeller stood adamant against accepting second place.

The Vice President asked me to go to Chicago as an advance troubleshooter to deal with any controversies or legal matters that might arise. Formally, I went as Counsel to the National Committee; informally, I was a member of a six-man strategy board which helped plan the Nixon campaign both before and after the convention. It was headed by Morton, the National Chairman, and it included three former Chairmen: Len Hall, who was Nixon's convention manager, Meade Alcorn, and myself. The other members were Undersecretary of the Treasury Fred C. Scribner, a politically astute Maine man, and Nixon's close friend Bob Finch, now Lieutenant Governor of California.

In Chicago before the convention began rumors were still afloat that a Nixon-Rockefeller slate could still be patched together. I doubted it, especially in view of the way work on the platform was going. To plaster over the party's continuing divisions, the 103-member Committee was aiming, under conservative prodding, for a compact document more notable for brevity than boldness, asserting lofty but generalized objectives.

The draft platform was hardly completed before Rockefeller denounced it as seriously lacking in "strength and specifics," [22] especially in the fields of foreign policy and defense. The statement was an invitation to showdown or compromise. Nixon chose the latter. Without discussions with his staff, he flew to New York to meet with the Governor in Rockefeller's apartment. The result was the celebrated "Treaty of Fifth Avenue" under which Nixon and

Rockefeller reached agreement on substantial revisions in the platform. The changes were relayed by telephone to Platform Committee Chairman Charles H. Percy * in Chicago, and moves began to incorporate them into the platform, despite private dissents by the more conservative Platform Committee members.

While some of the standpatters denounced the Fifth Avenue meeting as a "Munich," it did much to bring the party's progressives into the mainstream of the campaign. I was personally delighted by one of the by-products of the meeting, an agreement to revise the civil rights plank to commit the G.O.P. to "aggressive action to remove the remaining vestiges of segregation or discrimination in all areas of national life."

Pleased as I was with the decision on civil rights, I was one of the men in the middle on the matter of implementing the Nixon-Rockefeller agreement. The original rights plank was the deliberately generalized product of compromise, agreed to after much haggling with Southern delegates only a day before the "Treaty of Fifth Avenue" was achieved. The convention was already in its first day, but my assignment was now to see that the original work was undone and replaced.

As General Counsel to the National Committee, I found support in the rules for a finding that the Platform Committee could reconsider the civil rights plank and submit another one by a simple majority vote. Nixon forces embarked on a frankly high-pressure campaign to change enough votes. Some Committee members didn't have to be persuaded; some came around because Nixon wanted it that way. After a great deal of fevered discussion of differences, including one 22-hour Committee session, we got the remaining votes that clinched our case by pointing out that stubbornness would only bring on a divisive floor

* Now a United States Senator from Illinois.

fight in which Nixon's wishes were all but certain to prevail. The plank was changed. The resentment of those delegates who preferred a milder plank or who disliked Rockefeller—or both—was to smolder and, at the 1964 Convention, bring about a backtracking retreat from the party's strong civil rights stance.

Rockefeller's metamorphosis from a possible challenger
who just might try a blitz into a genuine noncandidate
left the track so clear for Nixon that the only suspense
was in the Vice Presidential race. As Chairman and nom-
inal Vice Presidential nominee of the Pennsylvania delegation, I was in a position to guide our big bloc of seventy
votes wherever Nixon wanted them to go. Nixon's final decision was not made until after his uncontested nomination, in which even Stassen joined.

Through four caucuses, the Pennsylvanians withheld
any Vice Presidential endorsement that went beyond their
early expression of support for me, which no one took seriously. Left to their own devices, most of them would have
gone for Rockefeller if he had been available. Otherwise,
they were ready to support Nixon's choice. That choice, I
told them hours before Nixon's nomination roared
through the convention, would most probably be United
Nations Ambassador Henry Cabot Lodge.

I knew Nixon had been leaning toward the former Massachusetts Senator who had become our tough, eloquent
spokesman in the U.N. After his own nomination, Nixon
called thirty-four Republican leaders representing the
gamut of party opinion to a closed midnight meeting in
the Sheraton-Blackstone Hotel. It was arranged as a secret session, and we all spoke freely. This frankness was
recorded with more enterprise than propiety by the Chicago *Sun-Times*, which managed to plant a reporter in a
closet hours before the meeting began. Any embarrassment resulting from the paper's sensational play of its ex-

clusive story was counterbalanced, however, by its demonstration that there was indeed a strong consensus at the meeting for the choice of Lodge. A very strong runner-up proved to be the popular Senator Thruston B. Morton of Kentucky.

Participants crossed the Republican spectrum, from Milton Eisenhower to the adept conservative Senator Styles Bridges of New Hampshire, from Thomas E. Dewey to former Ohio Senator John W. Bricker, the dedicated Taft man who had been Dewey's running mate in the uphill 1944 campaign. Five Cabinet members took part. I was there, along with Hall, Alcorn and Scribner, as a member of the Nixon strategy board.

Nixon told the meeting he felt the "only hope" for his campaign would be to concentrate the effort on foreign affairs, for Republicans could not compete by political auction in domestic programs against the Kennedy-Johnson ticket. Inevitably, Nixon said, the Democrats would "promise more."

Lodge was generally thought to be the best candidate to strengthen the ticket in this kind of contest, Nixon said, because his extensively-televised appearances as the U.S. champion at the U.N. had made him a symbol to the nation of continuous opposition to the Communist bloc. Nixon promised that he personally would take on presentation of domestic policy and would carry the campaign burden in the Farm Belt, where opposition to an Eastern Vice President was centered.

Nixon did not flatly dictate the choice of Lodge. He put Morton at the head of a list of three possible alternative candidates. He discussed the Kentucky Senator's appeal to middle-road voters and his broad national acceptability. The others to whom he gave top preference were Treasury Secretary Robert B. Anderson, who was known to stand high with President Eisenhower, and Representative Walter Judd of Minnesota, the Convention's eloquent keynoter. As a Texan, Anderson had potential sectional appeal, but he had little standing with party professionals. Judd, then nearly sixty-two, had already told Nixon he felt he lacked the stamina for the tough national campaign ahead. None of the top four prospects was asked to the meeting.

Some television viewers had tuned out the Convention to watch Lodge's devastating presentation before the Security Council of the case against the Soviets, who had cold-bloodedly shot down a U.S. Navy observation plane over the North Sea and held its six-man crew captive. Admiration for the U.N. Ambassador was high, and the 1,331 delegates went along to a man, with Goldwater blessing the new team along with Rockefeller.

Rockefeller introduced Nixon for the acceptance speech. The Vice President won a standing ovation when he vowed not to let the United States be "pushed around by anybody, any place" [23]—most especially not by Soviet Premier Nikita S. Khrushchev. To oppose Kennedy's still-fresh concept of the New Frontier, Nixon put forward a "grand new strategy" to reinforce U.S. leadership of the world's free peoples. It was a well-received speech, a fitting climax to a Convention in which Nixon had effectively seized and used an opportunity not only to run the party, but to lead it.

Nixon rightly foresaw the closest Presidential race of modern times. He stepped vigorously into the leadership job. Instead of naming the traditional campaign manager, he decided to work through his strategy board, now reinforced by Interior Secretary Fred Seaton, that had functioned for him during the Convention. He began planning for a campaign which he rather ambitiously—

perhaps incautiously—promised to carry into all fifty states. He began five days later in Hawaii, the fiftieth state.

As Nixon's acceptance speech had indicated, there was agreement that the Republican candidate should use all suitable opportunities to underscore his much-publicized differences with Khrushchev. Most Americans had viewed the Nixon-Khrushchev "kitchen debate" on television, and applauded Nixon's determined stand. Our strategy board felt that Kennedy had no comparably dramatic personal conflict with communism with which to counter this theme.

It was further agreed that Nixon should continue to encourage the kind of informal question-and-answer sessions with which he had effectively supplemented his campaign speeches while he was Vice President. The device loosened up his rather formal platform manner and gave him an opportunity to display the range of his experience and knowledge in fields familiar to individual audiences.

Resumption of the Congressional session on August 8 briefly converted the Senate floor into a national political arena, for neither Nixon nor Kennedy nor Johnson could slip away to campaign with the inconspicuous freedom they had enjoyed before they became national candidates. Lyndon Johnson had gone to Los Angeles as a Presidential contender: he returned as the Vice Presidential nominee, running the Senate where the Presidential candidate was a junior member. I tended to refer gently to J.F.K. as "the majority leader's leader" and L.B.J. loftily refused to take the bait. The post-convention session was an anticlimactic circus that did little to build the picture of a 2 to 1 Democratic majority united to carry out Kennedy's appealingly worded pledge to "get this country moving again."

Aside from the foreign aid money bill, the most sub-

stantial product of the postscript session was a watered-
down effort to provide health care for the aged. It was no
credit to anyone, but it appeared to be a debacle for Kennedy, who was strongly committed to a Democratic platform plank calling for a comprehensive Medicare program under Social Security. His plan, on which he had
proposed to wage a campaign fight, was rejected 51 to 44
—with nineteen Southern Democrats in opposition. I was
a Republican co-sponsor of an alternative based on voluntary contributions and direct Treasury aid. All Democrats opposed it and it lost 67 to 28. In the end, Congress
passed the minimal Kerr-Mills program, which made pub-
licly-assisted health care available to persons over 65 who
were, in effect, "medically indigent." It passed 91 to 2,
opposed only by Barry Goldwater and Strom Thurmond
of South Carolina, who was then still a Democrat. The
Kerr-Mills program worked reasonably well in Pennsylvania, but was not implemented in many states. It became
the forerunner of Title 19 in the later Medicare Bill,
known as "Medicaid."

In the debate that preceded defeat of Kennedy's bill,
the Democratic nominee called on "five or six" Republicans to provide the votes that were denied by his own
party. His answer came, most appropriately, from that
most independent of Republicans, Jack Javits.

"Sorry, sir, this is not the season for that," the New
Yorker replied. "The aged will have a splendid plan in the
next session, because the nominees of both parties are committed to medical care for the aged. But you cannot ask
liberal Republicans to just sign here when their ideals and
deeply held convictions are not reflected in the paper they
have been asked to sign."

In this uncompromising spirit the last of the Eisenhower Congresses ended. Until the election settled the air,
there could be no more forward motion.

Adjournment of the "sad little session" on September 1 turned me loose to work with a revived Republican Truth Squad. Once again, crisscrossing the country in the wake of Democratic candidates, we reminded voters of the aggregate experience and demonstrated capacity of our ticket, using facts to answer intimations that the United States was becoming a second-class power losing prestige in the world and influence in the U.N. Americans were prosperous and at peace, working in record numbers for sound dollars, whatever the opposition might say.

Possibly of more significance to the campaign's outcome, Nixon made an informal decision before he left Chicago to take part in a series of four nationally-televised debates with Senator Kennedy. It was a risk-filled gamble for Nixon, for the joint appearances would inevitably cut into the advantage in national exposure which he had built up during his two previous nationwide campaigns. But this loss would have been minor compared to the damage he would have suffered if he had appeared to be running away from Kennedy's challenge. The only thing to do was to accept, and work for a format as advantageous as possible for our candidate.

That the first debate went badly, from makeup to showdown, is now history. When a campaign event backfires, it is fashionable for the candidate's advisers to pass the word, long after the event, that they had privately advised against the hapless decision. In point of fact, I was among those who favored the idea of the debates and I joined in the general affirmation at a staff meeting in Nixon's presence. So far as I can recall, the only strategist to indicate doubt as to the advisability of TV confrontation was the cautious down-Easter, Fred Scribner.

Nixon, who always saves his heavy ammunition for a campaign's end, was toughening his attack when Mrs. Scott and I joined his party in early October for a 9-day swing through eleven states, from Pennsylvania west to South Dakota, north to Michigan, south to Louisiana and Mississippi.

I have a blurred recollection of airborne campaigning: eating barbecued buffalo-burger—and finding it not bad —with a large crowd under a broiling sun in Sullivan, Illinois; swelling with pride for my home state's organization when a large crowd in Wilkes-Barre stood firm to wait for our overdue plane in a downpour that wilted the roses on Pat Nixon's hat; riding behind a tractor through ankle-deep, incredibly rich black mud to hear Nixon's speech to a plowing contest at Sioux Falls, South Dakota; watching with incredulity as the Democratic Governor of congenitally Democratic Mississippi headed a reception for the Republican nominee that jammed the streets of downtown Jackson.

The crowds were big and they listened with the silence of students while Nixon made his carefully reasoned arguments on the questions of war and prosperity and human rights that were the issues of the campaign. There was applause, and plenty of it, for the openly partisan portions of his speeches, but the people were listening, listening intently. It was clear in mid-October that they had not made up their minds between the two vigorous young men who competed for their votes.

There were clear contrasts between the wittily pragmatic Kennedy, graceful as a matador on the offensive, and the more businesslike Nixon, only four years older but far more experienced in high office, obliged at once to defend the Administration of which he was a part and to show that Republicans, too, could grow with changing times.

There was a persuasive bite to Kennedy's much-repeated claim that he could best "get this country moving again." In that word "again," he left voters with the doubt that there had been motion in the Eisenhower years. The charge was hardly fair, but it was effective politics.

As they debated their new leader, the people made it clear that they still liked their old one. Ike picked Pittsburgh to make his last public appearance for the Nixon-Lodge ticket on the Friday night before the election. Escorting him, I saw wildly cheering crowds stretched all the way from the Greater Pittsburgh Airport to the downtown hotel where he spoke. The size of the turnout was gratifying to any Eisenhower Republican, but it was disturbing, too. The crowd was substantially larger than anything Pittsburgh had done to greet either Nixon or Kennedy. Pittsburgh had gone for Ike by 60,000 votes four years before, and it seemed in the mood to do the same again. How it would go for Nixon I didn't dare guess.

I did know that Kennedy and his people had been making hay in Pennsylvania with promises that a Kennedy Administration would go all the way to support an area redevelopment bill on the pattern of the Democratic measure Ike had vetoed for its pork barrel aspects.

To counter this effort, I had done much missionary work for a more realistic, but equally effective program to which Nixon was committed. Similarly committed to it was William W. Scranton, a gifted forty-three-year-old lawyer making his first race as Republican nominee for Congress in Pennsylvania's then Democratic 10th District, which took in some of the state's most depressed coal and manufacturing towns.

It all culminated in the wildly controversial election that won Kennedy the Presidency by a hairline margin of the popular vote. Even though my own state alone gave Kennedy an edge of 116,326 votes, our Republican Congressional candidates fought their way back into control of our delegation. Bill Scranton was elected to his first

term in the House. The Eighty-seventh turned out to be a
disappointing Congress: a lot of show, but no go. I remember commenting that never had so many people talked
so much and gotten so little accomplished. And so it was.

Despite healthy Democratic majorities, the new President was blocked on his tax reduction, school aid, Medicare and area redevelopment programs. The threat of
Southern rebellion postponed his effort to press ahead on
civil rights legislation until his hand was forced in 1963
by the Negro revolution. He seemed especially vulnerable
on foreign policy. Cuba was still a Communist beachhead;
the North Atlantic Alliance was coming unraveled; the
Congo was a seething issue among the Western Powers
and none of those powers was helping the U.S. effort to
prevent a Communist takeover in Vietnam.

During the pre-election period, Joe Clark and I had
joined forces once again in the cause of civil rights. With
more optimism than success, we entered with Republican
Senators Javits and Keating of New York and Democrats
Douglas of Illinois and Hart of Michigan into a six-
member bipartisan bloc seeking action on legislative recommendations of the Civil Rights Commission. As my
share of the effort, I reasserted the need for President
Kennedy to issue his long-promised executive order forbidding race discrimination in Federally-financed housing
and backed it up with proposed legislation to plug gaps
which the Presidential order could not touch. Clark moved
to insure equal employment opportunities, Keating for
added reinforcement of voting rights, Javits to speed
school desegregation and Hart to penalize violent interference with the exercise of civil rights. Except for the
ticklish fair housing issue, all these proposals foreshad-
owed provisions of the Civil Rights Act that was eventually
passed in 1964 by the Eighty-eighth Congress. The principal civil rights action of the Eighty-seventh Congress

was approval of the Twenty-fourth Amendment outlawing the poll tax as a prerequisite for voting.

President Kennedy scored one significant long-range victory with passage of the far-reaching Trade Expansion Act which gave the President broad authority to negotiate tariff reductions with other nations of the free world. Yet we approached the June 30 ending of the fiscal year without passage of a single one of the big appropriation bills without which new programs are impossible. Twenty-one of the President's major proposals were stalled in Congress, casualties of a divided Democratic majority.

Administration refusal to recognize that politics remained the art of the possible, even on the New Frontier, sometimes contributed to the negative record. The classic example was the bitter but sterile Senate battle over medical care for the aged. There was a majority in the chamber for development of a program to help aged persons meet high medical bills in the period of their lives when their earning power was reduced. But there were wide-open, bitter divisions over the President's plan to administer and finance the program through Social Security. Regulation, bureaucracy and compulsion were built into this approach. To reach the same end by a less restrictive road, Republicans proposed an amendment, for which I voted, that offered a broad-gauge voluntary program with the Federal share paid from general revenues instead of an earmarked tax. Administration forces beat the amendment, only to see the President's plan tabled 52 to 48.

There were enough sore spots in the Kennedy performance at home and abroad, including legislative rebuffs and the Cuban fiasco, to draw preliminary fire from Republicans warming up for the 1964 campaign. But Kennedy was personally magnetic and he had the advantages of incumbency in a time of general prosperity and technical peace. To have a chance of breaching the New Frontier, Republicans urgently needed a candidate equal to the challenge.

Luckily for my peace of mind, at this time I did not foresee the self-destructive division that was brutally to wound the Republican Party and prepare it to jump off the bridge.

VIII

PHOENIX TO ASHES

"Don't take it out of my time."
NELSON A. ROCKEFELLER

For Republicans, November 1964, began in trepidation and ended in recrimination. Everyone was angry: the lonesome survivors and the steamrollered victims, the right-wing purists who had wanted us all to rush lemming-like over the same abyss, and the traditionalists who had fought to hold the center of the road.

Woe-criers claimed to see in the G.O.P. the stigmata of internal factionalism and external opportunism that marked the hapless Whigs for extinction a century ago. The menacing parallel contributed to a torrent of self-criticism, a darkening of the political moon, that flowed from every sector of the party.

But could the disaster have been avoided? Were there signs along the road to San Francisco that Republicans had failed to read or respond to in time?

At first, and until the early summer of 1963, Nelson Rockefeller looked like the man to beat. As Governor of the Empire State, he had some political problems, but his

record was forceful and progressive—some said too much
so—and his ambition matched his wealth. Pollsters placed
him far in front of the Republican field, despite a 1962
divorce which did not seem to blight his chances. The reaction was delayed a year and a half, until the Governor's
remarriage on May 4, 1963, churned up a storm, then a
typhoon of protests from churchmen, community leaders
and most especially from middle-aged matrons. The hostility was reflected in Congressional mail and, more crucially for Rockefeller, in the polls. For the first time in
months, the New Yorker was displaced from his Number 1
position in the Gallup poll's ranking of Republican hope-
fuls. His successor was Arizona Senator Barry Goldwater,
the engaging, outspokenly conservative favorite of many
party regulars in the West, Midwest and, most particularly, the South.

Goldwater himself seemed to read less into the polls
than the zealous enthusiasts who were already boring in
with missionary zeal for the delegate putsch that reached
its climax thirteen months later in San Francisco. A scat-
tering—but growing number—of far-right extremists,
Birchers and archsegregationists among his fervent
backers appeared to embarrass Goldwater at this stage.
Several times in after-hours chats among Republican Senators, he stated his distaste for them with characteristic
bluntness. At the same time, he left the impression he
thought the Draft Goldwater people were wasting their
time. How was it possible, he would ask, for a Senator
from a state with four electoral votes to win a Presidential
nomination—especially when he didn't really want it?

I must confess that I, too, in these chats with him, was
inclined to discount my Arizona colleague's chances. I felt
that he had been built up in the minds of the party's wishful thinkers primarily because the decline in Rockefeller's
fortunes had left a vacuum that was as yet unfilled. Before

the summer ended, I assumed, the professionals in the big
industrial states that generally supply the votes and the
money to elect Republican Presidents would have reached
a collective judgment to rally behind a candidate with less
restricted appeal than Goldwater's. There were three obvious possibilities, but each was impeded by certain political liabilities.

Former Vice President Richard M. Nixon had come
within 119,000 votes of a popular plurality over John F.
Kennedy, and still had friends in the party. But his image
had been tarnished by his unfortunate losing race * for
the California Governorship in 1962 and he had abandoned his political base when he moved to New York to
practice corporation law.

Michigan's Governor George Romney ranked third in
the polls behind Goldwater and Rockefeller in mid-May.
The handsome, middle-road Governor's star was evidently
rising fast with the national public. But it was only half a
year since the election in which he broke a 12-year Democratic hold on the Michigan Governor's office, an election
in which he acquired a reputation as a loner that made
some professionals nervous. Before he reached unchal-
lenged national stature, there were unresolved battles with
the Michigan legislature which would affect his future.

Finally, there was my own Governor, William Scranton, an attractive, intelligent political centrist who won
his office the same day Romney won in Michigan, but
moved more swiftly than Romney (Scranton's first legislature was Republican) to wage and win a tax fight essential to his program. Scranton's success with a friendly leg-

---

* Nixon, prior to his decision, asked twenty-two of his political friends
for their advice as to whether he should make the California race
against Governor "Pat" Brown. Twenty-one of those present thought
he should run and that he would win. I was one of that mistaken "con-
census."

islature gave him the stature and the fiscal freedom to move forward as a national contender. Romney was not so fortunate; the Michigan legislature was far from cooperative.

I would have been obtuse indeed if I had failed to consider Scranton's potential in the vote-heavy industrial states generally and, specifically, in Pennsylvania.

That resounding triumph in Pennsylvania's 1962 gubernatorial election had rocketed Bill Scranton to first-magnitude stardom in the national Republican firmament. Even before he left for a post-election rest at his winter home at Hobe Sound, Florida, the cool, methodical young millionaire was forced by national speculation to deny that he had either intention or desire to enter the scramble for the Republican Presidential nomination in 1964.

"It's true I said a year ago I wasn't seeking the governorship," Scranton told one reporter in a post-election interview. "But when I saw the holocaust that hit this . . . party in Pennsylvania . . . I became concerned. If there were a similar concern nationally . . . well, who can tell." [1]

His hypothesis was prophetic, but none of us knew it. His principal concern was to lead his party to constructive use of the mandate it had won after eight years in the political wilderness.

It was a significant triumph over the Pennsylvania dinosaurs who had fought his nomination that Scranton had won his gubernatorial race in the cities where Democrats must score heavily to carry the state. Bill Scranton had been my choice from the very beginning.

I had fought for Scranton partly because he had what politicians call class—he looked and spoke like a winner. In my thirty years in politics, the Democratic Party had been stronger than its candidates, and the Republican Party correspondingly weaker. Polls show large groups of voters leaning to Democratic tickets because they have an affirmative concept of the Democratic Party. When they vote Republican, they vote for individuals, either because the Republican is extraordinarily good or the Democrat is excruciatingly bad. To put it another way, if all things are equal, the Democrats are the gainers from the straight-ticket vote. This can be quite an asset in Pennsylvania where the long-term trend in Republican registrations had, until recently, been down.

The obvious way out of this bind in 1962 lay in the choice of a strong, attractive Republican candidate who had appeal as an individual in all voting areas. Bill Scranton struck one as this kind of man.

We had been impressed by our young freshman colleague's role in the Eighty-eighth Congress. He seldom volunteered advice, but his views were sought, for he was well-informed, knew his own mind and had a way with words. He had won respect as a successful businessman and banker who had become the acknowledged leader of a resourceful campaign to reverse the declining industrial fortunes of Scranton, Pennsylvania, the old anthracite center that is named for his family. In Congress he had the natural makings of a leader; in political terms, once again, Scranton was a comer.

I had a personal reason for interest in the promising young Congressman. He was the son of Marion Margery Scranton, Pennsylvania's long-time Republican National Committeewoman, who was as popular and influential as she was politically shrewd. She was my valuable ally in Omaha in 1949. Even though illness kept her from the meeting, she worked by telephone to ease some of the pressure I faced as National Chairman. When Taft men accused me of appointing a "loaded" executive committee, she voluntarily resigned her place so I could name a pro-Taft successor. Three other women followed her example, and my opposition was temporarily mollified.

Bill Scranton had learned practical politics as the son

of Marion Margery Scranton, and was now ready to apply what he knew. Scion of a family to whom *noblesse oblige* was second nature and first duty, his philosophy was progressive, his viewpoint compassionate and his record that of a pragmatic, highly successful businessman. The definition of "Modern Republican" clothed him as neatly as his bought-off-the-rack ready-mades, which looked to those not in the know to be deftly tailor-made.

There was pressure from a number of party leaders for me to run. But in private conversations I held that it was still possible that Bill Scranton could be persuaded to make the race. Some of the party's top brass got in touch with General Eisenhower, a registered Pennsylvania Republican at his winter home in Palm Desert, California.

The next day in Gettysburg before the annual Lincoln Day dinner, the phone rang. "It's General Eisenhower calling you," the late State Attorney General Walter E. Alessandroni said.

Said the General, as I reached for a scratch pad: "Hugh, I've been talking to several of our mutual friends who told me about the news article saying you might be available to run. I'm convinced that you've got to run for Governor. It's the only way out of this situation, if we're going to win." I reminded the General that we had both tried to get Scranton to run at Ike's office in Gettysburg, and that he and former Defense Secretary Tom Gates had both refused. "I know," answered the General, "but if Scranton won't do it, I think you have to. It would be better for Bill to run so you could stay in the Senate, but if he won't, you know what you ought to do."

He delivered himself of some strong views regarding Old Guard habits of thinking and of their continuing reluctance to endorse the strongest candidates.

"We are doing very well with tickets in places like California and Michigan, and we have to show some sense in Pennsylvania."

Of these adjurations, I informed the press adding: "He [Eisenhower] told me he had hoped that Congressman Scranton would run for Governor so I could stay in the Senate."

There were more. Some of Ike's pungent diction that I later recalled might better have been left unsaid.

On the issue of his candidacy, Scranton was firm, but not unreasonable. He strongly preferred not to run but, he said privately, he might give the Governorship candidacy some consideration if all party factions united to support him. He assumed such unanimity to be impossible.

Scranton's terms were realistic, for he would have to surrender his House seat to run for Governor, and he regarded his chances of winning the statewide race as dim without a united party.

I laid down the final challenge to the neolithics at a Philadelphia press conference. I opened with a prepared statement that was as much an indictment as a declaration.

"As you will recall," I reminded, "a very small group of men—who represent a minority view in our party and who are afflicted with a contempt for public opinion—decided to dictate to the party who shall be its candidates. They did this without informing the officers of the party, without conferring with county chairmen and vice chairmen, without drawing upon the real grassroots strength of the Republican party in Pennsylvania.

"They offered a 'harmony' ticket, although the only things they harmonized were the personal ambitions of a few men. They spoke of 'victory,' although their candidates in the past have not known how to achieve victory.

"Many members of our party called . . . to help stop this . . . march . . . to another defeat [including] General Eisenhower." [2]

I pointed out that the former President had ignored heavy pressure to revise both his "frank and spirited com-

ments" and his expressions of confidence in me. I emphasized that I was doing "not what I *want*, but what I *must.*
. . . there are times in life when what we *have to do* com-
pels us to turn away from what we *love to do.*"

I announced my candidacy for Governor and promised
"a fighting campaign based upon the need for giving
Pennsylvania better and more economical government,
free of boss control." I said emphatically that I was "tired
of seeing losers pick new losers to lose again." [3]

My announcement triggered what one reporter called
the "Hugh Bomb," and it set off a chain reaction that
ended, to the satisfaction of Pennsylvania's moderates,
with the Old Guard also supporting Scranton.

Scranton's eviction of the Democrats who had ruled
Harrisburg for eight years was a triumph of organization
and personality. From the time he was nominated as a
"unity" candidate, he worked unceasingly and effectively
to weld party factions into a striking force sufficiently
vigorous to overcome the slight Democratic lead in registrations. It was up to Scranton himself to go on from
there to convince the independents who are the balance of
power in all genuine two-party states. In this he was brilliantly successful at the polls, partly because he stayed
true to his philosophy of liberalism on questions of human
rights and conservatism in money matters, partly because
he stayed unflappable throughout his bitter campaign
with his high-strung, albeit highly personable opponent
Dick Dilworth.

Because I believed in Scranton and the kind of Republicanism he represented, I voiced public hope early in
June 1963, that Scranton would "feel impelled" to accept the Presidential nomination "if he's called for higher
duty." The occasion was one of my bi-monthly telecasts
with Senator Clark.* I also said, to nobody's surprise,
that I saw nothing to prevent my running for a second

* The only regular TV program in the Senate conducted by Senators
of opposing parties.

term, with unemployment and the Kennedy record as my principal issues.

As he had before, Scranton soon disavowed any intention to run for the Presidency, and I privately promised not to pressure him toward a decision at that time. He did disclose that he was considering a "favorite son" candidacy if the race for the nomination appeared to be close. The device would give him early ballot control of our 64-vote convention delegation and, under some circumstances, it could be the balance of power.

But power is as power does, and in the summer of 1963 the strength of the majority was fragmented in the Republican Party. Only on the right wing was there effective forward motion. F. Clifton White's Draft Goldwater Committee had a mission, it had organization and, as its name implies, it had a candidate. Even before Rockefeller's remarriage, a postcard poll of delegates to the 1960 Republican Convention—most of them long-time party workers—showed Goldwater with the largest single bloc of support. He was the first choice of 481 of the 1,045 ex-delegates who responded to the poll by *Congressional Quarterly*. But it was significant that he won just forty-six per cent support in this sample. It was even more significant that the sample represented only thirty-nine per cent of the full roster of 2,662 delegates and alternates.

The old atavistic longing for the brand of "hold-the-line" conservatism that flowered in McKinley's era was still churning deep in the party. To convert it into a viable candidacy, Goldwater's supporters still had to offer a formula for victory over Kennedy that fitted the Arizona Senator better than any other Republican. They had contended for months that the 128 electoral votes of the South, when combined with claimed conservative support in states west of the Alleghenies, could be "the key to Republican success." The claim took on new meaning with the turbulent eruption of the revolution in civil rights in the summer of 1963. There was evidence, especially in blue-collar areas, that the Democrats would have to deal with the grotesque hobgoblin that has come to be known as "white backlash."

Segregationists were gravitating toward Goldwater. He was not yet a declared candidate and he was thus under no compulsion to comment on their support. But they plainly took no exception to a race-relations stand that was part of his particular brand of conservatism: while he supported school integration, he maintained (until convinced otherwise before he became an active candidate early in January, 1964) that the Constitution left the matter with the states. And he held that "The right of association . . . need not be disturbed in solving the problem of what we call civil rights. . . ." [4] It was not all-out segregation, and Goldwater's personal stance on human rights was decent and good, but it was enough for the principle's supporters, especially when it was merged into a brand of radical conservatism as unrealistic as it was archaic.

I encountered one of the first public collective frenzies of the New Right when I spoke on June 28, 1963, before the biennial convention of the Young Republicans in San Francisco—a prophetic site in view of later developments.

A majority of these youngsters were committed to Goldwater when they came to the meeting in the dignified ballroom of the old Sheraton-Palace Hotel. A sizable fraction of this majority vociferously favored extreme proposals espoused by some Goldwater supporters, such as the so-called "Liberty Amendment" that would have repealed the Federal income tax.

I had been invited by Leonard Nadasdy, the organization's outgoing president, to address the banquet session that normally winds up Y.R. conventions. I arrived at the

Palace Hotel at dinnertime and found Graustarkian
chaos. The beleaguered Nadasdy, a fair-minded moderate,
was near tears with frustration, for convention business
had ground to a standstill as factions and sub-factions
left the floor to caucus and conspire in rooms upstairs.

The banquet started hours late and it was half-past
midnight (in more ways than one) when I was finally
called on to speak to bleary-eyed delegates whose minds
were quite evidently on those caucuses still underway
above them. I gave them a speech that stressed basic Republican doctrine, but hardly the conservatism that was
capturing the convention. I tried as best I could to warn
against the party splitting menace of inflexible dogmatism.

"I am for a Republican victory next year," I said.
"You are for a Republican victory next year. But to beat
each other to bits now is a sure way to let our opposition
beat us once more at the polls. Let us leave lunacy to those
who would ride our money to the moon. Let us never forget who our real opponents are—the Democratic Administration. . . ." [5]

I might have been Canute addressing the tide. In a near-
riotous atmosphere, the delegates elected as their new
president Donald E. Lukens, an ardent Goldwater man.
He won by a margin of five votes out of 624 cast, the first
Young Republican leader in the organization's modern
history to take office publicly committed to a Presidential
hopeful.

Young Republicans are not party leaders. But the national press decided to use their 1963 convention as a kind
of Geiger counter of G.O.P. right wing conservatism. The
reporters prominently noted that no motion friendly to
the civil rights movement cleared the convention. (Chaos
on the floor mercifully prevented consideration of a pro-

posal approved by the Resolutions Committee that would have put the Y.R.s on record against both state and Federal laws forbidding race discrimination in public accommodations.)

The Y.R. meeting was the fuse that detonated a bitter Rockefeller blast on July 14 against infiltration of the party by the Radical Right. Rockefeller's statement did not name Goldwater, but it denounced the Southern Strategy that was basic to the campaign being waged in the Senator's name. Goldwater's people slashed back angrily at Rockefeller as a "party splitter." An inexorable process of polarization was under way, even though Goldwater himself was then giving first priority to party unity in his talks with an ever-widening circle of Republicans.

Now it was the Senator who looked like the man to beat. Late in July, I was asked if I would support my colleague from Arizona if he won the nomination.

"If you assume that I'll be a candidate," I replied, stating a widely-held assumption, "I'd have to run on my record, and mistakes . . . I would not consider myself bound totally to the views of the presidential candidate." [6]

Goldwater's continuous travels brought him to Pennsylvania on October 10 as the principal speaker at a $100-a-plate fund-raising dinner at Hershey. His appearance helped still charges of a Scranton-Scott "blackout" against the Senator, but its contribution to Republican unity was debatable. While the dinner was a financial success, a third of the 9,000-seat arena stayed empty. The Governor and I were present, but former President Eisenhower decided for reasons of his own not to essay the 40-mile drive from his Gettysburg farm to hear Goldwater.

Three weeks before that Hershey meeting, Goldwater was one of the eight Republican Senators to oppose the nuclear test ban treaty when it passed the Senate 80 to

19. With twenty-four other Republicans, I had voted for
ratification out of a feeling that "a balance of risks is better than a balance of terror."

The treaty was one of the relatively few substantial
products of a Congressional session that was drifting into
sterile deadlock. Southern Democrats slammed the brakes
on Kennedy's top-priority tax-reduction and civil rights
bills. Appropriations bills were stalled in a silly squabble
between committees. It was wordy, and it was dull.

This murky atmosphere was electrified overnight by the
resignation under fire of Robert G. Baker, the $19,600-a-
year secretary to the Senate's Democratic majority.
There were charges that he had used his strategic job to
advance his personal fortunes. As a member of the Senate
Committee on Rules and Administration, I found myself
part of the group assigned by the Senate to untangle
Bobby Baker's affairs. The Committee was made up of six
Democrats and three Republicans. By coincidence, my
Pennsylvania colleague Joe Clark was on the Committee's
majority side.

No case could be closer to the nerve center of the Senate
"establishment" than an inquiry into the activities of
Bobby Baker, who had risen as the protégé of the former
Majority Leader, Lyndon B. Johnson, then Vice President of the United States. It was Baker's job to keep
track of Senators and know their stands on pending issues. Most of them trusted him and worked with him.
Questions about Baker raised questions about the Senate
itself.

There was certainly no zeal for the Baker probe. With
the help of Joe Clark and my two Republican colleagues
on the Rules Committee, I succeeded in persuading five reluctant Democratic members that the inquiry would be
suspect unless we retained an outside counsel whom no one
could accuse of being on the Senate payroll.

The Baker investigation was settling down to business, amid partisan gunfire, when the shots that killed John Kennedy sent shock waves around the world. Nowhere in government outside the White House did they strike with more impact than in the Senate, where personal affection for old colleagues is not bounded by party lines. And nowhere was there deeper understanding for Lyndon Johnson as he faced the immense problems of transition.

On November 25, the day of the Kennedy funeral, I made a public proposal to Senator Leverett Saltonstall of Massachusetts, then Chairman of the Senate Republican Conference, that minority Senators declare a moratorium on political speeches for the balance of 1963 to give the new President a chance to get on with his overpowering job. The proposal was informally approved.

That same day, Saltonstall and I joined two Democrats, Senators John Pastore of Rhode Island and Henry Jackson of Washington in a bipartisan television symposium on the implications of the horror through which we had all passed. All four of us were shocked to numbness by the recent past, but hopeful for the future, primarily because of our confidence in the man we had known as Senate leader.

I had learned as a vigorous partisan how tough a party man Lyndon Johnson could be when the occasion required. But I also appreciated the skill with which he could prevail on Senators to "reason together" in the national interest. In that knowledge, I voiced hope that all American representatives abroad would tell a world that did not know our new President as the Senate knew him: ". . . you need have no concern about his patriotism, his firmness, his understanding of foreign policy, his alignment with freedom . . . ." [7]

We were still groping then for the twisted background that led Lee Harvey Oswald from lone-wolf Marxism to assassination. It was even then evident that overpowering hatred lay behind his deed, and that the dreadful outcome held a lesson for us all. "The next time you hear an expression of hatred . . . don't just laugh or snicker or be embarrassed or leave the room or get into a futile argument," I admonished a television audience. "It's our duty —all of us—to condemn . . . as a nation the kind of extremism that says . . . 'because you don't agree with me, you're a traitor.' " [8]

The real story of the 1964 Presidential election begins with the shots fired in Dallas on November 22, 1963. The assassination of President Kennedy was a national catastrophe with many ramifications, personal, national and international. Its effect on national politics was to put a new man in the White House, a new contender for election the following year. It had been axiomatic that the young, vigorous, eminently personable Kennedy would be a candidate to succeed himself.

The governmental transition wrought by the assassination was orderly by comparison with the upheaval Kennedy's passing brought in politics, especially Republican politics. Most of us thought it had arrested the Goldwater tide in mid-surge. As Robert S. Novak has pointed out in his excellent book, *The Agony of the G.O.P. 1964*,[9] such logic as there was in arguments for the Senator's nomination was not only nullified but reversed.

Goldwater's potential strength against Kennedy in the South seemed unlikely to hold well against Lyndon Johnson, the first Southern-born, Southern-bred President since another assassination ninety-eight years before threw the Presidency to another Johnson, Andrew, of Tennessee. At the same time, as I felt sure, Goldwater hardly seemed the type of Republican who could win back the big industrial states that had given Kennedy his winning margin.

Even Goldwater said it was "a new ball game with a new pitcher." [10] Rockefeller, who had announced his candidacy two weeks before the assassination, was girding for the primaries. The political seismographs in Harrisburg and Lansing showed new stirrings in the Scranton and Romney camps. Richard Nixon's credentials were restudied. There was a flurry of talk about Henry Cabot Lodge, Nixon's 1960 running mate, even though he was then serving the Democratic Administration as Ambassador to Saigon. It came to light that General Eisenhower had suggested that Lodge enter a field which the General hoped would include all promising Republicans.

But there was still no unity among the Republicans of the center. And Barry Goldwater's men never stopped working. Late in 1963, his partisans began stalking delegates. Their hunting grounds were the "convention states." There they bagged their game at the precinct and county conventions that picked the people who manned the state conventions which ultimately chose the delegations that would speak for the states at San Francisco. Where they could, they recruited the support of state and county leaders. When the effort failed, they scrapped protocol and inundated the generally-unnoticed little conventions with zealous volunteers to whom Goldwater was not a candidate but a cult leader. When these people won a place on a delegation, they went as disciples, irreconcilables, immune to conversion, persuasion or the logic of political compromise.

Their troops were commanded by hard-headed professionals who played politics for keeps. In New Mexico, the Goldwater people piled into the precinct meetings as soon as they began in December, 1963. In the counties they controlled, they arranged to split the delegate votes into quarters, so each vote at the state convention was represented by four people. When the state convention came in June, the key decisions were made by standing vote, with some Goldwater votes overstated four times. Some leading Republicans made public protests, but New Mexico's little fourteen-vote delegation went to San Francisco solid for Goldwater.* The Goldwater forces missed only three of the 108 delegates from the Mountain and Desert states.

In the South, where the Goldwater operation was led by hard-driving John Grenier of Alabama, 271 of 279 national delegates from the eleven states of the old Confederacy were captured for Goldwater. Most came willingly. Where there was resistance, Grenier usually bulled it through. In Madison County, Alabama, the site of Huntsville, Grenier refused to recognize the delegation chosen by 500 Madison Republicans, then overrode objections in the State Committee and replaced it with a more dependable group chosen at a mass meeting attended by 150 persons.

In Georgia, National Committeeman Robert Snodgrass had so successfully resisted racism in the party that fifty-eight per cent of the Negroes in his home Fulton County (Atlanta) voted for the Nixon-Lodge ticket in 1960. He and his moderate allies were ruthlessly steamrollered four years later. At the county conventions of March, 1964, Goldwater people captured eighteen of the twenty district delegates' seats. In May, the state convention, keynoted by Goldwater himself, picked four at-large delegates pledged to the Senator. Snodgrass was knocked out, and Georgia Republicanism turned lily-white. Goldwater won historically Democratic Georgia without any help from the Negroes.

Negro voters were pointedly ignored, too, when the North Carolina convention picked its solid twenty-six vote

* New Mexico elected centrist Republican David Cargo to succeed its Democratic Governor in 1966.

delegation in February. The Tarheel State, which had boasted one of the most promising Republican parties in the South, later rejected Goldwater by nearly 175,000 votes. But the party's most significant casualty in the state was its gubernatorial candidate, Robert Gavin, a progressive who held to the moderate position on civil rights. Even so, he received but three per cent of the 200,000 Negro votes cast.

"I believe as an American, as a Southerner and as a Republican," Gavin said as he recited these statistics later, "that our Party must be broad enough to support every American." [11]

It was not the year for the Gavins of the Republican Party. They were generally overwhelmed in the convention states; they fragmented their strength in the states whose primaries have so often served in the past as bellwethers of national convention sentiment.

Rockefeller sought to erase the political effects of his remarriage by waging the kind of battle he was equipped to fight: the long, tough route through the state primaries. It took money, endurance and innate optimism. Rockefeller had all three, but the combination failed to click.

Rockefeller met Goldwater head to head in New Hampshire's March 10 primary, the nation's first. Goldwater made some bad bobbles, including a suggestion that social security be made "voluntary," and Rockefeller tried to fight him on debating points. But the winner—on write-in votes—was Henry Cabot Lodge of Massachusetts, who was in Saigon, half a world away. Lodge won all fourteen delegates and thirty-five per cent of the vote to Goldwater's twenty-two per cent and Rockefeller's twenty-one. The Lodge victory may serve as a benchmark for future campaign planners. Two young Lodge rooters with little

money, some postcards and much zeal, derailed both the
Goldwater and Rockefeller organizations.

Failure to win even a quarter of the votes in the kickoff
primary led the Goldwater people to sidestep state popu-
larity contests wherever possible. There were exceptions:
where the cards were stacked in Goldwater's favor, as in
Illinois, which was avoided by other major contenders;
where withdrawal was impossible, as in Oregon, which
Goldwater all but wrote off, or where the stakes were too
large to ignore, as in California's June 2 jackpot, which
yielded Goldwater eighty-six pledged (and dedicated)
delegates and all but assured him the nomination.

June's realities seemed remote improbabilities when the
weary Eighty-eighth Congress reconvened for its second
session January 7—after a first session that ran to December 30. Rockefeller was crippled by his remarriage
and Goldwater was set back by Kennedy's assassination,
and there seemed to be an opening for a compromise candidate. My fourteen House colleagues on the Pennsylvania Republican delegation adopted a resolution with
which I concurred, urging Scranton to let others work for
him as a Presidential candidate. Meeting with the delegation, then with reporters on January 9, the Governor refused to take the plunge, but he tested the water. He
would, he said, be open to an honest and sincere draft, "if
such a thing is possible in the 'modern political system.' " [12]

Scranton's disclaimers, both public and private, seemed
to generate interest, rather than quench it. The Governor
told friends he was afraid he was "no longer master of the
situation." But he firmly refused to declare himself.

Through the long spring, it had seemed that Pennsylvania's big delegation would be used at San Francisco as a
strategic reserve to support the moderate champion—
whoever he might be. As Pennsylvania's favorite son and
delegation chairman, Scranton could count on the vast

majority of our sixty-four delegates to support that
champion—especially if he should be Bill Scranton.

But the Governor still remained aloof, even though he
had won 220,000 votes (58 per cent of the total) as a write-
in candidate in Pennsylvania's nonbinding Presidential
preference primary. The write-in, arranged and promoted
by Republican State Chairman Craig Truax, left Lodge,
Nixon, Goldwater and Rockefeller trailing in that order.
(All the results were write-ins, for there were no entries in
the Pennsylvania primary.)

On May 22, a month after the primary, Truax introduced the Governor to a delegation meeting as "the most
famous noncandidate in the United States." [13] But
Scranton still told a questioner: "For once and for all, I
don't want to be President or Vice President." [14]

Three days later, General Eisenhower gave new arguments to Scranton's backers when he sketched a pattern
for the ideal Republican nominee that seemed most eminently to fit Pennsylvania's Governor. Ike named no
names, but he said in a copyrighted article for the New
York *Herald Tribune* he hoped the candidate would sub-
scribe to the 1956 G.O.P. platform, as well as that to be
framed for 1964, would be a believer in "limited government," but a supporter of the United Nations who
shunned "impulsiveness" in foreign affairs. He stressed
the civil rights crisis and asserted a national obligation to
enact laws extending "the full benefit of citizenship" [15] to
all Americans.

Goldwater and Rockefeller, then battling it out in the
crucial California primary, each claimed to fit the Eisenhower specifications. It appeared to me that if the General
had a man in mind, he certainly was not Goldwater.
Scranton seemed to fill all the former President's require-
ments, and I so said.

In a race where two front-runners are as well estab-

lished as Goldwater and Rockefeller were in the late
spring of 1964, an outsider's chances depend mainly on a
convention deadlock between the leaders. Deadlock appeared to be more than a theoretical possibility if Rockefeller were to win the climactic June 2 test in California.
It was *the* race of the primary season: a costly, hard-
fought collision between champions from opposite poles of
the party, with all others excluded. The winner gained far
more than eighty-six pledged delegates, for both sides
agreed on one thing: the loser would be dead as a 1964
contender.

Rockefeller was rated narrowly ahead in polls taken
immediately after he pulled through the May 15 Oregon
primary at the head of a field of six. If the New Yorker
won, he would capture a bloc of delegates Goldwater badly
needed to keep his convention bandwagon rolling. Goldwater was already credited with about 500 delegate votes,
won in state conventions and lightly-contested primaries.
Arithmetically, victory in California would bring him
very near the 655 delegates required for the nomination.
Psychologically, if he won the Golden State, only a miracle could stop him.

The time to pass political miracles is before the votes
are cast. Those best qualified to help Rockefeller were the
men whose only chance for the nomination rested on a convention deadlock between Rockefeller and Goldwater if
Goldwater failed to win California. But, with the exception of Lodge, who turned over his organization to Rockefeller, all the representatives of the Republican center
regrettably stayed aloof, through most of the campaign.

In the final week, the three top contenders—Scranton,
Romney and Nixon—told the world, in effect, that it was
no concern of theirs if Goldwater won. The occasion was a
Rockefeller pamphlet which portrayed Goldwater as the
foe of policies endorsed not only by past Republican con-

ventions but by all the other contenders for the nomination. A vote for Rockefeller, the pamphlet implied, was a proxy vote for any of Goldwater's challengers. Goldwater counterattacked with wires to the three absentees, bluntly demanding to know whether they considered Rockefeller their representative in California. One by one, all three replied for the record that they favored no one in the key primary. These disavowals were massively advertised by the Goldwater people in the campaign's final week.

In fact, except for Lodge, I believe that Senator Clifford P. Case of New Jersey and I were the only national Republicans outside the Rockefeller organization who stated publicly that we hoped Rockefeller would win in California. Events might have been very different if Romney and Scranton and Nixon, instead of disassociating themselves from any stop-Goldwater movement, had issued more balanced statements which did not leave the impression it was all right with them if Goldwater won. They could, for instance, severally, or (even better) in concert, have drawn the issues between moderation and far-right conservatism clearly enough to make their own views evident. Unwilling to hang together, they faced the grim prospect of hanging separately.

The statements by the three absent candidates were exploited in every advertising medium and by the army of eager volunteers that swarmed out of Goldwater's Southern California power base. Then, three days before the election, they received another break: the birth of the first child of Rockefeller's second marriage. This widely-publicized blessed event reopened, too late to neutralize the impact, the welter of doubts and antipathies raised by the Governor's divorce and remarriage.

Goldwater won by only 68,000 votes out of 2.1 million, but it was winner take all. Forty days remained until the national convention opened. Production of a political miracle at this stage would require shock treatment, and the odds against its success were huge. At the same time, total failure to take a stand for moderation would be read by the nation, and rightly, as party-wide surrender to principles that were as grotesque as they were dangerous in a world of nuclear tension and race conflict.

To have the faintest chance, any effort to derail the Goldwater bandwagon would have to focus on a single candidate, and it would have to highlight the serious implications of a Goldwater candidacy. If these implications were brought home to enough rank-and-file Republicans and party professionals, there appeared to be an outside chance of swaying those delegates who were listed as "leaning" to Goldwater, but not formally committed to him. (Few of us who clung to this hope were yet able to comprehend fully the true believers' fervor that glued most Goldwater delegates to their candidate to the exclusion of all others.)

Four days after the California primary, I joined Representative Robert J. Corbett, our delegation's senior House member, in announcing formation of a Congressional committee to draft Scranton as a candidate who "represents the whole party, not one faction." We warned that the "divisive trend" in a Goldwater nomination could result in the loss of thirty House seats in November.[16] (We were optimists: Republicans actually elected thirty-eight fewer Congressmen in 1964 than in 1962—a loss which a more united party recouped with a vengeance in 1966.)

That same June 6, Scranton visited Gettysburg for a long talk with General Eisenhower. He later told reporters the General had urged him to become "more available" [17] for the nomination. He reported that Ike was concerned about the progressive tradition of the G.O.P. and urgently sought an "open" convention. News stories

construed Scranton's report as a sign that Ike was about
to commit his vast prestige to the preconvention battle.

The former President, who had encouraged all eligibles
to compete for the nomination, was jarred by the headlines suggesting that he had taken sides. He decided to set
Scranton straight with a telephone call. By coincidence,
his call reached Scranton at an acutely embarrassing
time.

It was Sunday morning, June 7th, and Scranton had
just arrived in Cleveland for the opening of the fifty-
sixth annual Governors' Conference. These affairs had
produced catalytic results in other Presidential years, and
1964 seemed to be no exception: Scranton's staff had
passed the word that something special could be expected
when the Governor appeared Sunday as the guest on the
national CBS panel show "Face The Nation."

Against this background, Scranton received the call
from the former President with whom he had talked so
cordially the day before, the one man whose endorsement
might—just might—be the equalizer in an uphill fight to
head off Goldwater. But the General made it clear on the
telephone that he was keeping out of the fight; he did not
want their conversation of Saturday construed to mean
that he was entering a "cabal" against anyone.

The results on television were slightly schizophrenic. At
one level, Scranton told a national audience, that had been
keyed up to expect much more, that he was ready to
serve if a majority of the delegates wanted him. At another, he declared "I don't plan to go out and try and
defeat Goldwater." He said at one point he feared the
party was "wedging itself away from . . . the principles of equal rights and unlimited opportunity," but later
told a reporter who suggested that he did not "want"
Senator Goldwater, he was "putting words in my mouth." [18]

In Washington, I was still working full tilt to move the

"Draft Scranton" drive out of Congress onto the national stage. I took what public encouragement I could from his statement on television that he was "ready to serve," but it alone plainly had not turned the trick.

In Cleveland, the press played Scranton's low-keyed performance against the barbed comments of two other Republican Governors. Romney saw "the suicidal destruction of the Republican Party as an effective instrument in meeting the nation's needs" [19] if the G.O.P. followed Goldwater's path. If Goldwater's views continued to diverge from the Republican heritage, Romney vowed, "I will do everything within my power to keep him from becoming the party's presidential candidate." [20]

Rockefeller, still embittered by the California returns, was openly scornful of Scranton's television performance. Asked if he would support Scranton, the New Yorker said he would "have to see where he stands." He had a two-word formula for what was needed: "More Romneys." [21]

There were no more at the Governors' Conference. And Romney himself showed no disposition to enter the lists against Goldwater, even though Richard Nixon flew to Cleveland on June 9 to urge the Michigan Governor to make the try.

But there were two significant events as the conference ended on June 10. With Romney as their spokesman, the moderate forces let it be known that they were ready to try a last-ditch stand, even though they still lacked a candidate. And in Washington, Barry Goldwater gave the nation concrete evidence of his philosophy by voting against cloture to end a filibuster that had stalled action for seventy-four days on the tough new civil rights bill pending before the Senate. And on June 19—less than a month before the convention, he broke with the overwhelming majority of his party and voted against the bill.

No single catalyst led William Scranton to the decision

to make his uphill race for the nomination. But certainly Goldwater's vote in defiance of Republican tradition and doctrine helped sway Scranton to a course he considered inescapable, however hopeless it might appear.

My first inkling that Scranton had done what I felt he was going to do came about 3 o'clock on the afternoon on Thursday, June 11, when Craig Truax telephoned me at my Senate office. The State Chairman wanted to know how quickly I could get to the Governor's official residence at Indiantown Gap, near Harrisburg. I was battling Senate business. "I'm very busy," I told Truax, "but if this involves action, I'll be there."

"This involves action," Truax replied.

I flew to Harrisburg in a chartered plane, then drove to the mansion in time for 7 o'clock dinner. The substantial party already gathered there included key members of the Governor's staff, George Bloom, Secretary of the Commonwealth, State Republican Finance Chairman Frank C. P. McGlinn and Malcolm Moos, a top White House speech writer in the Eisenhower era. It was hard to keep the conversation general during dinner.

Afterward, we settled over coffee in the living room. The Governor promptly brought the conversation to the point.

"We've been doing some talking," he said. "Have you anything of interest to tell us?"

I could think of no reply but the Biblical injunction and I came out with it. "He that would save his life must lose it." The Governor knew my attitude and understood my meaning: he might lose, but even a losing fight would do the party more ultimate good than no fight at all. There was a brief, brisk discussion of the wisdom of entering the race at this late date. The Governor listened in silence for a time, then leaned forward in his chair.

"I am going to run," he said. It was 8:05 P.M. He

promptly moved to the telephone and began placing calls
to advise prominent Republicans of his decision. The first
two went to Rockefeller and Romney.

A 4:00 A.M. call reached Nixon in London. "That's
good news, Hugh," said Dick. "I'll have a statement when
I reach New York this afternoon." The New York press
conference produced a "more the merrier" reaction from
the former Vice President. Other early morning calls by
McGlinn gleaned substantial financial backing.

The next morning, Moos and I drove to Gettysburg to
bring General Eisenhower up to date. Our ninety-minute
talk was frank and friendly. While we made it clear that
the fight was on, we neither requested nor received any
quotable comments from the former President.

Shortly after the Gettysburg meeting ended, Scranton
announced his decision loud and clear in a hastily-arranged
appearance before the Maryland State Republican convention in Baltimore (the most convenient forum immediately available).

"I have come to offer our party a real choice," Scranton
said in an apt inversion of a Goldwater slogan. "I reject
the echo we have thus far been handed—the echo of fear
and of reaction. . . ." [22]

It was a brave challenge, and it came nearer than any
action in recent months to unifying the Republican forces
not already committed to Goldwater. Nelson Rockefeller
generously turned over his entire highly professional national organization to the Pennsylvanian. Selflessly,
Cabot Lodge resigned his Saigon post to join the Scranton campaign. Eight Republican Senators, of whom I was
one, joined in a statement that urged an open convention
and, without attacking Goldwater directly, challenged
Goldwater's views on key issues. The Gallup poll found
after Scranton's announcement that the public favored

him over Goldwater, 55 per cent to 34, with 11 per cent undecided.

Delegates are not included in Dr. Gallup's general samples. But these developments, taken together, contributed to the optimistic tone of the frantic four weeks of airborne campaigning by which Scranton tried to make up for lost time. He found friends everywhere, but it was clear that too many professionals were already committed or neutralized. The Associated Press reported that the June crop of state conventions pushed Goldwater's delegate score over the 655 needed to win. We hoped and euphorically believed that perhaps a third of these were open to persuasion, but we had clear notice that we faced an uphill fight.

On June 30, Scranton took the long chance that he could make converts in the hard-shelled Illinois delegation. It was a tough test: Goldwater and Scranton each talked privately with the fifty-eight technically uncommitted delegates, and then the delegation was polled. The result: forty-eight public commitments for Goldwater— and none for Scranton.

Six days later, the grueling showdown began with the convening of the Platform Committee at the St. Francis Hotel halfway up San Francisco's spectacular Nob Hill.

I was there wearing two hats. Procedurally, I was there as Pennsylvania's representative on the 100-member Platform Committee; tactically, I was Scranton's representative and floor manager-to-be.

In extended consultations with the best brains in the Scranton and Rockefeller camps, it was decided that the 1964 confrontation, unlike the 1952 battle in Chicago, was not and should not be one of personalities, but one of issues. We had to ask delegates not, "Who are you for?" but "Where do you stand?" on the most vital issues facing the party, the nation and the world. The place to pose the questions was to be before the Platform Committee. What happened next would depend on the readiness of the Goldwater people to compromise.

I did not expect them to yield much. But I could hardly believe the degree of inflexibility I had encountered. The Platform Chairman, Representative Melvin R. Laird of Wisconsin, expected Goldwater to win and he was determined to keep the platform within the rigid confines acceptable to the Senator and repeatedly opposed attempts to broaden the document's appeal. It was evident early that the Goldwater people had the votes. We were even turned down on language committing the party to prompt "enforcement" of the Civil Rights Act. Representative John Rhodes of Arizona, one of Goldwater's men on the Platform Committee, questioned the word's impact in the South, and the civil rights plank accordingly committed the party only to "full implementation and faithful execution" * [23] of the Civil Rights Act, against which Goldwater had voted on July 2. Said Barry's men: "They will buy it in the South."

Those of us who considered ourselves traditional Republicans felt we had to dramatize publicly the losing battle that had thus far been bottled up behind closed doors. It was important to the party's survival to show that there was less than monolithic support for the kind of decisions being made in the Platform Committee.

We planned our strategy between the platform sessions in a two-room hideaway in the St. Francis, nine floors above the committee's meeting rooms. I presided as trusted friends, many from the East, some from the Midwest, a few from the Pacific Coast, came in to report on progress

---

* The "faithful execution" phrase was urged because it is to be found in the Presidential oath of office. So used in the platform, it committed a Republican President to do what he would swear to do, in any event.

on the platform that was rapidly becoming our only hope.

It was a rugged, command-post atmosphere. We installed extra telephone lines in the living room and the bedroom. Often, we had meetings going on in both rooms, and my staff assistants often had to carry the telephones into the bathroom between the two rooms, stretching the wires as far as they would go. We all came near to collapse with fatigue and when we could steal a few hours of sleep, we converted the bedroom back into a dormitory. I vaguely recall two staff men ejecting another from one of the beds so they could plant me there for a couple of hours. (I had a room at the Fairmont, atop Nob Hill, but I never seemed to get there, and I ate by snatching sandwiches from passing waiter's trays in the corridors.)

As the battle took shape, we faced two fundamental problems. First, we had to decide the issues on which we could most successfully wage a floor fight. Next, we had to determine which speakers could present those issues most effectively.

The Platform Committee majority's insistence on word-by-word acceptance of its Goldwater-oriented statement of principles raised three clear opportunities to offer substitute planks that would:

1. Repudiate "irresponsible" extremist groups, specifically including the Communist Party on the left and the Ku Klux Klan and the John Birch Society on the right.

2. Support full "enforcement" of the Civil Rights Act and assert the "constitutional responsibility" of the Federal government to insure the equality of voting rights of all Americans.

3. Affirm the exclusive authority of the President to control the use of nuclear weapons.

It was one thing to fix the issues, quite another to assure

their most effective presentation. In the first place, we were anxious to display as much breadth of support as we could as evidence that protests against the platform came from a substantial segment of party opinion. In addition, of course, we sought men of stature who possessed enough eloquence and presence of mind to deal with an audience that might well be less than friendly.

In the midst of this, someone at Scranton headquarters handed me a press release that had just been distributed to correspondents. It was the explosively controversial "Scranton letter," a now-notorious object lesson in bad political public relations. It was harsh and strident, and it savagely overstated the legitimate grounds for opposing Goldwater.

Scranton later said he neither saw nor signed the letter that went out over his name. Goldwater angrily returned it to Scranton without a reply. But his campaign staff first made copies and sent them to every delegate with a covering letter, terming it "an insult to every Republican in San Francisco." It added poison to an already rancorous atmosphere.

While we were working out the details of who was to speak for what amendment to the platform, I entered into negotiations with Mel Laird to develop the ground rules. We agreed that there would be three votes called, one a recorded roll call, the other two simple voice votes. Senator Morton of Kentucky and I were unable to persuade Laird to forego the reading of the entire platform, which would delay the debate on the critical amendments long past normal TV viewing time.

I remember driving to the Cow Palace for the showdown on Tuesday, July 14, the second night of the convention when the platform would be heard, debated, and voted upon. As I mulled over the sequence of votes and the order of speakers, trying to decide on the strongest combina-

tions, I remember saying that I felt like Casey Stengel
juggling a batting order before the game.

The other side was doing some juggling, too. They divided up the entire 8,500-word platform to be read by a
succession of speakers to the delegates before they were
asked to consider the moderates' amendments. It was a
tedious, two-hour process, all but guaranteed, as I had
urgently pointed out, to drive television viewers away
from their sets and quite possibly to bed. It was 8:54 P.M.
in the Cow Palace—six minutes to midnight on the East
Coast—before the reading clerk reached the last period in
the Goldwater Platform.

In my arranging of amendments and speakers, I remember saying to a staff assistant on the way to the Cow
Palace, "I have the feeling that Nelson is not too popular
with that crowd." But I was still shocked when I—along
with millions of people in the television and radio audience—discovered the extent of the bitterness against Governor Rockefeller in that convention hall.

Rockefeller spoke for our anti-extremism amendment.
It was a denunciation of the John Birch Society that
started the surly booing, a wordless chorus of hate that
drowned all other sound in the big arena. Rockefeller
stiffened, but kept his head and his courage until the din
subsided. As Chairman Thruston Morton angrily banged
for order, Rocky grinned: "Don't take it out of my time."
Goldwater lieutenants, fearful of the impact on the public, promptly passed word to their delegates to quiet down.
The delegates did, but the booing continued, wave on wave
of defiance to Rockefeller's brave, challenging sentences.
It was coming largely from the galleries, packed with
Goldwater's true believers. The wealthy, progressive,
Eastern Governor symbolized all they hated, with the Bib-
lical hatred of Jael.

The final roar came when the extremism amendment

was shouted down. The same fate befell the nuclear control amendment.

I called for a roll call vote on our civil rights proposal, in the hope that if we were able to shake loose any votes, it would be on this issue that was fundamental to the establishment of our party itself. We lost by a vote of 897 to 409, which was prophetic. It was a clear test of Goldwater strength and he won by just about that margin the next night.

I watched the tally from a vantage point on the platform below the speaker's rostrum, glumly recording decisions in delegation after delegation which I had come to expect, but did not yet accept.

We tried—how we tried—to cut our losses between the votes on each amendment. Through walkie-talkie men from our communications network, I would make connections with loyal friends from other days in desperate efforts to fight the tendency of delegates to go along with the winning side. Sometimes we shouted at one another through the platform rail while television reporters, garbed like frogmen, tried to catch stray words on their portable mikes. Sometimes, I scrambled down off the platform, onto the jammed press runway, then down to the chaotic floor. At other times, we called conferences in the closely guarded Scranton communications trailer alongside the Cow Palace. No one could enter the trailer who was not wearing a predetermined identification button. There was a brisk traffic in counterfeit buttons as there was in counterfeit tickets and floor passes.

So the game was to choose unlikely models from the novelty dealers who supplied them, and then wear them *under* the lapel except when they were needed as admission badges. Our button bore the white letters IRM on a dark field. Heaven knows whom they were originally made for but in the Scranton camp we called them "I Remember Mamma" buttons.

Forewarned though we were by the civil rights vote, the planning continued to the end in the Scranton trailer and in our headquarters on Nob Hill. The last lingering hope that General Eisenhower would abandon his determined neutrality vanished. But still, I felt, each vote for Scranton represented a vote of confidence in what I had known and believed in as Eisenhower Republicanism. It was tremendously important to show the surviving vitality of that spirit.

Milton Eisenhower made the nominating speech for William Scranton, a reasoned plea in a time of unreason. The seven-hour round of nominating speeches seemed endless, and I doubt that any of the speakers changed a single vote. The decision, reached at 10:39 P.M. on July 15 after a 25-minute first ballot, was mercifully quick: Goldwater, 883; Scranton, 214 (with 60 from Pennsylvania, the rest scattered across twenty-four delegations); Rockefeller, 114 (87 from New York); Romney, 41 (40 from Michigan); Senator Margaret Chase Smith of Maine, 27 (from seven states, with 14 from Maine); Representative Walter E. Judd of Minnesota, 22 (from three states); Senator Hiram Fong of Hawaii, 5 and Ambassador Lodge, 2.

An hour before the balloting started, Scranton and his advisers gathered in the communications trailer to prepare for the inevitable. When it came, he was ready. He went to the speaker's rostrum and moved to make the nomination unanimous.

I accompanied the Governor to the rostrum and stood by while he spoke. I envied his sportsmanship, but could not yet conquer my inability to share his sentiments. It would take me a while longer.

No unifying response in kind came from Goldwater. He delivered part of his answer when he picked Representative William E. Miller of New York, who had leaned toward Goldwater as National Chairman, as his running mate. He gave the rest of his reply the next day in his acceptance speech. Absent was the conventional olive branch, the customary promise to forget the family quarrel and get on with the assault on the political enemy. To the jubilation of his fevered followers in the Cow Palace, Goldwater put forward the tenets of hard-line conservatism as revealed truth. He underscored them with his reminder that ". . . extremism in the defense of liberty is no vice . . . moderation in the pursuit of justice is no virtue," phrases that shocked, angered and even frightened moderates.

Where Goldwater could have used his acceptance speech to call the party's factions back together, he turned it instead into a feckless challenge to all who disagreed with him to go elsewhere. Tragically for our party, all too many Republicans took him at his word.

Robert J. Donovan summarized the results in his perceptive book, *The Future of the Republican Party:*

> Goldwater's seeming defense of extremism made it just that much more impossible for Republicans like Keating, Romney, and Lindsay to endorse him or for those like Scott, Percy, Taft, Governor James A. Rhodes of Ohio, and many others to give him anything but the scantest recognition.
>
> Whereas Eisenhower had compromised with Taft on Morningside Heights and Nixon had compromised with Rockefeller on Fifth Avenue, Goldwater had delivered an uncompromising acceptance speech, after which he and his associates proceeded to rip the staff of the Republican National Committee to pieces to make sure that few were left who would have been discomfited by the tone of his remarks in San Francisco.[24]

After hearing Goldwater's acceptance speech, I certainly could not follow Scranton in donning a Goldwater button. I felt there was no place for me in picturesque San Francisco. That night, my wife and I checked out of our hotel and boarded a train for Vancouver to begin a long but relaxing trip aboard the Canadian Pacific back to the East Coast which Barry Goldwater had excommunicated.

The deliberately exclusionary acts and precepts of these newly-crowned Republican leaders posed serious problems for hundreds of Republican candidates. The oncoming right-wing crusade confronted them—and me— with a dilemma that was moral as well as political.

I was considering it in the light of hundreds of letters from my home state that urged, often demanded, that I repudiate Goldwater out of hand. And I weighed the future in the light of my nonexistent relations with the newly-reconstituted National Committee. From the convention through the election, I never received so much as a telephone call from National headquarters, and not a single offer, nor even a hint of aid. I did receive as much financial help from the Republican Senatorial Campaign Committee, headed by my colleague, Senator Thruston Morton, as could be garnered in virtual isolation from the National Committee.

On the other hand, I had been in Congress and on the National Committee well before most of the Goldwater crew entered politics. Over my quarter century in politics, it had become second nature to me to work for my party's success from top to bottom. Furthermore, I was covered by the rules of the Pennsylvania Republican State Committee, which require that all party officials must support the duly nominated candidates of the party. I was a member of the executive committee of the State Committee and by definition a "party official." Our county chairmen felt unanimously as the campaign started that they had no choice but to support the ticket.

Thus, the constituents who elected me were writing, all

but unanimously, "Don't do it," while my good friends among the county chairmen were telephoning, "Do it." (Nine-tenths of these pros were to change their minds before November.)

I felt I could not gear my personal campaign directly to a party platform with which I disagreed on such major points as immigration, education and civil rights. I knew I could not conform to the ideological passion for right-wing "purity" that was the hallmark of the national ticket.

A post-convention poll in Pennsylvania indicated that President Johnson would take the State by over one million votes. (The final result was half a million worse.) But this poll still showed me with a chance of winning.

My decision was expedited by a Republican "unity conference" in Harrisburg on August 7. I knew it would be attended by the other statewide candidates, all of whom had endorsed Goldwater, and by Scranton, who was dutifully fulfilling the promises of support he made at the convention.

Before our "unity" lunch, the Governor told me he still believed I would endorse the ticket, in my own time and in my own way. I promised to "say something very soon."

At the lunch, I leaned over my croquette and told the Governor, "I've decided to bite the bullet."

As Scranton predicted, I did it my own way, but State Committee members seemed greatly relieved when I announced to them that I would support the entire ticket "in compliance with the rules of the party." Truax obligingly announced that separate citizens' committees would handle the Goldwater and Scott campaigns in Pennsylvania.

On August 14, after it became probable that the courts would confirm Secretary of Internal Affairs, Miss Genevieve Blatt, the only Democrat in a statewide office, as my

COME TO THE PARTY

opponent, I kicked off my campaign with a luncheon speech before Lackawanna and Luzerne County leaders.

From the start, I professed confidence we would "carry Pennsylvania for the whole ticket," but this gambit did not ward off trouble. At meeting after meeting, I encountered heckling from quarrelsome right-wing ideologists who sought to substitute blind faith in their cause and its leader for the revealing process of genuine debate.

They were the same type of zealot whose demand for ideological "purity" produced the strange manifestations that speckled the 1964 campaign from coast to coast. Mostly young people, they attended political meetings as an act of faith, primarily to detect heresy. I was an arch-heretic because I held to the broadly centrist positions on which the Republican Party had grown great. Oblivious to party harmony, unhampered by good manners, they tried at every meeting to bully me into the Procrustean framework of their "purist" concepts—and damn the consequences.

The consequences were counter productive for them. The more these outriders of the right heckled me, the more determined I became to break away from them and from the cause they advocated so baldly—and so badly.

I took pains in every speech to make clear I was supporting the Republican Party and its candidates in accordance with party rules and because I felt I could do more good for the party within it than outside it. The hecklers could be counted on to ask the questions that allowed me to detail the policies and campaign tactics on which I could not go along with Senator Goldwater.

If it had depended only on the Goldwater record, the two-party system was doomed before election day. Therefore, I continued to stress the importance of returning Republican legislators to Washington and Harrisburg if the two-party system were to survive. As the campaign entered its crucial final weeks, the Republican Presidential candidate seemed oblivious to voter opinion. He criticized social security in St. Petersburg, Florida, a retirement haven for the elderly, and he blasted the Tennessee Valley Authority in Tennessee, where the Republican Senate candidates were "braggin' on" TVA. He came to a suburb of Philadelphia to air civil rights views that collided with mine and with those of 85 per cent of his colleagues in Congress. This last was the national ticket's sole contribution to my campaign.

I watched and catalogued the egregious follies of 1964 and feared that the National G.O.P. faced long-term trouble ahead. I privately predicted to Congressional colleagues that Goldwater would carry only the five states of the Deep South, Alabama, Mississippi, Louisiana, South Carolina and Georgia. I failed to reckon with the state pride that also gave him Arizona.

It was obvious that Goldwater was done for in Pennsylvania. As I traveled 40,000 miles by airplane, automobile, and helicopter to make 150 speeches in 66 of our 67 counties, the message came clear at almost every meeting— although it was sometimes not as loud as the shouted imprecations of the right wingers who did not like my style.

My style, evident to all observers of the campaign, was to appeal across party lines, trying to capitalize as much as I could on Pennsylvania's penchant for ticket splitting, without imperiling my standing as a Republican.

My opponent, Miss Blatt, was trying her resourceful best to rivet her campaign to President Johnson's and to persuade the voters that I had not removed mine sufficiently far from Goldwater's.

It was clear that a massive ticket split was under way. As I made my rounds from factory gates to street corner rallies and ladies' luncheons and county fairs, I got the

signal. It came in the knowing look and tone of countless
unidentified voters who would sidle up and say: "Senator,
I'm going to vote for *you*." There was a threat behind the
promise.

A few days before the November 3 election, Governor
Scranton told me the results of a consensus forecast based
on the findings of five leading polling organizations.
Their prediction for Pennsylvania: Johnson over Goldwater by 800,000 votes; Scott over Blatt by 800,000—a
switch of 1,600,000 votes.

"Do you believe it?" Scranton asked.

"No."

"Neither do I," said the Governor.

I personally suspected Johnson's lead was in the neigh-
borhood of a million votes. I felt I could still weather it,
with an assist from my ticket-splitting friends.

But voters need more than the will to divide their alle-
giances; they have to know the way, especially when they
are voting on machines which are designed to record a
straight party vote at the simple pull of a single lever.

As one cheerless poll after another predicted Goldwater's massive defeat in Pennsylvania, the danger of the
party lever registered on the state Republican organization. Straight ticket voting could kill our entire slate.
The way out, it occurred to the people in the Harrisburg
headquarters, was to encourage split-ticket voting for the
party's senior statewide candidate. If a Johnson voter
strayed off the Democratic line and voted for Scott, he
then could not vote a straight ticket and would have to
vote individually for all offices. This approach, Harrisburg argued, might just bail out some other Republicans,
especially State legislative candidates. Hopeful that
they might accomplish this, we volunteered a TV commercial pointed to achieve such an effect, more than pleased
that it had the State Committee's active blessing.

This 20-second film, geared to keep the potent Democratic Party lever from knocking down Republicans like a row of dominos, opened with a man in a voting booth, just about to pull a lever.

"Hey," says a firm but friendly offstage voice. "Don't touch that party lever."

"Why not?" our man asks, with no sign of concern at the unwanted intrusion.

"This election, each man has to stand on his own record," friendly voice replies, "That's why you want to vote for Senator Hugh Scott first."

"Right," our man responds, snapping his fingers to accent the pitch, "Pennsylvania needs a man like Senator Scott in Washington."

Persuasively turning back to the voting levers, he continues, "first Scott for Senator, and for President I'll vote for . . ." at which point the sound went dead.

The first time most people saw the commercial they thought the sound was faulty. People who saw it a second or third time got the point quickly, and it caused a lot of comment in the vote-heavy areas where it was being broadcast—a hearty plus for our side.

On Election Day, I did well in the urban, bituminous and anthracite areas. In this close election that was very likely my margin of victory. Split tickets saved, at the same time, about twenty Pennsylvania state legislators.

The next morning the news elsewhere was all too decisive. President Johnson had won our twenty-nine electoral votes and sixty-three of our sixty-seven counties by a margin of 1,457,000 votes for a majority of 64.9 per cent. I had been able to overcome the huge Johnson lead to win by 71,000 votes, carrying forty-two of our sixty-seven counties. The scale of his sweep more than doubled the previous state record set in 1936 when Franklin Roosevelt swamped Alf Landon by 663,000 votes. The pattern held good nationally. The recorded Johnson total was 43 million popular votes to Goldwater's 27 million.

A comparison of vote tallies is academic, especially when one has survived a landslide. The fact was that I was returning to the Senate as a member of a minority outnumbered 3 to 1, a ratio unequaled since New Deal days. The picture was equally dismal in the House, and there were only seventeen Republican governors left in the states. Our state picture was generally bleak but not as bad as that faced by many other Republican organizations. The elephant was scarred and dazed, deep in the woods. Had he lost his way altogether?

IX

THE ROAD BACK

"Together we can find a better way. . . ."
GEORGE ROMNEY *

POST-NOVEMBER 1964 was the dark of the political moon, the season when the long knives flashed, as I had learned so well at Omaha in 1949. After Dewey's defeat by less than three million votes, his foes in the party demanded my scalp as National Chairman because I was a symbol of discredited "Deweyism." Critics of the Goldwater campaign predictably made the same point in the wake of the 1964 disaster.

I had barely satisfied myself that I was indeed elected to a second Senate term before I predicted Dean Burch's removal from the Chairmanship to which the National Committee had elected him at Goldwater's bidding immediately after the San Francisco convention. Those who knew him—I never did—said they rather liked the 37-year-old Arizona lawyer; but his very existence in office symbolized a viewpoint the nation had rejected by an overwhelming majority. Burch had to go.

* Lansing, Michigan, June 20, 1967.

The Saturday after election a broadcast interview gave
me a chance at long last to state what I believed: that the
G.O.P. had just gone through "the worst managed campaign in American history, bar none." [1]

Our party was leaderless for the time being, but I predicted that the progressives, moderates and conservatives
who still held its center would agree soon on a course to
redeem its "beclouded" image.

"The party has been kidnaped," I said. ". . . the first
thing they did was take a good, decent and fine man like
Barry Goldwater and kidnap his mind and force upon him
many convictions which I think normally and on reflec-
tion, he might not have willingly conceived of himself." [2]

I could brush these things under the rug but I feel impelled by my duty to this account to speak with candor on
personalities of this period. I do so not to rub wet wounds
but to identify what to avoid next, lest chronic troubles be
repeated.

Republican rank-and-filers, I was sure, would refuse to
"pay ransom" to get their party back. And I warned
against repetition of the errors of judgment and of ego-
tism that allowed the party's capture by a fraction that
never represented more than a fifth of its membership.

That fraction's adherents were already trying to ra-
tionalize the setback with weird political arithmetic. They
somehow managed to find a mandate for the Right in the
twenty-seven million Republican votes, even though it has
been sixteen years since twenty-seven million votes * had
added up to victory in a Presidential campaign. To those
who argued that twenty-seven million voters couldn't be
wrong, wags retorted, if you believe that, go down to the
White House and say hello to President Goldwater.

Commenting on the unofficial totals I stated that although Barry Goldwater can hardly be blamed for his

* The final tally: 27,178,188.

still fond recall of those numbers, the vast majority of votes cast for the Republican candidate were indisputably cast by those who stuck loyally by the party label. Only a minor percentage of voters are, or ever have been, adherents of the philosophy of the radical right.[3]

I spoke with feeling, and it became evident in the days that followed that the feeling was widely shared. By mid-November, political commentators of every hue (and cry!) had drawn the ironic contrast between my position as the National Committee's fall guy in 1949 and my role in the chorus that demanded new leadership early in 1965.

I took my more-than-willing wife on a post-election ramble to the islands of the Pacific. It was no coincidence that I talked at Honolulu with assorted fellow survivors who felt the same need to relax the nerves and refresh the soul: by telephone with George Romney, newly—and impressively—re-elected Governor of Michigan, and personally with Hawaii's Senator Hiram Fong and attractive Daniel Evans, the promising moderate who weathered the Johnson tide to oust a Democrat from the Governorship of Washington State. I chatted with reporters, too, and predicted that my party, given half a chance, could regain fifty to sixty House seats from the vulnerable, over-extended Democrats in the 1966 mid-term elections.

By the end of November, I was ready to suggest some qualifications for the new man with whom I expected the National Committee to replace Burch after its scheduled January meeting in Chicago.

The new chairman, I told Earl C. Behrens, the veteran political editor of the San Francisco *Chronicle*, should be "a professional, acceptable to a broad consensus of the party and chosen for his ability to put together winning candidates and winning programs, rather than upholding some factional ideology." [4]

It was an idealized description, but I noted its application to one man: Ray C. Bliss, the Ohio State Chairman. While the Ohio organization remained in the Taft tradition, no one in the party questioned the professional competence or objectivity of the quiet-spoken technician who ran it. Months before the 1964 debacle proved his point, he drafted an incisive report that urged the G.O.P. to take timely action to correct its weakness with urban and surburban voters. He had rejected the national chairmanship in the past, but there was reason to believe he would respond to a new, party-wide appeal.

Goldwater predicted with apparent confidence that Burch's foes would not "have the votes" on the National Committee to replace his holdover Chairman. But the breadth of the demand for renovation of the party's top command became evident as the year neared its end. Strong sentiment for change was evident when the newly-formed Republican Governors Association met in Denver on December 4.

The Governors wisely did not presume to tell the National Committee what to do. They did make it abundantly clear that there was room in their kind of party for broad ranges of opinion. They committed themselves to a party of inclusion, not exclusion, and thereby began the process of dismantling the ideological barriers erected during the Goldwater campaign. They took steps to establish a national headquarters through which they hoped to speak more clearly to the nation and the party.

As the January 22 starting date for the National Committee meeting drew closer, it became evident that the lesson of 1949 was not lost on Burch. He tried at first to bargain: he offered his critics a chance to fill the $25,000-a-year post of executive director of the National Committee, then understandably vacant. And he let it be known that he would consider reshuffling of the National Com-

mittee's Executive Committee, which was overloaded with
Goldwater partisans. Burch's foes were not buying. Confident that they could command a majority of the National Committee's votes, they stood firm on their demand
for a new Chairman. They held to their stand despite—
and possibly because of—an open letter in which Goldwater insisted that replacement of Burch would amount
to "a repudiation of me." [5]

The Goldwater people claimed that Burch was given a
de facto contract when the National Committee elected
him for a four-year term. They kept trying for a face-
saving compromise. By a kind of poetic justice, I was in a
position to refute them, relying on precedent and logic.

My own experience at Omaha in 1949 was pretty con-
vincing evidence that compromise reached under such circumstances cannot long survive; even though I had won
the Omaha skirmish, I had found I had no choice but to
give back the chairmanship. By precedent and custom the
Chairman serves "at the pleasure of the committee" and
should be unseated any time the committee votes to declare
his seat vacant.

"He [Burch] should get out for his own sake and the
party's," I told Earl Mazo of *The New York Times* on
January 6 in a widely-reprinted interview. "Believe me,
I know—from experience."

Six days later, Dean Burch acting in the best interests
of the whole party announced in Phoenix that he would
submit his resignation to the Chicago meeting in the com-
mendably accurate belief that a showdown vote on the
issue would contribute nothing to party unity. In Ohio,
Ray Bliss disclosed his readiness to respond to the over-
tures that had deluged him.

Bliss' national target date was November 8, 1966, when
the mid-term contests for Congress and Governorships

would test the party's capacity for recovery. There would first be the municipal elections which many cities were to hold in November 1965. A dramatic showing in such local elections can build up priceless momentum for the next even-numbered year.

The 1965 returns were tonic for the anemic G.O.P., for they showed that determination, effort and responsiveness to genuine public needs can pay dividends for local and state organizations.

In Philadelphia, reigning Democrats had lost the fervor of the Clark-Dilworth days and their clanking machine was corroded with mediocrity, disunity and old-fashioned corruption. The election of famed investigator Arlen Specter as District Attorney on the Republican ticket was a triumph for a vigorous new generation that had moved into the seats of power in the victory-starved G.O.P. organization. As they applied fresh brains and talents to the problem of redressing the two-party balance, these new men took a fresh look at conventional political etiquette, notably the hard-line tradition of party loyalty. The case in point was Specter, a Democrat who had grown away from his party's shabby organization. The decision to nominate this discerning Democrat and support him through a winning campaign was but one product of the creative ferment bubbling through the party prior to the 1966 election.

The effects were visible in other municipal elections, notably in New York where Representative John V. Lindsay parlayed brains, personality and drive into the first Republican victory for the Mayoralty since the unorthodox F. H. LaGuardia won a third term in 1941. Gains cropped up in Louisville, St. Louis and other cities. Were they portents of more to come?

Even Lyndon Johnson conceded that the National Re-

publican Party "strengthened its position" in the 1966
mid-term elections. And this was just as well, for it was a
now-or-never test for the party that had backtracked into
a hole in 1964. Twice before, after the routs of 1912 and
1936, the party had risen to crisis and come back fighting
with strong, attractive candidates armed with generally
progressive platforms attuned to live issues. The 1966 returns were a heartening sign that there is a road back for
the G.O.P.

In Congress, Republicans netted forty-seven seats in
the House, their sharpest gain in twenty years, and the
Chamber's overall balance shifted back toward the center.
In the Senate, a net Republican gain of three seats restored the balance, sixty-four to thirty-six seats, that prevailed before the 1964 elections.

Resurgent Republicans netted eight Governorships,
winning Arkansas and Florida for the first time. The
sweep put Republican Governors in power in twenty-five
states, including seven of the "Big Ten": New York,
California, Pennsylvania, Ohio, Michigan, Massachusetts
and Florida, and Republican candidates captured 749
Democratic-held seats in state legislatures, losing only
192 seats, including seats lost through a reduction in the
size of certain legislatures following reapportionment. As
a result of the elections, Republicans controlled the Governorships of states with 109,563,000 population, while
Democrats held the Capitol in states with 85,468,000 persons. This constituted a major change from the 1964–66
period, when G.O.P. state administrations governed only
69,795,650 citizens, and Democratic Governors were in
control of states with populations totalling 108,763,569.

There is a special significance to the new Republican
upsurge in the states. It is by their performance at the
state level that parties build or demolish their rapport

with the voters. As Governors and legislators demonstrate their strength and responsibility, they directly enhance their party's future chances. And, as they represent administrations in power, they guide selection of national convention delegates. The restored strength of Republican Governors magnifies their already positive influence in the party's national councils.

The party cannot fail to benefit from the manifest ability and broad range of conviction of these twenty-five state executives. There are obvious national implications in George Romney's overwhelming re-election in Michigan, the comeback in Massachusetts of John Volpe, the nation's only Governor of Italian parentage, and the return of Nelson Rockefeller in New York and James A. Rhodes in Ohio will also help shape the 1968 picture.

The unanswered riddle of the election grows out of Ronald Reagan's whopping 965,000-vote win in California. He broke an 8-year Democratic hold on the Governorship and helped Republicans win four House seats. Some credit the size of his win to Reagan's magnetic personality, some to the persuasiveness of his brand of conservatism. His national success inescapably will be linked to his skill in accommodating his philosophy to the very real needs and justified aspirations of his fast-growing state.

The election broadened the Republican base in the Southern and border states, and in a most promising direction. The Nation as a whole gained by Winthrop Rockefeller's defeat of a blatant segregationist in Arkansas. Generally speaking, Republican victors in the South planted their banners nearer the center than did their Democratic opponents.

The G.O.P. advanced in 1966 at least partly because its best talents were applied at many levels to the problem of redressing the two-party balance.

At the party's summit, basic policy was periodically surveyed by the Republican Coordinating Committee, the representative leadership group formed early in 1965 to reunify our scattered battalions. Through the prestige of its members—all former Presidential candidates, Congressional leaders and representatives of the Republican Governors and the National Committee—its policy findings assured access to a wide audience.

In Congress, somber election post mortems produced a determination to make the most of the few resources available to a minority that was then outnumbered two to one. Even before Dean Burch was displaced as National Chairman, House Republicans moved to undo one of the most egregious of his doctrinaire blunders: they retained as their research director William Prendergast, the studiously objective political scientist whom Burch had fired as the National Committee's research chief. Professional research on issues, voting trends, voter attitudes, opposition strengths and weaknesses and the problems of minority groups is essential to the planning and execution of a modern campaign. Prendergast's abilities, which the Goldwater campaign could so well have used, have been increasingly reflected in the quality of recommendations offered by House Republicans.

There was study in the Senate, too. We were mindful of our Party's Eisenhower days of championing human rights, promoting record prosperity and keeping peace with all nations. So some of this Senate study was directed to development of constructive alternatives to President Johnson's highflying recommendations for the Great Society. We began from the premise that it is possible to agree with the goals of programs to strengthen equal rights, improve education or build social security, and still to disagree with methods that are ineffective, wasteful, au-

thoritarian or tinged with party politics. Republicans, for
the most part, found it possible to uphold the President in
his commitment to support South Vietnam in its struggle
against Communism—despite sniping from Democratic
ranks—and still to question the high priority in money
and effort assigned to the "moon race" with Russia.
Agreement with the goal of abolishing poverty still did
not silence Republicans when they saw bungling and politics in the Office of Economic Opportunity.

Senate researchers directed attention to the party's internal health in a brilliant report, "Where the Votes Are,"
produced after a year's study by the Senate Republican
Policy Committee. It began where any Republican realist
knew we stood: only 25 percent of the voters in 1964
classed themselves as Republicans, as against 38 percent
in 1940. With this division, Democrats could count on 54
percent of the national popular vote in a "normal" election where issues and candidates fall into customary patterns. Nationally, a permanent minority status loomed for
Republicans unless they succeeded in attracting "a lion's
share of independents and inducing unusual defections
among the less committed Democrats." [6] It was a formula
which we in Pennsylvania had proof-tested with some success.

The Committee's researchers went on to dig deeper, into
the fundamental changes that are taking place as the
products of the "baby boom" that followed World War II
take their places on the Nation's voting rolls. This new
generation, the report found, "offers Republicans their
first opportunity in nearly forty years" to regain majority status. During the next decade, the researchers reminded us, there will be a forty percent increase in fami-
lies under the age of thirty-five. Most of them will be living in metropolitan areas, struggling with the half-solved

problems—outdated schools, jammed traffic, festering slums, rampant crime, water and air pollution—that blight our suddenly crowded continent.

The report suggested that intelligent and compassionate Republican solutions to difficulties that beset the urban wage-earner can break the historic Democratic hammerlock on the votes of union members who are steadily growing more sophisticated and impatient with tradition for tradition's sake. Republican policies that effectively improve the Negro's chances in the job market will bring the party political opportunity as surely as they bring progress to the nation.[7]

As the new group strove for an open party of inclusion, the remnants of the far Right still bayed in the party's back alleys. I said with confidence in the summer of 1965 that I saw no likelihood that the party would return to the "Annapurna of Asininity" attained in the 1964 campaign, but some of the brothers kept trying.

Long-term success for Republicans clearly depends upon strengthening support for the policies of the Republican center. Continuance of ultraconservative "out groups" with allegedly "educational" missions was aimed at milking traditional Republican contributors for their money. There would be slim pickings for the regular party if these large donors actually filled the ambitious quotas set by such groups as Barry Goldwater's Free Society Association, the American Conservative Union and the United Republicans of America. Together, these organizations were seeking to raise over $3,000,000 for propaganda to promote their party-within-a-party and to back right-wing candidates, even where it hurt regular party tickets.

"All of these ultraconservative 'out' groups are seeking to raise more money than the Republican Party can hope to get," I warned the California Republican League in

December 1965. "They plan to use this money for their own independent objectives." [8]

In contrast with the citizens' organizations of the center, which serve the party by broadening participation in its affairs, these ultra-Right factions were patent political infiltrators, bent on remaking the party in their discredited image.

". . . these splinter groups are organizing people against today's party," I told the convention. "Their goal is to take the party over . . . and if it will not capitulate, to rob it of a significant part of its strength." [9]

I cannot too often or too highly praise the long record of idealism of Republican youth in the days of Presidents Lincoln, Theodore Roosevelt, Taft, Coolidge, Hoover, Eisenhower and now. And I join my young friends in exposing some recent trends in certain areas of their age groups. These young people rightly felt that no splinter group was more arrantly offensive to the principles of Republicanism—or Americanism, for that matter—than the self-styled "Rat Finks" who cropped up in the New Jersey Young Republican organization in the post-Goldwater period. They were, in effect, a suburban recrudescence of the Ku Klux Klan, racist bully boys who gloried in blatant bigotry against Negroes, Jews and Catholics.

The Y.R. leaders went into 1960 committed to Nixon, but after his defeat, the Goldwater forces saw an opportunity to exploit a leadership vacuum. They moved in and took over in state after state. Their well-planned campaign began at the county and state level, and was even more effective with the Y.R.s than it was with senior Republican groups. Where units proved invulnerable to normal democratic methods, they resorted to the tactics that worked so well with the regular organizations: come early (to organize) and stay late (to wear out the opposition). If it seemed worth while, delegations were provided with convention expense accounts; in some cases, "paper" clubs were established to generate extra votes needed to elect convention officers.

All this did a lot to perpetuate "Syndicate" control over the Y.R.'s and to train right-wingers for intra-party warfare. But it did precious little to increase Republican registrations or to elect Republicans to office.

As of this writing, the young crustaceans are still in defiant control of the national Y.R. organization. Rejecting cooperation with the national Republican Party, their articulate negativism continues to repel those young people who might otherwise enter the party through the door of its youth organization.

The number of new voters is increasing by arithmetic progression: 5,000,000 youngsters became eligible to vote between 1964 and 1966; another 7,000,000 will be enfranchised in the next two years preceding the crucial 1968 elections.* This huge reservoir of fine young citizens is by no means the captive of reactionary kooks. The Republican Party must reach them. How?

I suggest that the party can harvest millions of future votes if the national and state organizations work intelligently now to develop its potential membership of young voters and workers, especially since the national Democratic Party is having its troubles with its left-wing oriented Young Democrat groups.

The first step should be an assumption of responsibility for state and college Y.R. organizations by the appropriate Republican State Committees. The state committees should have final say over the selection of officers by these organizations. A state committee official, preferably a full-time paid worker, should be named as an advisor to work with the party's youth organizations.

* The "youthquake," according to House Minority Leader Gerald Ford.

At the national level, the Young Republican organization should be completely reorganized. The national president and vice president of the Young Republicans and of the college Y.R.'s should be named by the Republican National Committee, or by the National Chairman at the National Committee's direction. National Committee staff members assigned to the Y.R.'s—jobs now regarded as "patronage" for the youth leadership—should be replaced by a full-time youth advisor heading a Youth Division accountable to the National Chairman.

Inevitably, this program will be attacked as "undemocratic"—or should I say "un-Republican?" The charge implies that there is "democracy" in the present system, which is debatable. In rebuttal, I should point out that the National Chairman himself is elected by, and accountable to, the National Committee, and not to the party membership as a whole. The committeemen are chosen by a variety of methods under the party rules of the individual states. Moreover most top officials in government are not elected but appointed by a President or Governor.

If it were operated in the spirit in which it is proposed, such a system could and should enhance the quality of democracy in the individual Y.R. chapters and in the state Y.R. organizations, whose officials should continue to be elected by their membership. The free functioning of the individual clubs should also be protected against infiltration by party "fat cats" and other outside power cliques.

Fortunately, on college campuses, some college Republican groups, as well as the famous Ripon Society, have become the focus for creative thinking. They have turned up unfettered new approaches to the problems that concern the young voters and the young leaders whom the party needs so desperately if it is to be more than a permanent loyal opposition. Working toward the same end are other entities such as Republicans for Progress, the Committee for '68 and the National Republican Negro Assembly. As they have generated ideas, they have attracted recruits and encouraged the return of many who veered away from the dated dogmatism and the tired propaganda that passed for national Republicanism in 1964. These citizens' groups are the very yeast of our creative ferment and the recruiting office of our future state and national leaders.

What of the rights of minority members in Congress? My concern in this regard was whetted by my experience as a member of the Senate Rules Committee handling the Bobby Baker investigation, when Democrats seemed to be steering away from certain fields of inquiry.

We Republicans, outnumbered six to three, fought vainly for public hearings to explore the sensational closed-session testimony of Don B. Reynolds, the insurance man who said he took Baker's advice and provided a stereo phonograph as a kind of rebate for writing a $100,000 policy on the life of Lyndon B. Johnson while he was majority leader.

I had raised the obvious possibility of a "whitewash" in the Baker case on February 10th at the same Philadelphia news conference at which I formally announced that I was a candidate for re-election. At preprimary meetings, I found that the words "Bobby Baker" roused every Republican audience. I got things started by recounting a conversation with my wife following a White House reception at which the President had chosen to dance with her three times—once for her beauty, once for her charm and once because I was on the Rules Committee investigating Bobby Baker.

Majority members tiptoed around allegations of financial dealings between Baker and members of the Senate. Instead, they rammed down our throats an interim report recommending that fact-finding stop so the staff could work on a final report. On the Senate floor, Democrats did their part by killing proposals to extend the inquiry to look into activities of Senators, as well as their employees, and to review possibly "questionable" campaign contributions.

Later, the Senate ignored a section of the final report minority Senators supported in mid-May which proposed public disclosure of the financial interests of all Senators and their employees. But it did vote for the Cooper Resolution to create a six-member bipartisan "ethics committee" to look into allegations of misconduct. There was acute disinterest in a report by the Rules Committee's three minority Republicans which protested that the "full story" (of the Baker case) has not been disclosed . . . because the majority prevented the investigation from proceeding.

Inability of the minority to get off the ground in the Bobby Baker case is a cogent argument for increasing the staff assistance available to minority committee members. Genuinely "constructive alternatives" are sometimes more illusion than reality for a minority which must depend for its technical advice on staff members who owe their allegiance to the majority. Minority staff aides have been outnumbered by Democratic appointees as much as 10 to 1. On some, but not all, committees, even the power to hire and fire minority staff members is retained by the majority.

Truly expert assistance is essential for both sides, whichever party controls Congress. Unless its critical faculties are honed to a fine edge, Congress becomes a rubber stamp for the executive.

No one is more aware of the need for modernization of the machinery than a minority member, especially a junior one. His minority status deprives him of adequate staff help; his time in office lacks the seniority that gives clout in committee; archaic rules in committee and on the floor sometimes seem designed expressly to stultify him.

For years, programs advanced by Congressional juniors traded at a discount among G.O.P. leaders. The freshman Republican who had ideas to help his district through its growing pains was permitted by condescending seniors to "vote his district." But the seniors were based for the most part in rural-dominated districts that stayed safely Republican through the worst political upheavals. Seniority made them the quarterbacks of the Republican team, and they called "safe" signals tailored to "safe" districts. Safe this strategy was, for those who were, politically speaking, born safe. But it did nothing for the newcomers who had fought their way into the marginal seats that are the front-line salients in political warfare. They were treated as expendables, and many were picked off.

The juniors knew their constituents demanded action to deal with new problems—even if the solution, as yet, did not bear a Republican label. When senior party leaders opposed without offering improved alternatives, it was the marginal juniors who paid the piper.

There are welcome signs that this is changing—and more signs will be more welcome. Even though it was outnumbered two to one, the Republican leadership in the Eighty-ninth Congress worked with professional research staffs to develop and present constructive alternatives to Administration proposals. Some of those proposals have survived in finished legislation. One example is the Republican-sponsored voluntary medical insurance section of the Medicare Bill, which supplements the Administration's hospitalization plan.

Republicans can be proud of their responsible position on foreign policy under the Kennedy and Johnson Administrations. Their heavy support for the President's initial policies in Vietnam proved crucially important at a time when Democrats were publicly airing their doubts and differences about the jungle war. Republican refusal to play politics with the national interest helped our candidates across the victory line in the 1966 elections.

Money is the muscle of government and it is idle to talk of decentralizing responsibility unless revenues are redistributed. It is toward this end that Republicans have thoughtfully developed their plan for returning a portion of Federal income tax revenues to the states. It may be subject to improvement. It may not be the only solution and it may not be the final solution. But it deserves thorough analysis and consideration as a promising means to the larger end of helping our floundering urban localities to help themselves.

Congress can perform no greater service for the people it represents than to stimulate the processes of self-help in our cities. To the extent that Republicans take the lead in making this new kind of intergovernmental partnership workable, they will deserve and win public support.

Republicans must shun the lure of short-term gains that glimmer in the firewater jug labeled "Old Coalition." My party's past binges with the reactionary Southern Democrats have almost always left the Republicans nursing political hangovers.* Our bouts with the "conservative coalition" have visited us with censure in the press, dissension and distrust in our districts and, on too many occasions, defeat at the polls. The hardheaded Dixiecrats, meanwhile, have remained secure in their tenure and in their committee chairmanships, none of which seems to discourage some "senior safes" in my own party from urging the G.O.P. once again to reach for the reflected bone in the water.

* See Gerald Ford's speech of May 10, 1967 at Bowling Green University, Bowling Green, Ohio.

For decades, a wishful few on the fringes of both parties have advanced a simplistic plan for "reform" of our two-party system: realignment into "conservative" and "liberal" camps. It is a formula for chaos that ignores both logic and the facts of political life.

Arbitrary polarization would amount to "Operation Disinvite" for both parties. Imagine, for instance, the Democrats excommunicating the Western federalists, the Northern liberals or the Southern conservatives—or all three. Consider prospects for Republicans if they ostracized their urban liberals, their centrist moderates, their Midwestern conservatives or their Northwestern progressives.

Such a deliberate ideological cleavage would, as the physicists say, have a half life of six months. Indeed, it would hardly take half a year for both groupings to fragment into lukewarms and "red hots," into revisionists and "true believers."

What is actually happening in both parties is far more encouraging. Much as some Republicans sniff at L.B.J.'s strivings for "consensus," the stuff of victory is still breadth of backing, as successful Governors such as John Chafee in Rhode Island, John Volpe in Massachusetts, Dan Evans in Washington, and Ray Shafer in Pennsylvania have demonstrated. An effective appeal across a wide spectrum is what elects candidates. It worked for us Eisenhower Republicans in 1952 and for the Democrats in 1964. The Johnson approach to the Ninetieth Congress suggests that he hopes it will work again.

Republicans would be well advised to spend more time formulating attitudes, developing alternatives and grooming candidates to foster an appeal broad enough to win a consensus of our own. In good measure, that's what was done in the 1966 elections.

Some 4,000 candidates for Governor, Congress and legislatures formed their party groupings within the states. Whether they succeeded or not, most of those campaigns were party efforts, unified behind the party nominees. Few of those nominees were doctrinaire captives of ideological labelling. They were instead practical-minded individuals far more interested in solving the problems that beset their nation, states and districts than in proving rigid points of doctrine. Much more remains to be done, but the scope of the party's recovery has established a momentum that is growing. Because Republican newcomers have won such spectacular victories of late, there will be more Percys, Brookes, Hatfields, Bakers, Reagans and Lindsays tomorrow.

The potential for growth is particularly promising in the twenty-six Republican-run state administrations. The Republican Governors are building a modern party. Their record in seeking out solutions in education, urban problems, pollution control, fiscal policy and a dozen other fields, which is shaping the future of our citizens, warrants trust in Republican capacity to govern on the national level.

The search takes form, visible and viable. In Pennsylvania, Republican Governor Shafer surmounts ninety-three years of voter distrust and pushes through to a Constitutional Convention. In Maryland, Governor Spiro Agnew draws an opposition legislature into support of tax reform. In New York, Rockefeller innovates with the broadest transportation merger ever attempted at state level. Colorado's Governor John Love signs the most liberal abortion law in the United States.

In hard-boiled political terms, these twenty-six Governors wield real power through their control over state patronage. Their wishes will affect, and often control, the makeup of the delegations their states will send to the 1968 convention. There are rumblings from the right that as many as two-thirds of the delegates at the next convention will be the same people who were at San Francisco. On a simple numerical basis, as well as on precedent, I doubt it. Only 303 of the 1331 delegates at the 1960 Republican Convention had been delegates at the 1956 convention. Of the 1308 delegates at the 1964 convention only 250 had been delegates in 1960. From 1944 on, less than 25 percent of the delegates and alternates had attended the previous convention as delegates and alternates.[10]

Many, a great many, of the crew that shouted for Goldwater simply will not be selected next time. Those of the outshouted forty percent who stood up for Scranton and Rockefeller and the "favorite sons" of the center who come back can be expected to have profited from the experience.

Even among those who supported the 1964 nominee, there is an evident reluctance to repeat the ideological blunders of the Goldwater campaign. One of them is my colleague, Senator John Tower of Texas, who publicly told the 1966 post-election session of the National Committee that nondoctrinaire Republicanism works best in Texas, too. At the New Orleans meeting where he spoke, there was heartening attention to organizing for campaigns, developing affirmative issues and nominating attractive candidates.

As newly-elected Senator Howard Baker told the same meeting: "I decided I was a lot less concerned with what my old Democratic granddaddy might think of me and a lot more concerned with what my grandchildren must think of me." [11]

Republicans must remember their Senate Policy Committee's advice—to hunt "Where the votes are." In this increasingly urbanized—and suburbanized—country, fewer and fewer members of Congress speak for purely rural constituencies, and the party that ignores this reality pays the consequences.

What is politically possible was dramatically established when subservient majorities drove the Great Society program through Congress in indigestible hunks. The gap between promise and performance has been great, and even Administration Democrats concede the need to revise some of its more unworkable programs. The situation gives Republicans a built-in opportunity to put forward workable, acceptable proposals.

Republican responsibility is assumed even by Democrats, including President Johnson, whose international policies have been substantially better supported by the minority than by his own party. That same responsibility is reflected in the decisive support Republicans gave the procession of civil rights bills initiated under Eisenhower in 1957 and 1960 and continuing on to 1964 and 1965. None of these long overdue acts would have passed without vigorous support from the party that was born in the struggle for human rights.

The party must make a common determination to win elections rather than to risk any further invitations to squeeze itself into the mummy wraps of a narrow so-called "choice," as was offered in 1964—especially when that "choice" entails any trace of the indefensible "Southern Strategy" of that ill-fated foray.

The party's future in the South depends upon the growth of such rigorous challenges to the old Democratic hierarchies as we now find in Tennessee, Virginia, Florida, Arkansas and, to a growing degree, in a number of other Southern states. Southern Republican state organizations must be firm in forswearing racism and in espousing, through articulate and respectable candidates, policies of economic and social responsibility. The old one-party complacency will give way to healthy two-party competition to the extent that party policies develop national appeal.

In the states, Governors make party policy. In Congress, party policy should be established before divisive issues reach the legislative floor. There is machinery available for espousal of national policy in the Republican Coordinating Committee which has proven its worth in the policy development field and might well be more useful.

In 1965, the Committee confounded its critics—and some of its members—by issuing a series of well-researched, intelligently reasoned task force reports on emerging problems: foreign policy, human rights, federal-state relationships, job opportunities, fiscal policy. By election day, 1966, nineteen such papers had been released by the Co-ordinating Committee. Several received favorable press coverage, which never hurts a political cause. Of more moment to the partisan politician was the reception Republican professionals gave these constructive papers during the campaign. In a significant number of cases, they were used as source material, even as policy guides, by Republican candidates. As they helped some candidates make affirmative policy decisions, they steered others away from stating positions embarrassingly out of line with the national leadership. New position papers, advocating constructive solutions, continue to be released.

The right to dissent, even from the views of one's own party, is a cherished strength of the American system. But both the party and the dissenter are on stronger ground if a leadership consensus is available as the basis for reasoned argument.

In the absence of a group like the Coordinating Committee, members of the party out of power have two frequently conflicting reference points for individual policy decisions. One is the platform adopted by the last national convention, a document that tends to go stale with time. The other is the sum of the positions taken by the minority leadership in Congress. They are unreliable guides, for they are often tailored to legislative circumstance and they do not always coincide.

The Coordinating Committee device can meet both these objections. At its quarterly meetings, the committee deals with policy problems as they arise, so it is not forced to resort to the open-minded generalities that often dilute party platforms. At the same time, its policy papers are insulated from many of the pressures that are built into the legislative process.

The Coordinating Committee can be a forum for assessing the issues upcoming in future campaigns, thus welding a coherent philosophy acceptable to the party's broad center.

The Coordinating Committee is not being used as an arena for pre-convention politicking among supporters of aspiring Presidential contenders. Fear of such maneuvering brought dissolution of other attempts at between-convention policymaking, notably the promising movement that flowered briefly at Mackinac Island in 1943.

The Committee's members, shunning the intrigues that breed factionalism, are doing much useful spadework for the Platform Committee at the 1968 convention. To the extent that the platform strengthens the hands of our nominee in dealing with emerging issues—and doesn't hogtie him—it can contribute to the election of a Republican President.

And what of the Coordinating Committee then? Would a new Republican Administration look with favor on policy pronouncements by a senior party group, however well-reasoned? The answer is almost certainly no, because the White House is the powerhouse of any administration that hopes to lead. If the Coordinating Committee were continued with its role unchanged, it would be an innocuous fifth wheel at best. Under adverse conditions, it could become an embarrassing liability.

But parties, like football teams, revise assignments when the ball changes hands. When Republicans are on the political offensive, it should be possible to convert the Coordinating Committee into a kind of "National Policy Advisory Council" headed by the President, with the Vice President as his deputy. In this role, the Committee would report to the President on the political realities that inescapably intrude on major policy decisions.

The leaders of the new generation, the professionals and scientists and managers, have become incredibly adept at solving complex problems that arise in their own endeavors. They will demand no less of those whose profession is government. At home, they see inequities in education, snarls in mass transit, blighted neighborhoods, polluted streams and poisoned air. Abroad, they see alliances decline and enmities grow. They are seeking new solutions, and the quest grows more demanding by the month. The party that employs modern techniques to develop adequate responses to these challenges will speak for the younger generations which will dominate American politics in the last third of the Twentieth Century.

Republicans can be that party if they remain true to their responsible tradition and are, at the same time, responsive to the changing needs of a dynamic society.

There is room enough within the Republican Party for traditional conservatives, progressives, moderates and liberals. The common denominator of Republican commitment to more responsible and responsive government should serve to weld all party members of good will into a mutual determination to win elections. This centripetal phenomenon has heretofore been more commonly observed in our adversaries than in ourselves on Election Day.

The rigidity of the party line in 1964 and the resultant breakaway of moderates, liberals and independent voters proved disastrous.

I am reminded of the elephants in circus parades, swinging along, each elephant firmly holding with his trunk the tail of the elephant ahead. In one small town, the littlest elephant fell through an open manhole cover. Admitting responsibility, the town solicitor offered to pay for the value of the lost elephant.

"Oh, no!" countered the circus' representative. "The damage is very much greater than that."

"How can that be?" asked the town's lawyer.

"Well, you see, when that durned elephant fell down the manhole, he pulled the tails out of all the other elephants."

There is a secondary moral here, encased in a bad pun: a successful parade of elephants can be spoiled by too rigid adherence to details.

EPILOGUE

*Tempora mutantur et nos
mutamur in illis.*
(The times change and
we change with them.)

WE have seen how in 1964 my party suffered a new sort of isolation—and insulation—from the American people.

We have seen what alienation, obstruction, personality cults and coalitions—unproductive or inexpedient, or both—have done to the Republican Party. We have seen, too, as in the elections of 1966, that Republicans can profit from past mistakes.

Indeed, times do change, and parties, like people, must adapt to survive. The party has paid dearly for past errors: its long infatuation with Prohibition, its seduction by the Southern Democrats, its snipe hunts among the marsh lights of the left, its haring after the chimaeras of McCarthyism, and its lapses into blind obstructionism.

To modernize our appeal as the party with a future rather than the party with a past, temptations must be abjured, particularly the lure of fixed coalitions involving short-range compromise "victories" to the detriment of long-range party growth. This is not to say that Republican policies cannot be flexible enough to attract through missionary effort and persuasion varying—and changing —groups of Democrats to the support of Republican causes. Even so, the standard should be the merit of the proposal and its heft with the voters, rather than expedient joinder for the sheer satisfaction of minor statistical triumphs.

Success is the name of the game, but small tactical victories may lead to large strategic defeats. The well-being of the public must not be sacrificed to petty legislative surgery.

Republicans must also refuse, and publicly refuse at that, to follow dangerous trails blazed by dangerous people, such as the leadership of the John Birch Society, the Minute Men, the Liberty Lobby, and similar deceptively captioned pits.

Reapportionment has brought gains to Republicans which emphasize rather than deny their duty to remain faithful to basic tenets. Constituency alternations do require flexibility in adjustments to changing conditions and rising aspirations. These adaptations should involve compassionate and intelligent approaches without any loss to the principle of personal responsibility.

Constituency reshuffles are also bringing new men to Republican posts of duty: new men not shackled by ancient error, mouldy prejudice or ill-hallowed tradition. These new men are free from old feuds. Liberated by the party's new status and improving acceptance, they offer new opportunity for responsible achievement.

Responsible is the word. For the Republican Party *has* been responsible in foreign policy during these twenty post-Vandenberg years. The party has, barring a few aberrations, been responsible in its national fiscal policy. In its administration of state governments, it has left its adversary far behind. The party must now enlarge its reputation for reliability all the way across the political spectrum.

Being responsible is not enough. The party must also be *responsive* to the just and proper aspirations of the constituencies.

To deserve to win, then, Republicans must firmly establish with the voters clear conviction that they are both *responsible* in governing and *responsive* to the public welfare.

The Republican Party is no David forced to gamble on a single lucky shot to fell the opposition Goliath. The party is one of America's two great political armies—strong within itself and capable of applying that strength to win political victories; capable of righteous wrath, moral indignation and intelligent action.

There is room in such a party for a responsible left flank of innovators, just as there is for the steadfast types who have so long manned the artillery to the right. Linking the flanks with the main body of troops at the center, we can seize and hold the high road to national leadership.

Like a Gideon and his army of trumpeters, the party must adapt tactics to circumstance, but the whole army must accept a grand strategy that assures the future by recognizing the realities of the present and conserving the values of the past. To such a party national security entails more than military strength; domestic tranquillity more than stagnant order.

I propose open, continuing and co-operative re-examination by us Republicans of the stance of our own party and of the contentions—and intentions—of the opposition.

Together we can find a better way.

There are better responses to the needs and rights of

the governed than an infinitude of regulations imposed by a swarm of officeholders. The regulators of man's base impulses tend too often to restrict unduly man's natural rights. To guard against abuse of those rights carries no writ to deprive man of the just fruits of his toil. Order is not sword but shield: the shield of order to guard the sword of freedom. This must ever be the true stance of our party.

The Republican Party is essential to the two-party system. Quality of government improves when the two parties are in close and genuine competition.

We Republicans have failed to compete as effectively as we should have.

We are not yet competing as well as we must.

We must now do those things we ought to have done.

The Republican Party must face the future, for our country's sake and for its own good health, with an eye for excellence, a hand for the helpless, a head for the truth and a heart for the people.

Such a Republican Party can, if strong in resolution and secure in honorable purpose, deserve—and receive— the Nation's trust.

> *Vivat Respublica, vivantque*
> *qui illam regunt, et qui in*
> *temporibus futuris regent.*

> Long live the republic, and
> those who govern it and those
> who may in the future be
> called upon to govern it.

NOTES

Prologue

[1] Arthur Larson, *A Republican Looks At His Party* (New York: Harper & Brothers, 1956), p. 19.

Chapter I
Elwood, Indiana, U.S.A.

[1] Mary Earhart Dillon, *Wendell Willkie* (Philadelphia and New York: J. B. Lippincott Company, 1952), p. 119.

[2] *Ibid.*, p. 169.

[3] George H. Mayer, *The Republican Party, 1854–1954* (New York: Oxford University Press, 1964), p. 452.

Chapter II
Capitol Hill

[1] The United States Foreign Policy Document *Peace and War, 1931–1941,* published January 2, 1943 by the U.S. Department of State, p. 829.

[2] *The New York Times,* July 20, 1943.

Chapter III
Not Quite Washington

[1] *Fact On File Yearbook,* 1944, p. 305.

[2] "July 26 is considered the proper day to sow turnips in Missouri:

On the twenty-sixth of July
Sow turnips, wet or dry."

Harry S Truman, *Years of Trial and Hope* (Garden City, N.Y.: Doubleday & Co., 1956).

[3] Jules Abels, *Out of the Jaws of Victory* (New York: Holt, Rinehart & Winston, Inc., 1959), p. 177.

[4] Joseph C. Harsch, "State of the Nations: Republican Deployment," *The Christian Science Monitor,* January 17, 1956.

Chapter IV
The Battle of Omaha

[1] John Sherman Cooper, November 1948 Speech. (Quoted with his permission.)
[2] Boston *Traveler*, January 19, 1949.
[3] Omaha *World-Herald*, January 23, 1949.
[4] Omaha *World-Herald*, January 27, 1949.
[5] *Ibid.*
[6] *Proceedings of Republican National Committee*, Volume 2, January 27, 1949, pp. 235–6.
[7] Philadelphia *Evening Bulletin*, January 28, 1949.
[8] Santa Barbara, California, *News Press*, February 6, 1949.
[9] The Philadelphia *Inquirer*, July 10, 1949.
[10] Des Moines, Iowa, *Register*, August 22, 1949.

Chapter V
Portland to Portland

[1] William Shakespeare, *Julius Caesar*, Act IV, Scene 2.
[2] Charleston *Gazette*, February 12, 1950.
[3] Philadelphia *Evening Bulletin*, September 14, 1951.
[4] New York *Herald Tribune*, November 7, 1951.
[5] *The New York Times*, January 7, 1952.
[6] Raymond J. Blair, New York *Herald Tribune*, March 18, 1952.
[7] *Ibid.*
[8] *Ibid.*
[9] *Ibid.*
[10] Roscoe Drummond, *Christian Science Monitor*, March 14, 1952.
[11] Philip Geyelin, *Wall Street Journal*, June 19, 1952.
[12] *The New York Times*, July 3, 1952.
[13] *Ibid.*

Chapter VI
The Chicago Coup

[1] *The New York Times*, September 19, 1952.
[2] *The New York Times*, September 20, 1952.
[3] *The New York Times*, September 24, 1952.
[4] *Ibid.*

[5] *Ibid.*

[6] Sherman Adams, *First Hand Report* (New York: Harper & Brothers, 1961).

[7] *The New York Times,* September 25, 1952.

[8] Press release, October 27, 1952.

[9] *Ibid.*

[10] *The New York Times,* October 3, 1962.

[11] *The New York Times,* October 5, 1952.

[12] Philadelphia *Evening Bulletin,* September 9, 1952.

[13] *The New York Times,* October 25, 1952.

[14] *The New York Times,* October 30, 1952.

[15] *Ibid.*

[16]   A PRAYER FOR A FRIEND
Dear God—

In all things Thy will be done. If it please Thee that Thou shalt give to us the victory, help him to judge that which is surely good, to turn aside from all unworthiness.

Help him to share and to hold that faith shown bright in the eyes of the little children along the many places of his going.

Help him to follow after the ways that lead to peace, that by Thy grace the sounds of battle may be stilled, our sons returned to field or marketplace.

Help him, by high example, to bring our people together in friendly amity and tolerant accord that each may, in his own fashion, freely enjoy the fruits of a peaceful, happy land.

Help him, above all, O Lord, to be himself.

AMEN
[17] Philadelphia *Evening Bulletin,* November 18, 1952.

Chapter VII
The White House

[1] Los Angeles *Examiner,* August 27, 1953.

[2] *Congressional Record,* 83rd Congress, 1st Session, 1954.

[3] *Time* Magazine, September 27, 1954.

[4] Philadelphia *Evening Bulletin,* October 24, 1954.

[5] *Time* Magazine, October 10, 1955.

[6] Columbus *Dispatch,* February 12, 1956.

[7] Text of speech by Rep. Hugh Scott before the National Assembly on Civil Rights, Washington, D.C., March 5, 1956.

[8] *Official Report—26th Republican National Convention* (San Francisco: Republican National Committee, 1956), p. 208.

[9] *The New York Times,* November 15, 1956.

[10] *The New York Times,* September 23, 1956.

[11] *Ibid.*

[12] New York *Herald Tribune,* November 10, 1958.

[13] *Ibid.*

[14] *Ibid.*

[15] *Ibid.*

[16] New York *Herald Tribune,* November 7, 1958.

[17] *The New Methodology: A Study of Political Strategy and Tactics* (Washington, D.C., The American Institute For Political Communication, 1967), p. 34.

[18] Alan L. Otten, *Wall Street Journal,* September 16, 1959.

[19] Philadelphia *Daily News,* December 17, 1959.

[20] *The New York Times,* December 27, 1959.

[21] Open Letter to Senator John F. Kennedy, press release, Office of Senator Hugh Scott, June 19, 1960.

[22] Mayer, *The Republican Party, op. cit.,* p. 508.

[23] *Official Report—Republican National Convention* (Chicago: Republican National Committee, 1960), p. 351.

Chapter VIII
Phoenix to Ashes

[1] *Record Herald,* Waynesboro, Pa., November 8, 1962.

[2] The Philadelphia *Inquirer,* February 16, 1962.

[3] *Ibid.*

[4] Robert Novak, *The Agony of the G.O.P.* (New York: The Macmillan Company, 1965), p. 190.

[5] The Philadelphia *Inquirer,* June 29, 1963.

[6] Joseph R. Coyne, Somerset *Daily American,* Somerset, Pa., July 29, 1963.

[7] Broadcast with Senators Jackson, Pastore and Saltonstall, November 25, 1963.

[8] *Ibid.*

[9] Novak, *The Agony of the G.O.P.,* pp. 249ff.

[10] *Ibid.,* p. 265.

[11] The Washington *Post*, December 5, 1964.

[12] Harrisburg *Patriot*, January 10, 1964.

[13] Erie *Times*, May 23, 1964.

[14] *Ibid.*

[15] New York *Herald Tribune*, May 25, 1965.

[16] *The Sunday Star*, Washington, June 7, 1964.

[17] *The News*, Danville, Pa., June 8, 1964.

[18] "Face The Nation," June 7, 1964, as quoted in Novak, *The Agony of the G.O.P.*, pp. 430–1.

[19] *The New York Times*, June 8, 1964.

[20] *Ibid.*

[21] *Ibid.*

[22] *The New York Times*, June 13, 1964.

[23] *Official Report—28th Republican National Convention* (Washington: The Republican National Committee, 1964), p. 274.

[24] Robert J. Donovan, *The Future of the Republican Party* (New York: The New American Library of World Literature, Inc., 1964), p. 53.

Chapter IX
The Road Back

[1] The Philadelphia *Inquirer*, November 8, 1964.

[2] *Ibid.*

[3] *Ibid.*

[4] Easton (Pennsylvania) *Express*, November 30, 1964.

[5] *The New York Times*, January 7, 1965.

[6] *Where the Votes Are*, Prepared by the staff of the U.S. Senate Republican Policy Committee (Washington, D.C.: July 10, 1966), pp. 3–5.

[7] *Ibid.*, p. 79.

[8] Los Angeles *Times*, December 5, 1965.

[9] *Ibid.*

[10] David S. Broder, "Every Convention A New Deal for G.O.P. Delegates," The Washington *Post*, April 30, 1967.

[11] Text of speech by Senator Howard Baker before Republican National Committee, New Orleans, Louisiana, January 23, 1967.

INDEX

Smith, Dana C., Nixon fund and, 110-11, 113, 114
Smith, Howard W., 150
Smith, Margaret Chase, 71
  1964 convention and, 215
Sommers, Harry, 55
Snodgrass, Robert, racism and, 198
Spangler, Harrison, 55
  isolationism of, 25
  1952 support for Taft by, 67
Specter, Arlen, 229
Sprague, J. Russel, 1948 presidential campaign and, 37, 38
Stassen, Harold, 33, 147, 164, 171
  1952 Republican convention and, 104-6
  post-1948 party control and, 51
State conventions
  in 1952
    Eisenhower, 91-93
    Taft, 91-93
  in 1964, Goldwater supporters, 197-98, 200
  See also Primaries
States Rights Democrats, 44
Stevens, Robert T., 141
Stevens, Thomas E., 75-76
Stevenson, Adlai, 68, 108
  1949 contributions to, 114
  1952 elections and
    bet, 124
    campaign, 120, 122, 123
    defeat, 125-26
Strauss, Lewis L., 166
Summerfield, Arthur, 102, 104
  1952 campaign and, 110, 112
  Nixon fund and, 115
Symington, Stuart, 163

Taft, Robert A., 3, 10, 77, 129, 132, 162, 186
  death of, 137, 140
  failure of, 19
  1948 elections and, party control, 48, 50-51, 53, 60, 62-63, 65
  1952 elections and
    convention, 71, 95
    Eisenhower, 108-9, 112-13, 133-34, 216
    nomination, 74-77, 79-83, 97-105

opposition, 87, 95
  people's doubt, 94
  primaries, 89-91
  State conventions, 91-93
  supporters, 67-68, 71-72, 103
  Turnip Day, 40-41
  tradition of, 227
Taft, Seth, 216
Taft, William Howard, 99
Taft-Hartley Act, 142
Talbott, Harold E., 60
Taylor, M. Harvey, 155, 164
Television
  Clark-Scott debates on, 157-59, 189
  1952 elections and
    Nixon fund, 113-15
    Republican convention, 97-98, 101-2
  1960 Kennedy-Nixon debate on, 176
Thornton, Daniel, 89
  1952 support for Eisenhower by, 94
Thurmond, Strom, 44, 150
Tobey, Charlie, 53
Tower, John, 244
Trade Expansion Act, 180
Truax, Craig, 201
  1964 elections and
    campaign, 218
    Scranton, 207
Truman, Harry S, 34, 67, 77, 124, 138, 157
  criticized, 58
  1948 elections and
    campaign, 35, 38-43
    victory, 43-44
  1952 elections and, Eisenhower, 70, 80, 86, 94, 120-23, 125
  on Republicans, 63-64
Turnip Day, 40-41
Tuttle, Elbert, 88

Un-American Activities Committee, House, 30

Vandenberg, Arthur H., 10, 251
  failure of, 19
  Turnip Day and, 40-41
Volpe, John, 231, 242